For Our Children

A Dialogue of the American Dream

Tracy John Mollenkopf, MBA

A hundred years from now, everyone you know, everyone you've ever met, everyone you've ever heard of will be gone. The only thing that remains is a world...for our children.

WESTBOW
P R E S S
A DIVISION OF THOMAS NELSON

WestBow Press books may be ordered through booksellers or by contacting:

WestBow Press
A Division of Thomas Nelson
1663 Liberty Drive
Bloomington, IN 47403
www.westbowpress.com
1-(866) 928-1240

ISBN: 978-1-4497-7109-6 (e)
ISBN: 978-1-4497-7110-2 (sc)
ISBN: 978-1-4497-7111-9 (hc)

Library of Congress Control Number: 2012919872

Printed in the United States of America

WestBow Press rev. date: 10/18/2012

For every parent who so willingly sacrificed so their next generation could have a brighter future. God bless you. They will remember your struggle.

Epigraph

"And one more idea which may be laughed and sneered at in some supposedly sophisticated circles, but I just have to believe that the loving God who has blessed this land and thus made us a good and caring people should never have been expelled from America's classrooms. It's time to welcome Him back, because whenever we've opened ourselves and trusted in Him, we've gained not only moral courage but intellectual strength." - Ronald Reagan

"If religious books are not widely circulated among the masses in this country, I do not know what is going to become of us as a nation. If truth be not diffused, error will be; If God and His Word are not known and received, the devil and his works will gain the ascendancy; if the evangelical volume does not reach every hamlet, the pages of a corrupt and licentious literature will; If the power of the Gospel is not felt throughout the length and breadth of the land, anarchy and misrule, degradation and misery, corruption and darkness will reign without mitigation or end." - Daniel Webster

"Resistance to tyranny becomes the Christian and social duty of each individual. Continue steadfast and, with a proper sense of your dependence on God, nobly defend those rights which heaven gave, and no man ought to take from us." - John Hancock, the first signature on the Declaration of Independence

"Hold on, my friends, to the Constitution and to the Republic for which it stands. Miracles do not cluster, and what has happened once in 6,000 years, may not happen again. Hold on to the Constitution, for if the American Constitution should fail, there will be anarchy throughout the world." - Daniel Webster

Daniel Webster's description of the U.S. government as "made for the people, made by the people, and answerable to the people," was later paraphrased by Abraham Lincoln in the Gettysburg Address in the words "government of the people, by the people,for the people."

Contents

Preface

As the author, I highly recommend reading the final ten pages, first. Sincerely, grasping the ending will affect the way you read this story. As in life, your spiritual understanding of its devout conclusion directly affects the way you cope with every day of your life. For that reason, the same is true of this story. I am the alpha and omega, the first and the last, the beginning and the end. It is perfectly acceptable to be mindful of the conclusion; it's quite the revelation.

In 1962, I was born in Dallas, Texas. However, something more important happened that year. The Supreme Court of the United States voted 6 to 1 to remove the words "Almighty God" from the hallowed institutions of higher education in America. Since that day, violent crime, teenage pregnancies, and divorce have risen over four hundred percent. It occurred to me, in this dangerous world, that if a child did not attend his neighborhood church where could they receive the promise of salvation? It must come from the parents. This book is a gift that parents can give to their teenage children, young adults, and fifty-year-old sons and daughters with the hope that someday their hearts may receive peace. Long since after our voices had blown away on the wind. Moreover, those children will proudly give it to those who follow them.

Three integrated stories make up the novel with the single point of view from its narrator Gabriel, the archangel. Each part is a unique story representing a prayer for America, the answer to that prayer, and the journey or the prize, which we each must travel. Gabriel will provide the key that unlocks the promise of your child's salvation.

My promise to you; I will not sugar coat the world we live in. Seriously, that would be a disservice to you. Our world is often cold and hard. However, I will push the edge of the envelope. Some will say the adult themes of is book are not appropriate for children. They are correct; I agree. When the next generation does not have it better than their parents do; yes, our world has become inappropriate. America is an amazing collection of powerful emotions, daunting fears, and uncompromising hope for the future. It is always real and it is true; this sacred truth I will deliver.

Above all, this story is a message of hope for all those who follow after; I call them our children. So, read the last ten pages first.

PART I

The Prayer

A hundred years from now, everyone you know, everyone you've ever met, everyone you've ever heard of will be gone. The only thing that remains is a world...for our children. Therein rests the truth, for its own sake, as the single most important fundamental of a life's journey fulfilled. Therefore, what is this American promise of stewardship made over two hundred years ago by our founding fathers along with this nation of immigrants? We hold these truths to be self-evident, that all men are created equal, that they are endowed by their Creator with certain unalienable Rights that among these are the rights to Life, Liberty, and the pursuit of Happiness: no truer words have ever been written than our Declaration of Independence.

This right to life is the only fundamental right, from which all other rights are derived. What kind of life will remain in the world? What kind of liberty shall our children have? Liberty, the promise of tomorrow, simply means freedom from oppression. It does not mean freedom from the landlord, or freedom from the employer, or freedom from the laws of nature. It means freedom from the coercive power of the state, a foreign enemy, or any group that would seek oppression and tyranny, nothing else. You might wish for the pursuit of personal happiness. Perhaps not the kind of happiness that gold and silver might buy, but rather something from within. This right to the pursuit of happiness means man's right to live for himself, to choose what constitutes his own individual happiness and to work with a single mind for its achievement, so long as he respects the same right in others.

I see a Declaration of Independence that does not exist in any other place on Earth. Is America the last great hope of the Earth? Are we the prayer of God or just a dream? In spite of this, the real world is crushed with debt like never before in history. No ordinary debts, forged are these chains of debt called fiscal servitude. A kinder gentler word than "slavery" but oppression none the same, let us call this spade, a spade. The world is bankrupt, astray economically, politically, and religiously. A world without hope is a dangerous place.

In this dream, some will wither and some will fall, yet some will rise to fight for us all. Hence, on this most memorable of eves, the simple play began. Since I am the sole appointed guardian of God's children, the question posed so trustingly is 'What in the world will I do about it?' Thus began my love affair with America.

Opening Night

Here I stand, outside this lonely theater on a cold and dreary evening in New York City, a theater of broken hearts and shattered dreams longing for those who came before. But, this theater is not about the trials of failure, knocked down, and surrender. Rather, it is about how many times we are willing to rise and try again. Therein rests the secret of our inspired fame.

Inside I see a stage with velvet curtains, round lights in front of the orchestra pit, and a dark carpeted floor with lighted steps. The audience sits, in padded seats some lopsided and broken, as they eat popcorn and wait for the kids. A lonely theater attendant is walking slowly through the aisles with a flashlight. People are waving to each other for it is opening night, a see and be seen evening.

The story awaits the audience as they file into the theater like waves upon the shore, unaware of my impending gift for them. The world lies in the balance; their very souls are in play. A lonely playwright cautiously greets the audience as they enter the theater. As always, I take my rightful place in the wings. For I have the best ringside seat to the ultimate show of mankind.

"How are you?" An old friend extended a gracious hand in admiration.

"I am good," the playwright answered. "Thank you for coming."

The thrill of the opening night was perfectly intoxicating. When I first become a playwright, I had no idea of the state of mind involved in a production. I suppose I had led an ordinary life. Working week to week, paycheck to paycheck to make ends meet. Everyone else I knew was doing the same thing. I am a forty-year-old man carrying more credit card debt than I should, nothing special. I could probably lose twenty pounds but everyone else could too. Perhaps, if there wasn't a fast food joint on every street corner, it might be different. Oh well, I doubt I will ever write another play, so I will enjoy the moment to the fullest.

"This is your first show, isn't it," another friend said with anticipation. "You must be very excited."

"You can't imagine," the playwright grinned.

"Then, I'll see you after the play," the friend said.

"Of course, it is comforting to see those who know you and welcome you. Perhaps it is the tuxedo that gave me away," the playwright thought. "Dale, I'm so glad you made it."

"Great, this is my wife, Ginny," Dale replied.

"It's a pleasure to meet you, Ginny?" The playwright said kindly.

"It's a pleasure to meet you, too. Good luck, tonight," Ginny said with an air of excitement.

"Thank you," the playwright said. The long slow chime of the bell signaled the audience to be seated. The show is beginning. A tall young man with long blonde hair in a black rain drenched trench coat walks quietly past the playwright. The stranger looked directly at him, but the playwright intentionally ignored him. The house lights are going down, so the stranger continued into the theater. The stage is hit with the spotlight. The play is about to begin.

"Break a leg," the last fan said.

The air is thick with anticipation as the audience settled inside the theatre. The stage remains dark with the single spotlight on the scene. Inside a radio station sound booth, one man sits alone. The invisible orchestra began the night with their rendition of The Rolling Stones', *Sympathy for the Devil* as the play commenced. The lights go down, the curtain opened, and a silence fell over the audience; Mick Jagger would be so proud.

Upon the Stage

Dr. Mark Johnson is the forty-two-year-old radio host of a news talk show. He has not shaved in the last twenty-four hours. He is not dirty but looks tired, as if the weight of the world has been upon his shoulders for far too many years. He is a good-looking man, in a rough manly way; quick-witted with a silver tongue, but his better days are behind him. The station clock shows midnight as the "On the Air" sign flashed.

"When there's a two-thousand-pound elephant in the room, I believe it's wise to recognize it, before it causes any further damage," Mark said. He stopped to take another hit from his cigarette. Smoke slowly came out of his nose and mouth as he spoke.

"That's right boys and girls. My day of reckoning is upon us. I hope for the best; but alas, I fear, I prepare for the worse. It seems that tonight's broadcast of 'State of the Nation' will be our final show. Not because of the nation's demise, but rather my state of termination. However, I will not shrink from this tragic ending; I welcome it. Please excuse my unilateral over dramatization of the moment. It's just my...

style." Mark grinned. He is sitting comfortably in his chair addressing the overhead microphone as he has done a thousand times before.

"Here we are midnight to six in the morning one last time. Of course I'd rather go hunting with Dick Cheney, but here I am," he joked. He does look surprisingly calm for a man doing a live radio show.

"Since tonight's a rather special night, I think we should go out with a bang, not a whimper. I'm hereby officially tendering my resignation as an adult. All bets are off. What do you say to that? Are you with me? Of course, you are. Let the big dogs run; for tomorrow, we join the ranks of the unemployed, the destitute, and the morally bankrupt" he groaned. Casually, he opened a desk drawer to find a bottle of ten-year-old whiskey, unopened, and a cigar. There is a note attached to the bottle.

"Well, my two best friends," Mark rejoiced as he began to open the letter. "It truly is a special night. I wonder who gave me this?" The note read: *Dear Mark, this is your severance package; enjoy it. By the way, your producer quit, as well. You're flying solo tonight. Try not to do anything stupid; signed your former boss. P.S. Please don't drink during the show, again.* He looks at the label like an old friend he hasn't seen in years. "Well, boss, I wouldn't want to have it any other way," he grinned. He cracked open the bottle, smelled the top, and cleaned out his usual glass.

"For your listening pleasure, the new direction of the station will be to provide you with a classic rendition of easy listening music designed to sooth your soul, numb your mind, and absolutely bore you to tears," he said.

"It will, without malice, put you to sleep permanently. Valium's got nothing on what's coming your way. Perhaps, my fortunes are changing. I think I'd rather not be you," he said as he poured a drink. "I think I'd rather have a double."

"Am I a bitter man, I think not. I've enjoyed the last sixteen months of dead air that I'll never get back. So, tonight, on my last night, I get to say what I really think, what I really want, he sneered. "What are you going to do to me? Know what I mean?" He shots the half glass of whiskey in a single gulp. His face shrinks with pain as the fire burns all the way down to his toes.

"Oh, that tastes good. That'll make you feel alive. Are you ready, boys and girls? Let's do this crazy thing," he grunted as he looks around the desk for his local newspapers.

"KBRG in New York, proudly brings you the *"State of the Nation"* with, your host, Dr. Mark Johnson. Live and on the air with your state of the nation advisor on all economic and political events that shape our lives and sharpen our minds like a knife," he exclaimed. "The tongue is sharp like a knife, except it kills without drawing blood," as he laughed at his own joke.

"So, as always, the question of the day is, 'where do we go from here?'" he asked looking at his notes. "Please indulge me on this most auspicious of occasions. The mere thought of reporting these daily lies and propaganda, I mean *daily news*, is more than my heart can bear. Tonight, I will not insult you with more lies. Let's be brutally honest for once in our lives," he said. "They want me to tell you that today, July sixth, 2012; the Bureau of Labor Statistics released the Non-Farm Payrolls report. It showed eighty thousand new jobs have been created in the US economy. They tell me, I have to report this current event, but I can't. It's a lie. The real number is a loss of forty four thousand. Imagine where the markets would go, if they reported a loss of forty four thousand jobs, instead of the corrupted eighty thousand gains," he groaned in disgust. "I know this to be true because the birth/death adjustment for the month was a positive one hundred and twenty four thousand. This so-called adjustment accounts for jobs created or lost by small companies when they are born or die. How is it possible to arrive at such an adjustment? They guess, of course. See the problem, it's not real. It never was. How can you predict more new business openings than closings in such a depressed beaten down economy? Really, shouldn't it be just the opposite. Imagine if we dealt in reality, for a moment, instead of the fantasy of government adjustments and insane propaganda," he sighed. "The government can release any sort of number it wants but the rest of us wake up every day in the real world. You see, in China we doubt their press because it is a communist country," he stated.

"What does that say about us? If I recall, it was Thomas Jefferson that said the man who reads nothing at all is better educated than the man who reads nothing but newspapers."

"You see, it's a little white lie intended to make us feel better about ourselves. Why, because the battle for our minds has been lost for years. The truth no longer matters, only the soul and pocketbook remain. The battle for our soul is truly the last battle of the American Revolution," Mark exclaimed. "The trick in seeing the future is to look to the past. In 2006, a NYU economic professor named Nouriel Roubini warned us, and a skeptical IMF, that the United States was likely to face an once-in-a-lifetime housing bust, an oil shock, sharply declining consumer confidence, and ultimately a deep recession," he professed.

"One of his peers, a Nobel laureate named Paul Krugman said his once seemingly outlandish predictions have been matched or even exceeded by reality; which brings us to today," he consoled.

"In May 2012, Dr. Roubini predicted a perfect storm," he advised. "Stalling growth in the US, debt troubles in Europe, a slowdown in emerging markets, particularly China, and military conflict in Iran would come together to create a perfect storm for the entire global economy in 2013."

Roubini said, "this time around governments are running out of rabbits to pull out of the hat." Mark's face became serious at that point.

"Last week, Roubini told CNBC that there is 'virtually zero chance that pump-priming by central banks will succeed. It's like watching a slow motion train wreck.' Our destiny will unfold right before our eyes. At that point, there can be no more lies. The battle for the soul of America has begun since America represents the free world. Tyranny will become the ultimate adversary of our time. We will require extreme courage, strength, and God's wisdom on our side to win," Mark insisted. "And if we lose, then we shall witness, first hand, the second coming of the Dark Ages for our children."

"I know you don't want to hear it. The truth is depressing, it's so Kardashian," he consoled. "Yes, the woman got famous by making a sex tape, that's the truth. Her mother must be so proud; and in fact she actually is because society seems to embrace it. Of course, the truth hurts; it forced you to address your life and then deal with it. So please, for its own sake. Tonight, we shall not muzzle the dog. I think I'm getting excited."

"Now suppose, just suppose, what if the people running the government actually told you the truth? What a day that would be. I recall a poet that used this epitaph for his son who died in world war one. *If any question why we died, tell them, because our fathers lied.*

"It's still true, today. The founding fathers would be twisting in their grave to see the rhetoric that has evolved. Really, the unemployment rate is eight percent. We're not stupid," Mark seethed.

"The real unemployment rate is seventeen percent because it

actually counts everyone unemployed, not just the ones receiving benefits. The little white lie sounded better when you said eight percent. You'll sleep better at night not knowing the truth," he explained.

"Truth be told, if you just understand the lie; everything's better. But what if you don't, that's the problem," he questioned.

"Our politicians will always tell you, everything's fine. The economy's fine, Wall Street's fine, Main Street's fine. Even if they have to lie, everything is fine; until it's not fine. What if we're flying uncontrollably headlong into a train wreck," he warned? "What might that scenario look like?"

"Looting and pillaging, it's every man for himself. Live for the moment because tomorrow is meaningless. Forget our kids, forget our country, and forget everything that really matters. Nevertheless, we cannot have that. That wouldn't be happening now; would it," he insisted. "Not in America."

"What if you were the one in control and knew the party was over. Would you tell anybody? Would you say everything's fine? Then, loot like a pirate all the way to the bank. Enron did it cooking the books, Barclay's Libor scandal of lies, JP Morgan's London Whale rogue trader, Bernie Madoff's Ponzi scheme, and the list goes on and on. Yet somehow, CEO's compensation has tripled in the last decade. Why, because CEO's are the best liars of them all; it's called spin control and if you're good, bonuses in the billions. Where in the world does that money come from? Profits, doubtful, it came from duped investors. You and I, because we don't know the truth," he groaned. If you make money; you get a bonus. If you lose money; you get a bigger bonus."

"Which leads us to the billion dollar problem, what happens when there's nothing left to loot? The till is empty; now that's a tragedy," he revealed.

"So the question I'm asking is a simple one. Yes or no, have we actually hit the iceberg yet or not," he asked?

"I rarely ask a question to which I do not know the answer," he expressed. "Remember the Titanic; we could see it coming. It was right in front of us. But, once we hit that iceberg, it was all over. And right on cue, they said this ship is unsinkable. Everything's fine, we have nothing to worry about. Does that sound familiar; a few people knew the truth? Get those lifeboats going and by God I'm in one. Almost everyone thought it wouldn't sink, until it did. The sheep died, the wolves lived on to tell the tale," he replied with both hands on his head.

"So what's the truth? Tell me the truth, I can handle it. Such an honest gesture is not too much to ask; truth for its own sake.

"I'm reminded of a man I met in my youth. I was playing in the street when I saw the elderly man planting a tree in his front yard. I stopped to watch. After a moment, I asked, "Hey mister, what are you doing?"

"I'm planting a peach tree," the old man said.

"Why," Mark recalled?

"For the peaches, of course," the old man said.

"But, it's so small," I explained.

"Yeah," the old man said.

"And you're so old," I questioned.

"Bummer huh," the old man said.

"You'll never be able to eat any of those peaches," I replied.

"It's not for me," the old man said.

"Then who's it for," I said?

"It's for you," the old man said.

"Me," I questioned?

"Son, I've eaten a lot of peaches in my day. Peach jam, peach pie, peach ice cream, I enjoyed them all. When I was your age someone planted a peach tree for me. I hope someday; you'll do the same," the old man implored.

"I'll never forget that day. The idea that a man would do something like that amazed me. Why would he do that? I was just a child, too young to understand, but that idea had remained with me all my life. It wasn't until I became a man that I realized there is something bigger in the world than just me. It's our mark left upon the world, our families, and our legacy. Evidence that we were here," Mark expressed.

"I always thought it was easy to do the right thing; I was wrong. I know I can't save the world; but maybe I can save a little piece of it," Mark assumed as he puts on his walking headset.

"I want to talk for a moment about something I recently read. *Time Magazine*, June 11, 2012. The cover reads, *'How to Die'*. Sincerely, they intend to tell me how to die, as if people haven't been doing that for a million years. As if it was any of their business.

"They seem to be pushing a death agenda that devalued the lives of the elderly and actually encouraged adults to have their own parents killed in order to reduce medical costs.

"In fact, as *Time Magazine* said, organizations that embraced these 'outcome-based' death panels, actually receive a cash bonus when they save money by pulling the plug on Granny! Life has become cost effective.

"That's the answer to health care in America, you see. It's about killing your elders and then convincing yourself that you're compassionate for making sure they die sooner rather than later.

"We have the Geisinger Health System to thank. It is a system that many health care experts see as a model, a way to save significant amounts of money while providing better care," Joe Klein wrote.

"Over time, it became clear that quality health care can be provided in a way that made patients happy, for less money," Mr. Klein wrote. "After moving his parents to the Geisinger Health System, Mr. Klein wrote about how people stopped sticking needles in his parents during their last months of life. They stopped performing unnecessary and duplicative tests and procedures and they started speaking to him in a candid, yet humane, manner about the best way to let his parents pass on," he wrote.

"It's trendy to kill your parents off, didn't you know? It's good for the economy! And it's good for society! Death to grandma! For God's sake, if this is the battle for our soul, we will lose it, as well," Mark exclaimed. He walks over to the window to see the city lights at night.

"You must understand this story is personal for me. I've tried to live an honest life. A life without regrets, but the single most difficult thing I have ever had to do in my life is deal with the passing of my mother," Mark expressed with a somber voice.

"Do I regret what I did, yes? Did it have to be done, yes? Was it difficult to pull the plug on my mother, yes? But it was like a drop of water in an ocean of tears, compared to...having to watch her die before my eyes," Marks quivered with emotion.

"Having to sit and watch the woman that raised me, changed my diapers, and taught me how to become a man. She was the most important person in my life, ever. And I could do nothing but watch, knowing what I did, knowing what had to be done. Watching her die was unbearable.

"It is the only thing I've ever regretted in my life. When I close my eyes, I can still see her. It never goes away. Nothing else even came within a thousand miles of that day. That's the day you come to terms with your maker, forever, for what you did.

"Some people will do it because they see the light, some because they feel the heat. Regardless, I will never forget it as long as I live. On that day, when your heart died, your soul was in play," Mark paused for a moment of sadness causing dead air.

"I'm sorry; I did not intent to have dead air, tonight. I cannot help but remember the late great George Carlin's view of life. He said, "Life's journey is not to arrive at the grave safely in a well preserved body, but rather to skid in sideways, totally worn out, shouting what a ride!" He laughed a sympathetic laugh.

"Life is not measured by the breaths we take, but by moments that take our breath away. George was the man. Therefore, the lesson here is, or should I say the point is be careful what you wish for, all you trendies, because eventually, you'll be old, too!

"And if you create a society in which pulling the plug is the socially-acceptable way to kill off all the 'old and useless people'. Well then... don't be surprised when they cut off your feeding tube, too, and you'll suffer a long, slow, painful death while your own children cheer about how socially responsible they are," Mark said frankly. He returned to his chair and used the overhead microphone to adjust his demeanor to the audience.

"Sorry about that, I don't mean to be such a drama queen. It is just my style. See, that's not even the truth, I'm not sorry," Mark sneered.

"Perhaps a love story gone tragically bad, that would be uplifting. A few weeks ago, there was a man named Dominique Strauss Kahn. He was the head of a very powerful world organization simply called the IMF. The International Monetary Fund is an organization of a hundred and fifty countries, working to foster global monetary cooperation, secure financial stability, facilitate international trade, promote high employment and sustainable economic growth, and reduce poverty around the world.

"Sounds pretty good, doesn't it. Well, it's bull. They are the lender of last resort, when all else fails. These very powerful individuals oversee hundreds of billions of dollars given out in loans to the underprivileged of the world.

"This is a very influential man who, much to his dismay, had a long and drunken night in his New York hotel room. He saw his one true love, a thirty two year old immigrant chambermaid from Guinea, fleeing down the hotel corridor. She was screaming for help, with Dominique somehow still in his room, so they say." Mark enjoys his sarcastic look of disbelief.

"Suddenly, the police are on the scene and Dominique is accused of sexual assault with a million dollar bail bond. What a monster," he shuttered as he moved closer to the microphone.

"But, the plot thickens, it appears there is more to the story, a much different story at hand. So the question we should be asking, is why? Try to follow me on this, it gets complicated.

"What's important is Dominique made a bad decision. Oh, not with the chambermaid. He made it perfectly clear, he wanted the International Monetary Fund SDR's to be accepted as the currency of trade and commerce for the world. No longer would the US dollar hold that coveted role, such a fatal mistake.

"In just one moment of decision, one thought, in a single statement, Dominique managed to completely piss off three hundred million Americans, all by himself. I mean, you really have to try hard to piss off three hundred million people, it's no small feat," Mark insisted. He graciously lights up his cigar like a Cuban refugee landing at Miami Beach.

"Inevitably, the situation got worse. With great sadness, he resigned his position to avoid further embarrassment to the organization. The drama was over and a new head of the IMF took his place. Her name is Christine Lagarde," Mark smiled with his cigar in his cheek. "A very American friendly girl, the kind of girl you want to take home to mother, a girl that loved America.

"And this is where it gets really crazy. Suddenly, out of nowhere, the charges were dropped. It's was like a Christmas miracle. Dominique is declared innocent of all charges. A tremendous victory for a man wrongly accused. The system works, all hail the system.

"Not quite. Oh, he's free alright, but not enough to get his old job back as one of the most powerful and influential men in the world. He was finished because of a chambermaid from Guinea.

"I can't make this stuff up; really, I don't have that much imagination. He gently scratched his head in disbelief.

"So here's my point. Believe everything that's written. Don't rock the boat or think for yourself, for that matter. Just enjoy your life and be healthy consumers. It's under control, don't worry, be happy.

"Now, if you walk through life with blinders on, one thing is for sure. You're going to miss the hurt, but you'll feel the pain. It's been said that, ignorance is bliss, but knowledge is power. Yes, ignorance is bliss until the Mack truck is headed at you. Then it behooved you to know how to get out of the way. Knowledge has consequences and can be a burden, but which is better, a gun out there or my own gun here with me?

"The point is, when someone says to you the point is, they are trying to break down something very complicated into something that a third grader can understand. However, it's quite difficult to take something complicated and make it simple. There are a thousand idiots out there, more than willing to take something simple and make it complicated. The point, the moral to the story, the climax to the show is a simple, life is a gift," Mark graciously said with a smile to the audience. "Freedom is a simple gift, but it must be protected at all costs for it to last. And it is earned, it's certainly not free."

"Speaking of protecting it, I can't say enough about our friends over in the Middle East. Aren't they the best? We find oil in their country, set them up with refineries and distributors all over the world. We make them millions upon millions of dollars; that's simple, isn't it? What do we get in return for our pleasure; hate and oppression, price control and contempt for our efforts.

"Unbelievable, pardon my rant, but I have to get this out of my system. Seriously, when the stock market goes up, so does the price of oil. How is it that the price of oil is directly related to the Dow Jones Industrial average? Hey, America's doing great; let's charge them more for oil. They can afford it. What are they going to do about it, stop driving?

"Four dollars per gallon of gasoline kills the economy. It drains our purchasing power and puts American business, out of business. It is criminal, it is oppression. People have less money to spend on our advertisers and my show gets canned like a tuna," he bellowed.

"But, it doesn't stop there. The Dow Jones crashed because they sucked the life out of the country and suddenly, like a gift from God, the price of oil drops. The average gas price has come down about forty cents since the peak near four dollars a gallon in early April. With US drivers expected to use a hundred and thirty billion gallons of gasoline this year, the forty cent price break works out to about fifty three billion dollars in annual savings, fifty three billion dollars.

"With fifty two weeks in the year, you do the math. That's not pocket change. Money pours back into the economy and pop, it starts all over again. What do we make of this modern day miracle," Mark scolded.

"We're being played, played by our enemies, and played by the people that would like nothing better than to destroy us. They call us the Great Satan for a reason, they hate our guts. I don't know why, but they do, that's for sure. The Great Satan, are you kidding? Get a life.

"Our enemies are tyrants, nothing more. They want to oppress and control us because they can, nothing more. It's been that way for centuries. They have the supply and we need it. We will pay whatever price they demand for it, even if that price is freedom.

"We don't even care. We don't do anything about it, but cry. They tell us, they're our friends. They pat us on the back, so they know where to stab us. And we just roll over and take it. For God's sake, somebody grow a spine.

"As bad as it is, it's nothing compared to being played by your friends, betrayed by the people we live with. I'm talking about the mother of all mortgage melt downs, the crash of 2008," Mark stopped a moment to take a shot of whiskey. He seemed to be almost punishing himself. "Oh, it's going to be a bad night. Where was I? Oh yeah, stealing a blind man's pencils."

"Try this on for size; sell a mortgage to a guy that doesn't even have a job. Then, put all those failed mortgages together and package them. Pay off a few rating agencies to stamp a triple 'A' rating on it. Sell the investments all over the world; commissions will be outrageous. Seriously, we'll be richer than your wildest dream. And when eight out of ten houses on Sesame Street are in foreclosure, the portfolios crash, and investors lose their shirt. Who cares, we'll be on a beach in Aruba. We'll be the tannest white men in the Caribbean. Oh man, that sounds good. And you won't believe the best part, no one went to jail. The rules of government regulation protect them.

"Steal a little, go you jail. Steal a lot, go to Congress. Incredibly, the government bailed everyone out. And where does the government get its money, from you. It's completely over the top. You paid for it, idiot.

"They're drinking rum on the beach with your money. You want to know the really sad part, you don't even care. You let them do it. You let them walk away," Mark screamed as he sits back in his chair and puts his hands on his head. He took a moment to get back under control.

"And now, the entire country is sixteen trillion in debt, not counting social security and health care under funding. We owe more money than any country in the history of the world, ever," Mark revealed with a sarcastic attitude.

"I mean no one is even close. We spend a trillion dollars a year more than we bring in. That's like losing three billion dollars a day, down the drain. We could care less, you know why? Because, we have the magic money printing machine to print as much money as we need. We don't have to earn it, it's free. We are the luckiest country on the planet Earth, while it lasts. Now, you understand why Dominique got fired. Just imagine what I could do with a magic money machine? It would be Vegas every night, baby. The party would never end. We could do anything, anywhere. I'd be the tannest white man in the Caribbean," Mark laughed and knocked a few papers off his desk and finds another cigar under the stack.

"Nice, but seriously, I like to say, but seriously because what I'm about to say next is going to be completely out of control.

"But seriously, in 2008, the stock market crashed and burned, it made the depression look like a day in the park. Parents in Beverly Hills started considering raising their own kids. I even saw the CEO of Wal-Mart shopping at Wal-Mart. Hot Wheels stock was trading higher than General Motors.

"Then, like a raging bull fighter, the treasury went to work printing money; we're talking an unprecedented rate in the history of the world type of printing money, billions upon billions. Talk about stimulus, it was heroin. But what's really mad is, we haven't stopped, haven't even slowed down. We pumped over two trillion into the market, that's with a capital "T", and it roared back like never before, then seven hundred billion in bailouts and eight hundred billion more in another stimulus. Brother, the debt business was booming, Jack.

"It was completely and utterly market manipulation on the grandest scale and it worked. We did it, Helicopter Ben to the rescue. Did we pay any of our debt; are you crazy, of course not! The five trillion dollar party was back on, unbelievable. Vegas, baby, and we were back on top," Mark arrogantly lit his new cigar.

"I don't mean to be cynical. It's just a house of cards and everybody knows it. If you're not part of the solution; you are the problem.

"I recall the Tea Party and Occupy Wall Street movement trying to do something about it. If you're young, that's the place to be. Trust me; they have your interests at heart. But, special interest groups are buying politicians with millions in campaign donations. They just can't compete.

"Riddle me this. What do you get for eight hundred thousand dollars in campaign donations," Mark expressed? "You're the ambassador to Aruba and the tannest white man in the Caribbean."

"Let me be clear on this point, I'm not against America, I'm not putting it down. Quite the contrary, I believe it's the greatest country ever known to mankind, blessed by God. There was a time when we said to the kings of the world, no more.

"America is an experiment in freedom. The likes the world has never seen before. We have so much to be grateful for, so many advantages. It just tears my heart out to see it being abused. The greed and corruption that run ramped today is not what the founding fathers envisioned for America or the way God intended it to be.

"It's the land of the free and home of the brave. Give us your huddled masses, yearning to live free. A government of the people, by the people, for the people, there are heroes among us, everywhere you look. We have nothing to fear but fear itself and a date that will live in infamy. We are famous for our strength.

"Is it possible that we still have enemies, of course. How would they attack us? Militarily, they would never stand a chance. Economically, that's how we defeated communism in the Soviet Union, remember. It's not been that long ago. I love this country, I believe it is God's favorite, too. If we were ever under attack, I would fight with every last drop of blood to defend it.

"The government, however, is massive, complex, and difficult to understand, it may seem like Chinese, but if you look at it like a single household. It actually makes a lot of sense.

"What do we owe, what do we have, and what's coming in. Keep it simple. The average American family makes about forty thousand a year. With a married couple, both working, let's be generous, call it eighty thousand. So, what do we owe? A house payment, two cars, insurance, utilities, food, clothing, kids, it goes on and on. Don't forget, Keeping up with the Jones, not the Kardashians, just the Jones.

"At the end of the day, what do you have, nothing. The bank owns the house for thirty years. By the time you own your car, it's trashed. No savings to speak of. But, let's not forget credit card debt, the blood suckering drug dealers that tempt us to extreme.

"The average American is into them for about eight grand. That's the average. What if you lose your job or a pay cut reduces your income? You're in a tight spot. You have to cut back on expenses, find another job, something to make ends meet. It's not that hard to understand. A five year old gets it. The government, however, doesn't have a clue.

"We call it, living within your means. Governments call it austerity. I know you've heard that word before but you're not exactly sure what it means. Well, boys and girls, it's called responsibility. You won't find that word in government.

"Every presidential candidate, in the last hundred years, that's run on that platform has lost, miserably. So politicians say we're not in a recession. That's what they are selling and that's what we want to hear. Do you buy it?

"Approximately one-fourth of all American children are enrolled in the food stamp program. The number of Americans on food stamps has increased from thirty two million to forty six million in recent years. In fact, approximately half of all U.S. college graduates under the age of twenty five were either unemployed or underemployed last year. America's trillion dollar student loan crisis is failing, not because of the debt, because of a lack of jobs.

"What I mean is, at this point, one out of every four American workers has a job that pays ten dollars an hour or less. As a result, approximately twenty five million American adults are living with their parents.

"As the middle class shrinks, the ranks of the poor continue to expand. Sadly, at this point half of all Americans are either considered to be low income or are living in poverty. Forty two percent of all American workers are currently living paycheck to paycheck, almost half of America," Mark professed. "The land of the free and the home of the brave, that's a hundred and thirty million people."

"It was reported that twenty thousand people applied for just nine hundred jobs at a Hyundai plant in Montgomery, Alabama. Are you kidding me! So, let me ask you this? Does this look like prosperity to you? Stop and think. Does it seem like we're at war or might I be an idiot? And the government is nowhere to be found.

"At some point, money from Heaven will be the path to destruction. We can print money, until we run out of trees, it won't help. Governments and central bankers are not going to do anything until there's a serious crisis. That's the point. Beware the politicians, everywhere. In school, they excelled in recess but have excelled at little since," Mark warned.

"You want to see a serious crisis. Remember the IMF, that wonderful benevolent organization, they just bought Greece. Yes, Greece can you imagine. They just bought a country. Did you see that coming, because it has never happened before?

"Greece is stone cold broke, just like the future of America, and that's a serious crisis. They owe more money than they will ever be able to pay back and now, they can't make the interest payments on their debt. That's the crisis, the interest payment not the debt. They can't get a loan to pay the interest on the debt. The real problem is the pending default on all that debt we read about in the papers.

"Just like a house that can no longer make its payments; it's foreclosure city. The bank owns your house buddy, and you can bet the ranch, that the IMF owns Greece. They bought and settled the Greek debts, paid off their creditors with pennies on the dollar, and took over the country. Any decision the Greek government wants to make must be approved by the IMF; no more freedom," Mark groaned looking for his bottle of ten-year-old whiskey. He took another shot to ease the pain of his conscience.

"Now, I know you didn't see that coming. Last time I checked when a government is owned by an individual, a group, or a party. It's called Fascism and brother, that's not a good thing.

"Why is that so hard to understand? I am beside myself with grief over the loss of something we cherish so much. You wake up one day and it's gone. How can you choose oppression over freedom? What in the world is wrong with you?

"All those wars fought, young men died, countries ravaged and all for naught. All those soldiers died in vain when on a single day, freedom died and oppression won," Mark barked as the liquor starts to show its effects.

"And it doesn't stop there; countries like Spain, Portugal, Ireland, and Italy are all in the same leaking boat. What's happened in this crazy old world," he slurred his words before breaking into song, "Momma, don't let your babies grow up to be Fascists. Don't let them live free and vote like they want, make them be tyrants and lawyers and such," Mark stopped singing much to the appreciation of the audience. "I'm sorry Willie, that's wrong on so many different levels. I don't know what came over me. I suppose a monetary lapse of freedom will do that to you."

"Maybe I need another drink. I just broke my own heart, if I actually had one," Mark sniveled while pouring another drink. "I just lost it when Greece and France voted down capitalism and the ability to live within your means in favor of socialism. It seems the lure of living on other people's money is more than any Euro trash can resist. They have surrendered liberty for a lifetime of servitude.

"Such is life, C'est la vies, welcome to socialism," he mourned. "I suppose Benjamin Franklin said it best; those who would give up an essential liberty for temporary security deserve neither liberty nor security. Ultimately, man will be governed by God or by tyrants. Viva La France."

"Regrettably, we're forced to look austerity straight in the eye. Greece is living it, right now. If you want to know what America is up against, this is it. Here it comes, right in your face, Uncle Sam.

"It's time for our nightly top ten. Tonight, from CNBC news, we examine the top ten austerity measures that the country of Greece is implementing, or should I say imploding. Here you go; this is what it looks like.

"Number ten, Taxes will Increase - In Greece, taxes increase by two billion euros this year and three billion the next year. There will be higher property taxes and an increase in the value-added tax. Break out your wallet folks, the government needs your money.

"Number nine, Luxury taxes will be introduced on yachts, pools, and cars with special levies on profitable firms, high-value properties, and people with high incomes. It doesn't pay to be rich in Greece anymore. Who really needs a yacht, anyway? If you're rich enough to have a yacht, why choose Greece. Just use it to winter on the Riviera.

"Number eight, excise taxes on fuel, cigarettes and alcohol will rise by one-third. That takes all the fun out of it. This party is over. But that's okay; you don't have enough money to drive to the store, anyway. I'd better have another drink before it is too late," he giggled.

"Number six, defense spending will be cut by two hundred million euros in 2012 and three hundred million each year from 2013 to 2015. I mean really, go ahead, attack us, take us over, payoff our debt, please, hurry up we surrender.

"Number seven, public sector wages will be cut by fifteen percent. So, with prices going through the roof, you have even less to spend. The fun just never stops. We're half way there and we haven't even hit to the good stuff.

"Number six; I thought I already said number six. Sorry my bad; okay no more whiskey, yeah right."

"Number five, education spending will be cut by closing or merging two thousand schools. Why do you need an education if there aren't any jobs? What's the point, get it. I told you it was getting better.

"Number four, Social Security will be cut by one billion euros this year, one billion in 2012, one billion in 2013, another billion in 2014 and seven hundred million in 2015, if you can hold out that long. The retirement age will be raised to sixty five from sixty one, as well. Get back to work you slacker. You're never going to retire, anyway. You can't afford it. You're right, grandma, I would like fries with that burger.

"If you think I'm kidding, you're going to love this. Number three, the Greek government will privatize a number of its enterprises, including the gambling monopoly, several port operations, Hellenic Telecom and sell its stake in Athens Water, Hellenic Petroleum, PPC electric utility and Greek lender ATE bank, as well as state land and mining rights. Privatize, that's a nice way of saying, fire sale. A century old country, up for sale, maybe they could build an Indian reservation in a casino. I mean gambling, telecom, electricity, state land. Come on over, it's your chance to own a piece of Greece; it is completely out of control. You think they would sell the Grand Canyon. I'd sell West Virginia, five million people, fifteen last names. You ever been there, it sucks.

"Number two, only one in ten civil servants retiring this year will be replaced and one in five in coming years. I heard Exxon lay off twenty five Congressmen. No more free rides, who'd really want to work for a bankrupt government, Maestro, drum roll please.

"And the number one reason why austerity in Greece really sucks, health care spending will be cut by three hundred million euros this year and two billion euros from 2012 to 2015. Don't get sick in a hospital in Greece, you'll check in, but you won't check out," Mark rejoiced. The audience applauded.

"It's not a pretty picture, to say the least. It's actually quite sad. It doesn't have a happy ending either. Here it is America, are you ready? An elderly Greek man, who lost his government pension, walked into the Athens parliament square, pulled a gun and shot himself in front of hundreds of people," Mark said sadly.

"A woman heard the man say 'I don't want to leave my debts to my children.' After yelling it to the crowd, he pulled the trigger. He left a note behind saying, 'I have debts, and I can't stand this anymore. The government had annihilated any hope for my survival and I could not get any justice. I cannot find any other form of struggle except a dignified end, before I have to start scrounging for food from the trash,' he said in the note.

"His lesson to the world was, don't depend on anyone but yourself. The government has its own agenda and it's not yours," Mark added.

"So what do you do? No political candidate is going to go anywhere near that, not now, not ever. It's the United States of Europe in your face, can you say Storm the Bastille.

"Greek and American politicians have the same idea on how to handle the situation, just get another credit card. Seriously, get another credit card to pay their bills with. And when that card is done, get another and another and another. It's insane and entirely shameful.

"That's the plan until their term is up and can no longer run for office. Retire on a beach, get it. But here's the downside, remember the civil war, when the southern states seceded from the union. It got bloody. Greece wants out, they're done. Spain's right behind them.

"The point is, when you leave the Euro zone, you will default on all country to country debts. For Germany, that's about two hundred billion lost, gone, in an instant. The rich countries get richer and the poor get poorer unless the poor don't pay anything back. Then, everyone is poorer. When that happens, it's going to get bloody. You don't believe me. Yesterday, Greece sold four billion dollars of Greek bonds to the Greece Central Bank. The bank stole the money from Germany when German BMW's were sold in Greece. The money for the BMW's went to the Greece Central Bank and was supposed to go back to the German manufacturer. But it never got there. It stayed in Greece and now the government has it. They desperately need it to run the country. Yeah, it's going to get bloody, very bloody before we're done.

"So it boils down to just three options. First, austerity, cost cutting, and payoff your debt. Bite the bullet, work harder, it's going to hurt. By the way, good luck getting elected. You'll need it.

"Option two, throw money at the problem until it stopped being a problem. Your sole job is to spend money with reckless abandon. I could do that job in my sleep. If you gave me ten thousand dollars and told me it was my job to go and spend it, could I do it? Oh, yeah. I'd be the top spending producer of other people's money in the world. A one man stimulus programs to jump start the economy. That would be so easy. However, what's difficult is making money. Oh, what a concept. That might take some skill.

"So, when you consider electing the next President of the United States. Ask him if he knows how to spend money, because that's all he wants to do. You don't believe me, in the eight years George Bush was president, and we spent four trillion dollars that we didn't even have. We were forced to get a new credit card, and we did.

"But that's nothing. In just the first four years of Barrack Obama, we spent five trillion that we didn't have, either. Just like its monopoly money. There's no skill in that.

"In the first two hundred and twenty four years of American history, we ran up six trillion in debt. Since the year two thousand, we're now sixteen trillion in debt and growing, it's unprecedented. We're not just spending money we don't have, we're gushing it. It is completely out of control.

"So, the billion dollar question is, if the government of the United States of America is spending money that they don't have, then why can't I?

"You can't, because that would be irresponsible. You can't," a pause of dead air fills the theater. "Where's the fun in that. It's time for a commercial break. I think I need to throw up, now," Mark looks exhausted and beaten down. The spotlight faded to black. The stage is silent for a moment, then a violent roar, like a man calling up the dinosaurs of old. The spotlight came back on and he has returned to the microphone.

"I used to be indecisive. Now I'm not sure. However, I do feel better about our third and final option, to do zilch. It doesn't seem like much, but when you consider option one and two. Doing nothing started looking pretty good.

"Option three is to kick the can down the road. I know you've heard that before. By kicking the can down the road, we create a very comfortable today, but unfortunately, sacrifice the future in doing so. Someday, someone's children and grandchildren will have to pay our bills. But not today, that's the beauty of it, that's the point.

"Live for today, live for the moment. You know the drill. Life goes on; everything's fine, until it's not fine. You can only keep the wolves at bay for so long. Perhaps, on that day, a leader will come along to save us all. I hope he's a good man. He'll need to be," he grumbled as he adjusts his overhead microphone.

"So back to my point, before I was rudely interrupted. The point is, the American Dream is being systematically devastated right before of our eyes and most Americans don't even realize what's happening.

"Back in the day, if you worked hard and played by the rules you could always find a good job. That good job would enable you to buy a house, buy at least one car and support a family. It would also enable you to take a couple of vacations each year and buy some nice things for your family.

"After working for thirty or forty years you would look forward to a comfortable retirement. Nostalgia isn't what it used to be. As I said, that was back in the day, not today's American Dream.

"Once upon a time, the United States had the largest and most prosperous middle class in the history of the world, but now that's changing at a breathtaking pace. Our economy isn't producing nearly enough jobs for all of us anymore.

"The cost of living continues to rise steadily every single year while wages do not. Millions more Americans are falling into poverty and dependence on the government is at an all-time high.

"Something is fundamentally wrong with our economy. It's not working the way it used to and the middle class is being absolutely shredded.

"There's a good man, a Nobel laureate named Joseph Stieglitz, a Columbia University professor, who wrote a book about the current inequality of America. He says that we are no longer the land of opportunity. Imagine that. He must be a genius. He also says that the American Dream is a myth that it never really existed.

"All the hope of the world, the dream of a better life, a world free of oppression to worship God in his own way, it never happened. The sea to shining sea was just a myth," Mark stopped to look at his smoking cigar and shake his head.

"He explains his point of view by saying, in short, the status you're born into, rich or poor, is more likely to be the status of your adult life in America, even more likely than Old Europe.

"Perhaps, he doesn't understand the meaning of the American

Dream. Perhaps, he seeks the material comfort of wealth and power, the opportunity for prosperity and success regardless of social class or circumstances of birth. Maybe it's the notion that our social, economic, and political system makes success possible for every individual. I think not.

"I think the American Dream is more. It is rooted in the Declaration of Independence which admirably states that all men are created equal and endowed by their creator with certain inalienable rights such as Life, Liberty, and the Pursuit of Happiness.

"What about these conceits? Such things cannot be touched or obtained with money. They must be felt, experienced, and treasured. It's the very nature of man to yearn to be free. Is this not the American Dream promised to us all?

"So what are we to do with Mr. Stieglitz? How do we understand such a man? Truth is I'm afraid he might not be wrong. With over forty nine million Americans who can't feed themselves or their family, America had to spend sixty five billion dollars, just to survive. The founding fathers did not intend America to be a welfare state. Rather, a land of opportunity.

Mr. Stieglitz would say that means forty nine million kids will grow up to be adults, alas, depending on food stamps just to survive.

"We desperately need the strength and wisdom to triumph over our fears and give us the courage to do what is right. We must come to the understanding, the understanding that our worth is something more than paper and coin.

"This is who we are as American's, like nothing the world has ever seen. We're endowed by our creator for something more. The President of the United States must understand this is our destiny," Mark pleaded.

"Most American families are finding it harder and harder to make it through each passing year, and unless a 'miracle' happens, things are going to continue to get even harder.

"I cannot emphasize it enough, we need a miracle and we need a president. Ronald Reagan, Theodore Roosevelt, Abraham Lincoln, the greats. The men, who molded America, made it great. Bottom line, we're in way over our head and without real leadership, forget it. It's not happening.

"The president, first and foremost, needs experience in government, but not Washington, DC. The political world, special interest groups, and the desire to protect your job at all costs have stained him. I heard Obama changed his slogan to *Maybe We Can*."

"Secondly, you have to be committed to making money. Losing money is no longer acceptable. The government must stop the deficits. Sustainable growth and controlled expenses lead to a surplus, thus paying down the debt. I cannot remember a president who actually made money. I saw Bill and Hillary traveling together, and they actually shared a room," Mark sneered. "The point is you have to be pro-business. That's what we do. Not just in America, all over the world. Free trade goes hand in hand with free democracy. One does not exist without the other."

"Finally, the president must unite the country, both republican and democrat. He must speak to both parties to do what's in the best interest of America. I know it's huge. No one has done that in decades; however, it is critical. If you can't overhaul the government, you're not the ideal candidate for the future. Maybe it can't be done," Mark said reluctantly. "He must be right for the job and the job must be right for him. It's our only hope," he paused to reflect on his thoughts. "We need a man who plants an entire rainforest full of peach trees. God bless you, we need you now, more than you know."

"For the record, I will not be part of a generation that corrupted the best thing that ever happened to the world. Are we clear on that? The children of America have the right to a free country. They have to right to opportunity, to liberty, and to the pursuit of happiness. The same as you had growing up. Sixteen trillion in national debt and rising will rob them of these gifts. This debt will cause incomes to fall and prices to rise, crushing the middle class into economic slavery. That's not a threat, it's a promise. So, if I get a little bent out of shape, that's why," Mark explained as he organized his desk to take callers. "I will thankfully sacrifice whatever I need in order to guarantee this country's freedom for this generation and the next."

"It's time to open up the phone lines and talk to America. What's on your mind, I'm here. Pick up the phone and make that call this morning. I promise I won't laugh, much. We have our first caller," Mark expressed with excitement. "Good morning, you're on KBRG live radio, *State of the Nation*, have we hit the iceberg yet or not?"

"You're a liar, I'm glad you're getting canned. Would you like some cheese with that whine," said a young man on the other end of the phone.

"Hey, I know you, you're that suicidal twin that killed his brother by mistake," Mark snapped.

"I did not," the first caller barked.

"Judging from your voice, I'll say your twenty years old and you're just getting off work at two in the morning. That would probably mean you work at Jack-in-the-Box. And let's see, you're the guy who works the fries," Mark pointed out with a sharp tongue.

"Hey, I work the grill. I haven't worked fries in over six months," the first caller gripped. "I'm moving up, dude."

"Oh, definitely Generation Y, maybe Generation X but they're too old for you. Or should I just say echo boomer," Mark said.

"Am not," the first caller blurted.

"Really, your parents are divorced because your father worked sixty hours a week and was never home for you," Mark explained. "You sat around the house saying, I want my MTV. So, you can't get a decent job and you have a tattoo. The longest you've held a job is a year and a half. You value time over money and relationships over work, hence the reason you can't hold a job. Your parents must be so proud," Mark boasted with an exaggerated sense of irony.

"Who do you think you are, my dad," the first caller cried.

"I'm sorry, I didn't mean it. I'm speaking in generalities. I'm sure you're not like that. So, before you get stoned, do you mind if I ask you a few questions," Mark suggested?

"Dude," the first caller bellowed in anger.

"Dude, have you stopped beating your girlfriend, yet," Mark said?

"What," the first caller said.

"So how much do you make a year? Can you even get a date on twenty-five thousand dollars a year? Tell me what the hot chicks do at Jack," Mark said.

"The register, that's where the money is; those chicks are all about the money," the first caller expressed with attitude.

"At Jack," Mark said?

"Yeah," the first caller said.

"Do you think most chicks are all about the money," Mark questioned?

"Yeah, it's America. Make some coin and be the tannest white man in the Caribbean. You said it, bro," the first caller said.

"You do realize that there is absolutely impossible for you to ever go anywhere near the Caribbean. You're twenty, no college, no skills, no goals and nothing to hang your hat on as an accomplishment. I mean, dude, where do you see yourself in five years, the morgue," Mark argued.

"I'm going to be manager," the first caller blurted.

"Of a Jack, no way, come on. Do you think someone is going to turn a million dollar a year restaurant operation over to a kid without a clue," Mark insisted.

"You don't know anything," the first caller cried out.

"I've a Ph.D. in economics. You're lucky you graduated high school. But, no you're right. You got it all figured out. You're on top of the world," Mark consoled.

"I'm so glad you're getting canned," the first caller laughed.

"Well I'm glad my show getting cancelled is making you feel better about yourself. Let me give you a clue. The highest paying job you'll ever get is jury duty. You'll be crossing over the Mexican border looking for a job. Someday, you'll wake up and you'll be a sixty-year-old. Guess what you'll have seen? Over the next forty years, the world's population will outgrow its water supply, which means less food can be grown, less meat for your burgers. The price of food blows off the charts, dude. When you order a burger, some kid is going to ask, if you can afford fries with that. You'll have to start eating regular brownies, dude," Mark preached.

"What do you know," the first caller said.

"If I were to agree with you, we'd both be wrong. But that's okay because the world's oil supply will be gone. India and China's increased demand along with the end of locating easy oil will cause the price of oil to kill your dream of ever owning a car. I've got you a bicycle with the word 'dude' on it," Mark laughs.

"You're so uncool," the first caller said.

"Oh yes, and you're going to see it all, first hand, through your bloodshot eyes. You see kid, nothing stays the same. It either gets better or it gets worse. Maybe Michael Phelps will share his bong with you. Buddy, you have no one to blame but yourself," Mark stated.

"What's wrong with you? You just hate people. You hate everybody," the first caller yelled.

"I don't hate people, just stupid people. Hey, it's not your fault. You're the most protected generation in history. Have you ever ridden a bike without a helmet, or sat in a car without being secured by a seat belt. Of course not, you've been hovered over by your 'helicopter parents'. You're like a trophy kid," Mark instructed.

"Trophy kid," the first caller said.

"Yeah, when you were growing up, you played sports, right. Did you get a trophy for just showing up? Of course, you did. You didn't earn it. You didn't achieve anything or work for it. It was given to you. Buddy, that's not how it works in the real world. I'm sorry, but if you don't do your job or do it badly, somebody else comes along and does it better. You're out," Mark preached.

"I'm not the one getting canned," the first caller screamed.

"No you're not, yet. You were pampered, nurtured, and given everything they needed or simply wanted. It's no wonder you grew up with a sense of entitlement. How much credit card debt do you have," Mark said?

"That's none of your business," the first caller complained.

"That much, so you're technically savvy but financially illiterate. This reflects an attitude of apathy or I'll worry about it later mentality. That's very common," Mark said.

"Why are you so mad at me," the first caller cried?

"Because you still have time, time to get it right. Aristotle argued that the young men often brought change and complained that it was for the worse. Yet, this change occurred because of the energy of young people. He also recognized the value of wisdom in older people. Together, you could become unstoppable. The wisdom of age is education. Aristotle believed that the educated differ from the uneducated as much as the living from the dead," Mark professed.

"Education is an ornament in prosperity and a refuge in adversity. It is the best provision for the journey to old age. He said it is the mark of an educated mind to be able to entertain a thought without accepting it."

"I hate you," the first caller blurted.

"What lies in our power to do, rest in our power not to do," Mark said.

"I hate you, even more," the first caller grumbled.

"Anybody can become angry, that's easy, but to be angry with the right person and to the right degree and at the right time and for the right purpose, and in the right way, now that is not easy. Thank you, Aristotle my friend," Mark explained. "The point is you still have time to educate yourself, to listen to someone. You don't have to listen to me, but find someone you admire. A good man you trust. I know a man, I think you might like. His name is Jim Rogers."

"Never heard of him," the first caller snapped.

"Jim is a legendary investor who co-founded the Quantum Fund with George Soros in 1970; it returned four thousand percent while the S&P five hundred did only fifty percent. In 1980, he retired at the age of thirty-seven. He bought a motorcycle and spent a number of years traveling across China and six continents. He's taught at Columbia University and authored an amazing bestselling book called *A Gift for my Children*," Mark revealed. "They call him the Indiana Jones of Finance. I think you would actually like him."

"In his book, he gave fatherly advice to his two young daughters. This advice is meant for any child looking to make their way in this modern world," Mark explained.

"He says, swim your own races. Do not let others do your thinking for you; rely on your own intelligence; it's important to decide for yourself what's important and what you want to do before you turn to others. Be who you are; be original; be bold; and above all, be ethical.

"When it comes to education, there's no such thing as *enough*. No finish line! He says, educate yourself to the world, and let it be a part of your perspective. Do not rely on just books; go and see the world; experience life as they do; see the world from the ground up.

"Understand this, if everyone saw himself as a citizen of the world rather than his own town, city, or country, the world would be a much more peaceful place. Keep an open mind and be a world citizen.

"Philosophy will teach you how to think for yourself; you must learn to think at a profound level if you want to understand yourself and what's important to you. You must know yourself if you want to accomplish anything in life.

"Think outside the established framework, to examine things independently, this is true philosophy. Draw conclusions from your observations as well as on the basis of logic.

"Nothing is really new. What is happening now has happened before and will happen again. Learn from it; use it to your advantage.

"Above all, he says, discover your passion. Age is irrelevant when you're passionate about a goal; when you find something that interests you, just do it! The quickest way to success is to do what you like and give your best; dedicate yourself to what you feel passionate about; try as many things as you can, then pursue the one about which you're passionate.

"Live your life with a dream; if you continue to be passionate and work hard at what you truly love to do, you eventually find that dream.

"His advice to the world, anything that is a must-see, must-try, must-read, must certainly be avoided, especially if it's popular. Once you do get to know and understand yourself, remember who you are and stay with it; and don't be greedy. If you let vanity and self-importance take over, you will lose all that you have achieved.

"If you're looking for success, be quick to start something new, something that no one else has tried; the more certain something is, the less likely it is to be profitable; if anyone laughs at your idea, view it as a sign of potential success. Attention to details is what separates success from failure; the devil in life is in the details.

"However, he left us with a warning shot across our bow. He says, with all sincerity, people need to stop spending money they don't have. The solution to too much debt is not more debt."

"Just because you have a way to get the banks to lend you money, doesn't solve the problem, it made the problem worse," Mark insisted. "Governments need to stop coming to the rescue of failing banks. We're going to have financial Armageddon, anyway, when the rest of the world stopped giving those people more money."

"Jim concluded by asking, what are you going to do in two, three, four years when the market suddenly says *no more money* and the Germans don't have the money and the American debt has gone completely through the roof?

"Quite a question," Mark said. "Are you still with me, son."

"Yeah," the first caller sneered.

"Oh yeah, and he says, don't get married until you are at least twenty eight and know a bit more about yourself and the world. What do you think about that," Mark grinned with a half smirk cigar smile.

"Whatever," the first caller said.

"We are talking about your future, you know. I hope this helps. Oh well, it's been so good talking with you, son. Good luck and the best to you in the future," Mark said as he puts his finger down on the disconnect button creating a dial tone.

"There's always something magical about two in the morning. Ladies and gentlemen, the future of the country is in solid hands. You have nothing to worry about," Mark proclaimed. "Who's next? Hello, we have another caller."

"Good morning, you're on KBRG live radio, *State of the Nation*, have we hit the iceberg yet or not," Mark repeated?

"I'm worried about social security," the second caller said.

"You're a boomer. I love boomers," Mark rejoiced. "Boomers gave us, a man on the moon, Vietnam, Hula Hoops, Woodstock, civil rights on the front lines of social change, the Pill, the Battle on Michigan Avenue, Tune in, Turn on, and Drop out, Watergate, The Feminine Mystique, Easy Rider, Cocaine, Muhammad Ali, The Who, The Seeker and Bob Dylan. God, I love Bob Dylan. 'All I can do is be me, whoever that is,' Bob said that.

"You should be worried about social security. After decades of 'selfish' prosperity, many boomers now worry they'll outlive their savings, and wonder if they might be to blame. The recession couldn't have come at a worse time for the oldest of them, who turned sixty five in 2011," Mark explained.

I'm eligible to take it next month, but they tell me to wait until later," the second caller stated. "It will be more money then."

"If you're still alive, it will. Waiting to take it until your older helps the government reduce the number of years it has to payout. That's good for them but not for you. Think about it. Consider the source when taking advice. The government expects you to pass away at seventy two. That's why they want you to start taking payments later. But, they still have to pay out a portion to your spouse. But how long is she going to be around without a husband, get it." Mark indicated. "Which bodes another question, why do husbands always die before their wives?

"I don't know," the second caller said.

"Because they want to," Mark laughed. "I can't believe you're a boomer. What's on your mind?"

"Some say we'll run out of money and there won't be any social security," the second caller groaned with concern.

"Are you having an out-of-money experience? Don't worry, it'll never happen. They'll just print more money if needed. You can't have a million eighty year old men standing on street corners with a tin cups. It's not good business. Now with that being said, you have to understand. Old people don't spend money. That's not really a good thing for the economy. They save their money for a surgery or procedure or whatever," Mark comforted.

"I know," the second caller said.

"But you've given us so much. The boomers, for good or bad, are the economic motor that has driven the economy of the United States of America, if not the entire world for the last twenty years," Mark bragged. "As we decide which cars we're going to buy, and which clothes we're going to wear, and what food we're going to eat, we've absolutely had the power. Seventy seven million baby boomers have led this country out of the three television network station eras."

"Yeah," the second caller said.

"And now you're old, older than dirt. All the things you've learned, the things you know, all that knowledge. And you've absolutely have no idea what to do.

"What do you suggest," the second caller said?

"Seventy seven million baby boomers could elect a president, elect a congress, and elect a house of representatives to do absolutely everything they dreamed of doing. All you have to do is just one thing, organize. Organize your vote. The republicans have their elephant, the democrats their donkey. Why can't the boomers have their man? You know they'd win. But, you had better hurry. You're not getting any younger.

"I hear you," the second caller said.

"No you don't. Where it really gets ugly, is the trend. It is against you. Ten thousand boomers a day turn sixty five in this country, every day for the next nineteen years. The baby boomers generation is getting old," Mark proclaimed. "I want what's mine, and I want it now! That was quite the battle cry for an entire generation. I don't think they'll be quite so gung ho on their way out. Don't expect the market to rally on that news. Take your money and get out. It's the end of an era. Seriously, there will come a day when the last baby boomer will pass away from this Earth forever. The generation will be just a distant memory."

"You make it sound so cold," the second caller mumbled.

"Unfortunately, the truth usually is. What if we simply don't have an answer, as a society, to the problem of a very large number of relatively unhealthy people who live into their eighties and nineties? And what we end up doing is either place them in warehouses, supposed care facilities for the elderly, though they're nothing more than dying motels. Or this scenario one sometimes hears, we end up exporting them, against their will. That cold enough for you," Mark emphasized.

"I can't imagine," the second caller fumed. "This is a nightmare. What can we do to stop it?"

"If we really want to end it right, I suggest we get back to the ideals, the fire, which we started life with. We have to realize that our last obligation is not to put an unconscionable burden on our children and grandchildren. We need to go out serving," Mark explained.

"Serving, I'm far too old to serve. When my wife says, let's go upstairs and make love. My answer is, Honey, I can't do both," the second caller laughed.

"That's funny," Mark grinned.

"Getting lucky means you find your car in the parking lot," the second caller laughs again.

"Where's the beef," Mark grinned again. "Seriously, but serving doesn't have to be hard. It can be fun. It can be the adventure of a lifetime."

"I afraid I don't have any adventure left," the second caller said. "Thanks, I'll be sorry to see you go."

"Hold on. Look, I like you, so what's your name," Mark asked?

"Bob," the second caller said.

"Bob, I'd like to help you. Get a pencil, you're going to want to write this down," Mark said.

"Okay, let me get one," Bob said.

"While we have a moment, I want to thank everyone that has

helped make *State of the Nation* a memorable part of my life. It's been a privilege and a pleasure. I feel the need to give something in return. That's what we're doing now," Mark explained.

"I'm back," Bob said.

"Good Bob, you're from generation that asked 'What's in it for me', right. Well, 'what's in it for you' is this. Have you ever considered becoming an ex-pat," Mark asked.

"Ex what," Bob said.

"An ex-pat is an expatriate who now lives abroad, usually retired," Mark said. "It's considered an alternative to retiring in America."

"I could never do that. It's too expensive," Bob said.

"Actually Bob, it's not, it is incredible affordable. You're the baby boomer generation, Bob, remember that fire is part of you," Mark expressed. "There's an entire generation waiting to retire. You need to know what's out there, you have options."

"What do you mean," Bob questioned.

"Once upon a time, many years ago, there was a very poor country called Mexico. Then, someone got the idea to build resorts in some of the most beautiful scenery you have ever seen. While, Mexico is still quite poor, there are pockets of resort towns that are nothing short of paradise. Over the years, these resort towns have no longer become affordable as places to live," Mark explained. "But now, Bob, you have to think bigger, okay. Are you with me?"

"Yes," Bob said.

"This idea has taken root in many other undeveloped countries. Beautiful countries with beach front property, ocean views, and mountain ranges, all at insanely affordable prices. We live in unusual times, my friend," Mark professed. "But, Bob, here's the best part. They want you to come. They need you, badly. So, they've built a very nice health care system. Some countries know what they are doing and do it very well. This is a unique opportunity that has never existed in the history of the world."

"But I don't think I want to leave. I like it here," Bob said.

"Bob, you know how I feel about America. It's the greatest country in the world. I'm not asking you to leave it because the cost of living is tough here," Mark pointed out. "I'm saying you've been here all your life. You've worked very hard, sacrificed to make a home and a life for your wife and children. You deserve to live your golden years like a king in paradise, not some suburban box in Toledo. Do you understand me, Bob? It's important."

"I do," Bob assured.

"Do you want something more? Is this something you might be interested in," Mark questioned? "There are three serious rules to becoming an official ex-pat. Actually they are more like guidelines, but I had to say that."

"I'm listening," Bob said.

"Don't just listen, Bob, write this down. Rule number one is health care, find a doctor, get acquainted, get him your records, and know the hospital closest to you. Remember you're old," Mark urged. "Invite your doctor to dinner, every two weeks. It's important. Ask his wife for referrals with any domestic help you might need. She knows the lay of the land. She's your friend."

"I can do that," Bob said.

"That takes me to rule number two. Friendship, Bob, join a Christian church, preferably full of ex-pats just like you. Again ask your doctor. You've something in common with the other ex-pats; you're both Christian ex-pats. Make friends, remember you're old, you know how to make friends, don't you," Mark grinned. "Be a friend, you've been doing it your whole life right."

"I can do that," Bob stated.

"I thought you could. And of course, the most important rule, number three. Money, you own a home by now, right. Hire a management company and rent it to some stressed out yuppie chasing quotas," Mark explained. Take your rent, what little savings you have, plus social security and go relax. For the first time since you were five years old, relax."

"That's cool," Bob said.

"It's the goal of every Ex-pat to do one thing, relax. When you're not stressed out every single minute of every single day chasing quotas, you might not need all seven medications you're currently taking," Mark emphasized. "Tune in, turn on, and drop out one last time."

"That sounds awesome," Bob said with hesitation. "Can I really afford it?"

"That depends; some places are more expensive than others. There are a dozen undiscovered beachfront paradises just begging you to come. It all depends of your preference, what you want," Mark asked. "We're talking about the entire world, remember."

"What if I need work," Bob said.

"If you really want a job, teach people to speak English. You speak English, don't you Bob," Mark answered.

"Yeah," Bob giggled.

"Good, let's start down south, South America at the northern end. Ecuador, it is crowded with ex-pats. This is basically Florida or Arizona for the ex-pat community. The country's retirement benefits package included fifty percent off transportation, utility bills, international round-trip flights originating in Ecuador and tickets for cultural and sporting events. Foreigners can also enroll in Ecuador's Social Security medical program for fifty seven dollars a month. Those over sixty five years of age pay lower income tax," Mark explained. "Penthouse suites and beach front condos go for fifty thousand, while beach front rentals hover around five hundred a month."

"A retiree's entire cost of living rounds out to roughly eight hundred to fifteen hundred a month, and the neighbors more often than not are either ex-pats or English-speaking locals," Mark professed. "We'll warn you that this isn't exactly undiscovered country among retirees, but its several steps up from the costly retirement kennels and golf carts of more costly American hot spots."

"Fifteen hundred a month, that's nothing," Bob bragged.

"I'm with you. Let's move up the coast a little closer to home, Central America. Nicaragua, a visit to the doctor is fifteen dollars. Health care can cost as much as sixty percent less than the U.S. A huge ex-pat population in the colonial city of Granada spends about twelve hundred a month to live, considering a small house can be five hundred to a thousand a month to rent," Mark said.

"The best steak dinner in town runs about thirteen, while regular meals go for half that and local meals are two or three bucks. Local beer, meanwhile, runs between seventy five cents and a buck fifty. This makes Florida's cost of living look like Manhattan's.

"Is it safe," Bob feared?

"Is it safe to live in east LA? South Dallas," Mark insisted? "It all depends on where you live. There are places in every country that are unsafe to live. And true, some countries are safer than others. It all depends on what you can handle."

"Panama has Ex-pat discounts called The Pensionado. A retiree has it pretty sweet in Panama. International Living magazine says retirees can live like kings here for fifteen hundred to two thousand a month and score apartments for less than five hundred a month or buy waterfront condos for less than two hundred thousand dollars. Pensionado, meanwhile, gives users fifteen percent off fast food, hospitals and clinics, professional services used in Panama. You get twenty five percent off the price of food eaten in a sit-down restaurant, public transport and fifty percent off movies, theater tickets and sporting events," Mark explained. "And there's no age limit for the service."

"But what about my children and friends," Bob stammered. "I won't be able to see them."

"Facebook, you can speak to them on Facebook and Twitter daily," Mark said. "You know, Bob, your children look up to you. You're the example. Do you want to be the grumpy old man in Toledo or the rocking dad on a beach in paradise?"

"I don't know," Bob said.

"If you really want to have fun, try Honduras, it's the closest to America. They have lots of things to do on the water."

"I like the water," Bob revealed.

"The benefits offered to retirees beyond the three-hour flights back to see the kids are fairly substantial, especially considering that ex-pats living on beach front property can do well on less than fifteen hundred a month," Mark acknowledged. They have scuba diving, fishing, and sailing, kayaking, snorkeling and surfing. When the kids come to visit, they won't leave, really. You're the coolest dad in the world, ever."

"That would be really cool," Bob laughed.

"If you want the adventure of a lifetime, there's Malaysia in Southeast Asia. The country's 'My Second Home' retirement benefits program for all foreigners is a great draw, but so is the quality Internet access, cellphone coverage and roads. It also helps that it's dirt cheap," Mark said. "A sea-view apartment with a pool and gym on Penang Island goes for a thousand a month, and big-budget movies usually premiere here, shown in English, and go for about four bucks. Oh, there's plenty of English being spoken as well."

"It's really a small world, isn't it," Bob acknowledged. "But, I have a brother-in-law who is completely broke. He lived on social security alone. He's going to get kicked out of America or worse.

"I'm sorry but he's way too expensive to maintain with the cost of health care. Since he has no money; they'll pull the plug on him, first," Mark preached. "As soon as they have the opportunity, he's history. Seventy million baby boomers are unmanageable, to say the least. It's unattainable, it's unapproachable, it's just plain unsustainable. No matter how you look at it, it's going to be horrible. I'm so sorry."

"I understand," Bob groaned. "Where is the cheapest place in the world to live?"

"Thailand, about five hundred a month is enough to score a nice new home just about anywhere in Thailand," Mark reassured. "One of International Living magazines contributors pays just two hundred a month for a beach side bungalow with air conditioning, hot water, Wi-Fi and a refrigerator."

"Altogether, the cost of living in Thailand sets retirees back only about a thousand a month while giving them great amenities and vibrant cultural and entertainment options. Bangkok still gets pretty wild, but there are lots of ex-pats and English speakers to help ease the transition."

"Bangkok would be too wild for me, remember I'm old," Bob admitted.

"Yeah, but Bob you're not dead," Mark observed. "You're more of a nice island country guy somewhere in the south pacific, right."

"Right," Bob said.

"In New Zealand, the English speaking certainly helps but so do the winters that come during an American summer. That's some pretty costly snow birding, so maybe the low cost of every day amenities should be seen as long-term investments. New Zealand's reputation for healthy living and near-absent pollution should appeal to those who want to extend retirement as long as possible," Mark explained. "It's the most conservative of all the islands."

"You're forgetting one thing, my wife. How will she ever agree to do something this crazy," Bob complained.

"How do you sell this adventure of a lifetime to your wife? You'd better write this down. Why do you want to be an ex-pat? Sincerely, this is what you say," Mark directed. "Honey, I've given it a lot of thought. I haven't always been the best husband, provider, or friend to you, I'm sorry. I did my best, because I love you."

"I could never give you the best, but I wish I could," he said. "I want to spend my golden years with you, in paradise, living like a king because you deserve it. Will you come away with me?"

"That's pretty good," Bob approved.

"It's great," Mark insisted.

"Ok, what's next," Bob asked.

"Make a list of all the geographic possibilities and why, list each country's strengths and weaknesses. Let her make the choice," Mark requested. "You can always live in more than one place by renting. This is important. You do not have to make the commitment of buying a property. Rent a condo on the beach for six months. Try it out; play it safe. Maybe your renters moved out and you need to go back home, no problem. Maybe you just want to see all the best places in this amazing world. It's easy to rent a condo for six months, move around, and travel light to see the world. It's so much more fun when you know what you're doing."

"What if she doesn't like it," Bob moaned.

"Move back home, kick out the renters, pour a tall one and she is back in the good ole US of A," Mark said. "No harm, no foul."

"It's a big step," Bob said.

"Start with a vacation, visit a few places to see what's available. Go on the internet, it's all good," Mark consoled.

"I like all good," Bob giggled.

"Find a doctor, find a church, rent the house, and be a friend. Think it over, pack your Bible and serve, it's your calling," Mark preached. "Do you have any idea the difference seventy million boomers could do in this amazing world. It's incredibly good."

"You're crazy," Bob said.

"Why do you think I'm on at four o'clock in the morning," Mark said? "My friend, Toledo will do fine without you. Know who you are and imagine the fun."

"I think I understand, keep an open mind and be a world citizen. God bless you," Bob acknowledged.

"Thanks, it's not easy being a tortured soul; I'm just hoping God grades on the curve. Farewell my friend; normally my producer would be here to say, whose next. I'll try it. Who's next," Mark barked. The playwright, alone in the darkness, is watching the play from backstage. Mark looks at the control booth to prepare for another caller but no one is there.

Enter the Devil

"Good morning, you're on KBRG live radio, *State of the Nation*, have we hit the iceberg yet or not?" Mark repeated again.

"One Nation under God, you never say that anymore," said the third caller. "Why's that?"

"Because that's a dangerous subject," Mark said.

The playwright is still watching from backstage when the stranger in the black trench coat walked up behind him. The playwright had no idea he was there. They watched the play together.

"What's dangerous about it," the third caller said.

"Everything," Mark warned.

"What are you afraid of," the third caller questioned?

"You call me up at three in the morning to talk religion," Mark said impatiently. "Okay, here's the deal. A Christian has one foot in this world and one in the next. When you speak to a person that has both feet in this world, there will always be misunderstandings and miscommunication. What one person thinks is important will not be remotely significant to the other. Do you really want to talk religion at three o'clock in the morning?"

"It's my favorite subject or rather the lack of it," the third caller demanded.

"What's the matter, God didn't let you win the Lotto," Mark said.

"God, do you believe in God," the third caller repeated?

Our playwright is still standing in the same place watching the play, but the stranger in the black trench coat has disappeared.

"I believe in the hereafter," Mark expressed.

"I'm sorry, did I touch a nerve,' the third caller said sarcastically.

"Sometimes, good things fall into the wrong hands and become bad things," Mark explained.

"Is that a problem," the third caller said?

"When you do it for all the wrong reasons," Mark exclaimed. "You had best choose your words wisely."

"Why, does it bother you," the third caller replied?

"Every day is a battle between good and evil," Mark stated. "Most days good wins. Some days it doesn't. What day is it for you, sir?"

"Oh, it's a good day," the third caller remarked with attitude.

"Right," Mark said.

"You sound skeptical," the third caller said.

"Who am I talking to," Mark questioned?

"You don't know me," the third caller assumed.

"Why, should I," Mark said?

"I've had so many names over the years," the third caller admitted.

"Why is it at three in the morning, I get all the jack wagons," Mark pointed out. "Is it something about me that brings out the best in people? You're not stupid are you, I really hate stupid people."

"You never answered my question, Dr. Johnson," the third caller reminded. "Do you believe in God?"

"That again, okay, let's play your little game," Mark said. "Yes, I believe in God."

"Then you must believe in the devil, too," the third caller affirmed.

"Like I said, it's a day to day battle. I've seen the devil in my day. What have you seen," Mark said?

"Oh, I've seen all the days of thunder, days of pain, the days of glory of my reign. I tempted Adam with a taste. I kissed upon the cross of fate, and cast the doubt upon his face. You see, I've seen both here and there, I've seen it all from everywhere. I know the answer before you ask. I seek men's soul, that's my task. Come to the dark side, young Jedi. I am your father," the third caller crooned as the audience laughed.

"I know, by day, you masquerade as the angel of light, that's your story," Mark professed. "By night, you're just another wolf in sheep's clothing."

"I do assure you that I am not so dishonest, as I look. Yes, I lie when it benefits me. I tell the truth when it benefits me," the third caller explained. "At least I'm honest; you rationalize your lies are just excuses for your lack of bravado."

"You don't know me. You just want to friend me on Facebook," Mark grinned.

"Of course I do, but I know what you really want. You want your radio show back," the third caller announced. "And I can give it to you."

"I recall you tempted our savior and lost," Mark pointed out.

"You actually doubt my power, remarkable. Look at all I've done with your precious *State of the Nation*," the third caller said. "The economy of the whole world hangs by a thread. I'm so excited, just giddy."

"How do you manage to do that," Mark requested?

"The truth, which is what you want so desperately this evening, isn't it? You live in a world not directed by industry and innovation, but rather by what a few people want to see happen next," the third caller lectured. "So, you gave them the power to do it, with your wallet. It doesn't matter who you are, if you have a wallet full of cash, you're in. My people live in the institutions that wield the currency like a weapon. That weapon, like a gun, is argued to be used in self-defense. That's my deception. My people so eloquently speak of using the gun to attack slow economic growth or decline, and to bolster real employment. They're defending the people!"

"But some people demand to know the costs of your plan," Mark said seriously.

"Yeah, I hate that. There should be no informed decisions. When you deviate from my plan, there will be consequences," the third caller ordered. "You see, I'm the prince of this world, the power of darkness, and the angel of the abyss."

"And man is given no quarter," Mark acknowledged.

"I prefer the way your President Lincoln said it. The money powers prey upon the nation in times of peace and conspire against it in times of adversity. The banking powers are more despotic than a monarchy, more insolent than autocracy, more selfish than bureaucracy. They denounce as public enemies all who question their methods or throw light upon their crimes. I have two great enemies, the Southern Army in front of me and the bankers in the rear. Of the two, the one at my rear is my greatest foe. Your vision, Mr. Johnson is a gift," the third caller said. "I am impressed."

"More like a curse," Mark admitted.

"I know you understand; in every country around the world, humanity chased the same goal...treasure. Therefore, I must maintain the status quo. Zombie banks and bad debts must be propped up, at all costs. Unfortunately, if those who are responsible and understanding are lost along the way, then so be it," the third caller warned. "Their downfall will be for the greater good Mr. Lincoln. Did you see that coming?"

"Like a bunch of drug addicts that run out of crack. Then suddenly, a tyrant walks through the door with a bag full of crack," Mark said in disgust. "The new political party raged on. Are we that stupid?"

"Just naïve," the third caller admitted. "It's important that a tyrant put on the appearance of uncommon devotion to religion. Sheep are less apprehensive of evil from a ruler whom they consider god-fearing and pious. On the other hand, they do less easily move against him, believing that he has the gods on his side. You're friend Aristotle sold me that one. Would you like to meet him?"

"Not just yet," Mark replied.

"Then tell me what you are afraid of? What do you want to know," the third caller repeated?

"Greece is a mirror for America, isn't it," Mark asked? "They've more debt than they can ever pay off, too."

"Did you see my article in the New York Times, on January 10th? I reported a story on Greek disability payouts creating acrimony. It seems the Greek government has expanded the disabilities that are recognized to include pedophilia, exhibitionism, and kleptomania. My kind of place," the third caller laughed.

"What," Mark said?

"To make a long story short, the Greek government is negotiating how much not to pay their bills, while it demands more bailout money from its neighbors," the third caller advised. "And now, this is a place where habitual stealing is a disability. Seriously, this stuff can't be made up; no one would believe it."

"So, the entire country can now file a disability claim," Mark acknowledged. "This is how world war's got started. Everything collapsed, we blamed the foreigners, and tyrants ride in on white horses. Are they on our side, not likely?"

"The instinctive reaction to pain is to find a cause or scapegoat to blame. I made that trick up myself," the third caller said. "The surprise isn't that Greek Neo-Nazi's captured seven percent of the popular vote in Greece's election last Sunday, but rather that it took so long for it to happen. I love it when history repeats itself."

"Human nature always remains the same," Mark answered.

"I do so love human nature. It's so poetic. I think I'll call you peaches," the third caller laughed. "You still never answered my question. What kind of man are you, peaches? Do you want to help others?"

"Why do you think I'm on the radio," Mark snapped?

"Because, I put you there," the third caller stated.

"Enough, did you escape from a padded room? Are the guys in little white suits looking for you," Mark said? "I really don't believe a word you say."

"You doubt my power of illusion and deception," the third caller scolded.

"Oh, you'll definitely have to prove yourself," Mark said.

"1962," the third caller replied.

"What happened in 1962," Mark questioned.

"That was my best year, my best trick, ever," the third caller boasted.

"The suspense is killing me," Mark said.

"I convinced the most god fearing nation in the world to take 'Almighty God' out of their schools," the third caller bragged. "I, with the unconditional support of the Supreme Court, brought the single largest educational institution in the world to its knees. With my help, this Supreme Court of the United States ended God's reign by an overwhelming margin of 6 to 1. This landmark vote was just 6 to 1 because before the decision could be announced, Justice Felix Frankfurter suffered a cerebral stroke, my bad, that forced him to retire. Justice Byron White took no part in the case. He was such a tough nut to crack."

"With your help," Mark replied.

"Yes, but it gets better. What an amazing turn of events that followed. Once God was out of the equation, the rest was easy," the third caller pointed out. "Since 1962, violent crime, divorce, teenage pregnancies are all up over four hundred percent. The list goes on and on. You need more proof than that, Doctor Johnson."

"Answer this one question, and I'll not doubt you again, I promise," Mark requested. "What is evil?"

"It's whatever you want it to be," the third caller said quickly.

"That's not good enough. You can do better," Mark said skeptically.

"The nature of evil," the third caller professed.

"Do your worst," Mark said.

"To give up, to surrender what is yours. Idle hands, vanity, greed, pride. Evil is all around you, you don't even have to look for it. It's right in your face," the third caller exclaimed. "Cigarettes kill more people than all the guns in the world combined. You do it willfully, joyfully, and without my influence at all. It's all about me. What's in it for me?"

"So you're just an innocent bystander," Mark suggested.

"Sometimes, I get more credit than I deserve," the third caller said. "Some people are just mean and hurtful. Much of that is from human nature. I'm just good at causing chaos. I must admit, the human spirit can get pretty low, even without my help."

"I'll give you credit, you're pretty good," Mark acknowledged. "But, that's not the answer. The answer has always been turning from God. That's all you have. Without that, you're nothing."

"You think you know," the third caller stammered.

"Yeah, I do. Evil is mankind's failure to realize its ultimate promise of salvation," Mark commanded.

"That's good," the third caller said.

"Speaking of good, you were an archangel at one time, weren't you," Mark recalled, "a created being inferior to God, right."

"That's a long time ago, you wouldn't understand. I got tired of taking orders. I wanted to do my own thing, be the boss," the third caller sputtered. "Haven't you ever felt like that?"

"We're not talking about me, Lucifer," Mark assured.

"You think you know me, don't you, peaches," the third caller said? "You want to determine your own life, your own fate. That's the first step away from God, isn't it? I used that same spirit against mankind to get them away, too."

"So clever, it must be so empty for you, and don't call me peaches," Mark scolded.

"Quite the contrary, peaches, have you ever stepped on an ant," the third caller said. "It wasn't going to hurt you, but you did it for no reason. I step on people's hopes and dreams, joys and peace, life and health, prosperity and harmony. I love it, that's what I do, peaches."

"You're sick," Mark sneered with disgust.

"I'm sick, you know the difference between right and wrong, and still do wrong with no regret. That's so twisted," the third caller laughed.

"We are sinners," Mark said.

"I know every cop is a criminal," the third caller said.

"No one said it was easy," Mark replied.

"The path is narrow to Heaven and few will be able to see it, but my path is a six lane highway with an HOV lane and free toll tag," the third caller laughed. "I can solve all your problems and make your Earthly dreams come true. Then, I lay your soul to waste."

"Whatever, I've played along because it's late. I've no sympathy for the devil," Mark said.

"What's confusing you is the nature of my game," the third caller advised.

"You've been a good sport and I appreciate it, but it's time to say good night," Mark beseeched. "It's getting late."

"Do you mind me asking one last question," the third caller said?

"If you must, make it short," Mark complained.

"What's a soul is worth," the third caller bargained?

"What do you mean," Mark said?

"What would you do to save a soul? How far would you go," the third caller said? "What would you be willing to do?"

"I would do whatever it took to save a life," Mark admitted.

"That's not what I said," the third caller screamed.

"Then say what you mean," Mark barked.

"I said a soul," the third caller repeated. "Lives come and go, they mean nothing to me. Everyone dies sooner or later, but a soul is forever. A man's soul is eternity."

"Bring it on. I can do this all night," Mark snapped.

"Oh, you're a rare one. This is going to be fun. You and me, for a soul, that's old school," the third caller stated. "A confrontation of Good and Evil, on the ultimate battleground, a human soul hangs in the balance for the fight for dominion over man. Let's put it to the test. You think you're up to it."

"You're a funny man," Mark said. "Our belief in God and the Devil is a construct of the human mind and that all people contain within them both good and evil. We attempt to conjure the devil to prove our might. But the most disturbing theme is his claims that only by following him can people find real happiness. He wants us to believe that God is a brutal, jealous bully. He tells us the same lie enough times until eventually we believe it. As God and Devil battle for a soul, we must remember that the devil is the true master of all lies."

"I am compelled to warn you, I never quit. No matter how many times you turn down my offer, I'm not giving up. A battle to the death for a soul," the third caller repeated. "I told you it was going to be a good day."

"You know you can't win. In Revelations, you're defeated," Mark explained. "In the Millennium, when the beast and the false prophet are cast into the lake of fire. You are imprisoned in the bottomless pit for a thousand years. The resurrected martyrs live and reign with Christ. After the thousand years, you were released and made war against the people of God, but you are defeated and cast into the lake of burning sulfur."

"And finally, the Last Judgment of the wicked, along with death and Hades, are cast into the lake of fire. There is a new Heaven and Earth; they replace the old. There is no more suffering or death. God came to dwell with humanity in the New Jerusalem. The river and tree of life appear for the healing of the nations. The curse is ended. Christ's reassurance that his coming is imminent," Mark professed. "I'm sorry to disappoint you, but I do know who created me and you will never have my soul."

"I'm not talking about yours." The devil laughed.

A dial tone is heard as Mark looks into the microphone. He has a strange curious look on his face. He prepared for the next caller, but this time he moved a little slower.

"That wasn't creepy, no, not at all," Mark mumbled as he looked over his shoulder. "I want to go on the record as saying that the devil, hatred, evil or whatever form it may come in is oppression. History has taught us that tyrants have brought down evil and oppression upon their people since the beginning of mankind. Where would the world be without America to stop the oppression and end the wars to end all wars? There is only one force of history that can break the reign of hatred and resentment, and expose the pretensions of tyrants, reward the hopes of the decent and tolerant, and that is the force of human freedom. That is the force of America."

"It was George Bush that said, 'we are led, by events and common sense, to one conclusion: The survival of liberty in our land increasingly depends on the success of liberty in other lands. The best hope for peace in our world is the expansion of freedom in the entire world. So, it is the policy of the United States to seek and support the growth of democratic movements and institutions in every nation and culture, with the ultimate goal of ending tyranny in our world.' Well-spoken George, sometime presidents surprise you," Mark admitted.

"We have confidence because freedom is the permanent hope of mankind, the hunger in dark places, the longing of the soul," Mark said. "When our Founders declared a new order of the ages; when soldiers died in wave upon wave for a union based on liberty; when citizens marched in peaceful outrage under the banner 'Freedom Now', they were acting on an ancient hope that is meant to be fulfilled. History has an ebb and flow of justice, but history also has a visible direction, set by liberty and the Author of Liberty, God."

"In the long run, there is no justice without freedom, and there can be no human rights without human liberty. Are we clear on that," Mark said? "The devil hates our freedom, our freedom to choose, because we always choose God over him, when we are free to choose."

"Good morning, you're on KBRG live radio, *State of the Nation*, have we hit the iceberg yet or not," Mark repeated again?

"You're an idiot," the fourth caller shouted.

"Oh, come on," Mark snapped slamming his finger down on the disconnect button creating a dial tone. "Oh, that felt good. Is this the best you can do? No point or intelligent rhetoric for America. Please, don't cut government spending on education. We're only ranked twenty five in the world on the education of our youth. Congratulations America, you've come so far." He looks at his half empty bottle of whiskey.

"I need another drink, if I am to get through this day," he pleaded as he pours a drink and slams it down. "That's better. Okay, let's check the board. Only one caller left, awesome," Mark expressed impatiently to the point of a meltdown.

"Good morning, you're on KBRG live radio, *State of the Nation*, have we hit the iceberg yet or not," Mark repeated again?

"Yes...," the last caller stated in a female voice.

"Finally, someone is paying attention. Thank you very much, what's on your mind this morning," Mark asked.

"You're right," the last caller said meekly.

"I love that," Mark admitted. "If she tried that just once, who knows what might have happened."

"Now miss, I'm right about a lot of things," he bragged. "Not to blow my own horn, but can you be a bit more specific? My ego would appreciate it."

"You're right about the world. It's full of hate and...," the last caller stammered.

"I hear what you're saying, darling. We're surrounded by the greed and corruption that steals our freedom. The world is full of hate and people that just want to bring you down. They hate everything so they want you to feel the same way. They want to control you. They want to own you," Mark explained. "But you can't give in to their hate. What's on your mind?"

"I can't do it anymore. I just can't," the last caller sniveled.

"What do you mean? Can't what," Mark said impatiently.

"The thought of living one more day in this world is more than I can bear," the last caller professed.

"Oh please, come on, honey. It can't be that bad. It's rough all over. You know, there's a support group out there for people who don't like their job, it's called everybody," Mark laughed. "I want to die in my sleep, like my grandmother, not screaming in terror like the passengers in her car." The audience laughed along with Mark.

"You...," the last caller sputtered.

"Nobody promised you happiness in this world. It's up to you. You have to want it, you have to try," Mark exclaimed. "Get off your back and make something happen. Take charge of your life. We live in unusual times."

"You're not listening," the last caller cried.

"I've heard it before. That's what's wrong with America. Everyone wants a free ride. Take it easy, let the governments take care of me. Nobody wants to pick themselves up by the bootstraps and make a living. Hey, when the going gets tough, just throw in the towel," Mark complained. "That's what I'm hearing."

"Why are you saying this," the last caller wept?

"Because this is America, the land of the free, home of the brave," Mark expressed, "the brave, darling."

"I'm not brave. I'm scared," the last caller cried.

"You're right about that. Tomorrow, I'll be out of a job. I'm scared too, but you don't see me throwing in the towel. You're a coward," Mark shouted.

"You don't know me," the last caller cried out.

"Oh, I know you all too well. You want to quit. End your life because things are a little tough. Well, sister, I've got news for you. The economy sucks, people are out of work, fifty million people on food stamps just to survive," Mark protested. "I saw where Martha Stewart wrote a book on creative recipes for food stamps. But, I don't see them jumping off a bridge. And now you're crying, wonderful. A woman's tears are such a weapon."

"You don't believe me. You don't know," the last caller cried out in tears.

"Know what. We don't even know your name. Tell the listeners your name, darling," Mark directed.

"Pleasure," the last caller said quietly.

"Pleasure, what are you a stripper," Mark acknowledged.

"Escort, I'm a call girl," the last caller explained.

"I can't call you Pleasure. What's your real name," Mark said?

"Rebecca," she sniveled.

"Well, Rebecca. I'm sorry. I can't imagine anyone wanting a life like that. Can you tell me what happened," Mark asked?

"He left me," Rebecca said.

"Who left you," Mark said?

"My husband, he beat me, and then left me," Rebecca said sadly.

"Did you go to the police," Mark said.

"For what, so they could bring him back and beat me some more. Are you serious," Rebecca snapped.

"Then what," Mark said softly.

"What do you mean, then what? I had no money, no job, and no skills. I lost my house, my friends, I lost everything," Rebecca babbled.

"Is that when you started turning tricks," Mark said.

"No, I started as a stripper. They gave me drugs. They were easy to get," Rebecca professed.

"Are you still using," Mark replied?

"Yes," Rebecca stammered.

"Why," Mark said?

"It takes away the pain, so I can feel nothing," Rebecca said.

"Then you owed more money," Mark added.

"Yes, they wanted me to do porn. I had to do it," Rebecca bawled.

"They kept feeding you more and more until you became addicted, it was too late," Mark said. "It's an old story. I'm sorry to say."

"That's when I become a call girl. Now you know me. Do you want to hang up, now," Rebecca said? A long slow pause of dead air fills the stage.

"Of course not, do you have any children," Mark asked?

"When I was twenty, I had an abortion," Rebecca sniveled. "I murdered my baby because my boyfriend told me to. Today, I have no one. I would never bring a child into this world."

"What about family," Mark said.

"My mother's gone. My father might as well be. He's been an alcoholic since she died. He doesn't know I'm alive," Rebecca cried.

"I don't know what to say," Mark said.

"I've been with two men and a woman tonight," Rebecca admitted.

"I'm sorry," Mark reassured.

"I can't do it anymore," Rebecca exclaimed as a strong voice of despair came through the radio.

"Very well, where are you? I'll have someone come for you," Mark said.

"You're not listening," Rebecca repeated. "I don't want to see another sun rise in this god forsaken world. I don't want anything from you."

"There are people that can help you," Mark advised.

"You want to know where I am. I'm on the roof of a twenty story building. I have a gun and a bottle of pills. I have everything I need," Rebecca explained. "I don't need your help."

"You can't do this," Mark implored.

"Why not, I'm supposed to be working, right now. If Raul finds me here, he'll beat me," Rebecca said.

"Who is Raul," Mark asked?

"Seriously," Rebecca yelled.

"Okay, I get it. But killing yourself won't solve anything, it's not the answer, it's pointless," Mark pleaded.

"Sure it can, I listen to your show all the time. I'm awake from midnight to six in the morning every day, remember. I listen during downtime between Johns. Sometimes, I even listen while I'm working, too. It made me forget my problems for a minute," Rebecca explained. "Some people have it worse, even more than me. I think I would like to live in Ecuador."

"Thank you," Mark said. "But nothing is so bad, that it can't be fixed."

"Why won't you listen to me," Rebecca cried out in anger? "I'm done with this world; you've shown me there's no place in it for me."

"You can't blame me for the world. I didn't cause it. It's not my fault. How dare you make me the scapegoat for your life," Mark shouted? "You want me to feel sorry for you. Fine, I get that. But you can't use me as your reason to throw it all away, I won't do it."

"What are you doing up here," an angry voice shouted in the background. "I've been looking all over for you. You're supposed to be working. I told you what would happen if I caught you, again."

"Leave me alone Raul," Rebecca shouted in fear.

"I told you," Raul said as he beats her.

"Don't," Rebecca wept hysterically.

"What the...," the pimp shrieked as a single gunshot is fired. A body hits the ground, followed by total silence.

"Rebecca, Rebecca! Mark yelled. The radio is filled with dead air followed by uncontrollable crying. "Rebecca, are you alright?" She began screaming incoherent gibberish. "Rebecca, can you hear me, breathe just breathe?"

"I can't," Rebecca shuddered in tears.

"What happened," Mark shouted as he finds himself standing, yelling into the microphone?

"He's not moving," Rebecca stammered.

"Is he dead," Mark said?

"I don't know," Rebecca cried out.

"Is he breathing," Mark replied softly?

"No," Rebecca said.

"Rebecca," Mark consoled.

"When they find out, they're going to kill me. I'm dead," Rebecca wept in tears again.

"Look, you're in over your head," Mark advised. "You have to turn yourself in."

"You're so stupid. Do you not understand the business I'm in? He's not alone," Rebecca barked.

"Look, the police can protect you," Mark exclaimed.

"He's dead. I can see him. He's right in front of me," Rebecca explained. "He's staring right at me."

"Listen to me, you killed a pimp. It was self-defense," Mark stated "I'll testify to that, you're doing the police a favor."

"They won't believe a prostitute," Rebecca snapped.

"Rebecca, the phone lines are going crazy. I have a hundred phone messages," Mark revealed. "Everyone knows you're innocent."

"Don't leave me," Rebecca begged.

"I'll never leave you, I promise," Mark consoled.

"But, they always do. If I put this gun in my mouth, it will finally be over," Rebecca pleaded. "No more pain."

"Stop, please. Talk to me, just talk to me," Mark begged. "Can you do that for me?"

"No more talking," Rebecca restated.

"Okay, okay I get it. Can you just listen to me for a few minutes," Mark begged. "If you still want to take your life, I can't stop you. But can you just listen to me for a minute."

"Maybe," Rebecca said reluctantly.

"Rebecca, do you believe in God," Mark said? The sound of a gun being cocked back, ready to fire, echo throughout the theater. A sobering moment of dead air embraced the audience. "I'm sorry, I didn't believe you. I'm an idiot. I didn't mean it, not a word of it. You're right, the world sucks. We've screwed up everything good we were given. We take everything, do nothing, and proclaim our success to everyone. We think we're Gods, but we're not. I know you're just sick and tired of being sick and tired, we all are."

"Hmmm...," she mumbled.

"There is a light in this world. A light that holds us, heals us, and saves us," Mark said compassionately. "He offers a life without pain and suffering. He died on the cross to take away our pain. He just wants to help us. I know you don't understand but he cares for you and everything you've been through. Let me prove it; I can Google it, please just wait. There was a prostitute named Mary Magdalene. She washed his feet and rolled away the rock that closed his tomb. She was at the trial and witnessed his crucifixion. She was part of everything important he did for us; she was a prostitute, too."

"No," she cried.

"I have it, Luke 7:38," Mark exclaimed. "As she stood behind him at his feet weeping, she began to wet his feet with her tears. Then she wiped them with her hair, kissed them and poured perfume on them." Then he said to her, "Your sins are forgiven. Your faith has saved you; go in peace."

"Stop," she wept.

"Rebecca, he knows your struggle. You're not alone," Mark preached. "I know I rant about the world's injustice, I know there's little hope left in this country. But, I still recognize the two thousand pound elephant in the room. I know it can be saved. A man of god will lead us out of this abyss. Don't let this world stain your soul; don't let them win. If we possessed a President of the United States that truly believed the only way to save our country was by the grace of God. We could turn it around, turn around our lives, our world."

"A hundred years from now, everyone you know, everyone you've ever met, everyone you've ever heard of, will be gone. All that remains is a world for our children," Mark prayed. "That's our job. We need good people with both feet in the next world and a President, a true man of God, with a huge pair of...between his legs. It will get better but we're running out of time. It's almost six o'clock. Don't quit, it's always darkest before the dawn. We need you. There is good and virtue in this world. The truest friend to the liberty of this country tries most to promote its virtue, if we would most truly enjoy this gift of Heaven, let us become a virtuous people. Please, see the sunrise with me, one more time."

"I quit," she cried.

"I know a place at the corner of seventy fifth and Main. It's a great little spot for waffles, have breakfast with me. I'm buying. It's the best in town, please. I need a friend, too." Mark admitted hoping for a response, but nothing. His desperation is coming through his voice. "Rebecca, with God's help, we can do this together. Can you do that for me? Will you do it for us?"

Then, as quickly as it came, another gunshot blasted over the radio. The shot echoed throughout the theater, again, you could hear a pin drop.

"Rebecca," Mark pleaded. The silence was deafening, he fell back into his chair. The radio sign, "On the Air" goes dark. The show is over. The clock on the wall read six in the morning. The stage lights dim and the curtain closed.

As the curtains slowly reopened, Mark sits alone in a booth eating waffles. He awkwardly reached for his coffee and knocked it off the table. It spilled on the floor. As he reached down to pick up the broken cup, a woman bends over to help him. The spotlight slowly panned upward to show the woman's body, then her face. She looked exhausted, but managed to create a very sad smile.

"Hello," Mark sputtered.

"Hi," Rebecca responded with a shy voice as they look each other with disbelief. She has a beautiful face, but the years have been hard on her. She is blonde but not a platinum fake blonde that you might expect. She has a nice smile in spite of the long night of cruelty she just endured. It was a comfortable moment. The kind of moment where you feel safe, then Mark's text message ring tone goes off, the awkward silence is broken.

"Uh, that's my phone," Mark stammered a little better this time.

"What's it say," Rebecca said quietly?

"You win peaches, this time," Mark spoke clearly this time in an understanding tone. He looked up at her and realized what just happened. It was her soul. It was the battle for her soul and he has won the day. They both sat at the booth and began to talk. The waitress brought another plate of waffles.

The final curtain closed, the play has ended, and the audience applauded with approval. All the actors come on stage and bow to the audience. They applaud again. The crowd began to exit past the playwright.

The Interview

A few close friends greet him after the show. "Wonderful, see you at the after party," a friend said.

"Thank you very much," the playwright replied.

"Simply marvelous, young man," a friend boasted.

"I'm glad you liked it," the playwright said with appreciation.

"I loved it. I hope to see you again," another friend added.

"You are too kind. Thank you," the playwright expressed as they shook hands.

"Sir, a few questions please," a reporter asked.

"Of course," the playwright said.

"Can you tell us your motivation behind this wonderful play," the reporter questioned?

"A cry in the wilderness," the playwright answered.

"What does that mean," the reporter said?

"It's a prayer for America," the playwright acknowledged. "I think of movies as the greatest of all the media. They may even carry an actual message through a speech spoken by some character, perhaps, of America's true calling in the world."

"This success will vault you into fame and prosperity for an unknown playwright," the reporter explained. "You might be famous, how does it feel?"

"Let's give credit where credit is due," the playwright responded. "All glory goes to God. I'm just a simple messenger."

"How do you do it, how do you write with such passion and conviction," the reporter exclaimed?

"A writer took a blank sheet of paper, created a universe, and fashioned a world. He populated that world with hopes and dreams. He made it the way he thinks it should be," the playwright admitted. "Inevitably, you fall hopelessly in love with it. You experience a crushing need to see it come to fruition, to nurture and care for it. It becomes part of you. This experience has given me a valuable insight and understanding that I never had before."

"What is that," the reporter asked?

"God created the Heavens and the Earth from a blank universe. In seven days, his script was written. Millions of years later, he is still working to fruition. He created a world and made it the way it should be. He fell in love with us. He is part of us. Only now have I come to realize, just why he truly loves us so much," the playwright professed. "Thank you for the interview, that's all I have to say. I hope you understand. I must be going." He shook a few more hands as they left.

The Storm

"Can I give you a ride to the after party," another friend said.

"No thank you, I'd rather walk. I'll see you there," the playwright replied.

"Okay," another friend said. The playwright walked alone on Broadway and 38th Street. The famous stretch near Times Square, where Broadway crossed Seventh Avenue in midtown Manhattan, is the home of many Broadway theatres, large-scale plays, particularly musicals. This area of Manhattan called the Theater District or the Great White Way, a nickname originating in the headline "Found on the Great White Way" in 1902. The journalistic nickname was inspired by the millions of lights on theater marquees and billboard advertisements that illuminate the area.

He saw the stranger in front of him waiting, but pretended not to notice him and looked away. The stranger spoke, but does not seem to move his mouth.

"Do not be afraid. Few men will have the greatness to bend history itself. Each time a man stands up for an ideal or strike out against injustice, he sends forth a tiny ripple of hope. Those ripples build a current that can sweep down the mightiest walls of oppression. Do you have the courage to enter the moral conflict? The future doesn't belong to those who are content with today, timid and fearful in the face of bold endeavors. Rather, it belongs to those who can blend vision, reason, and courage in a personal commitment to the ideals and great enterprises of the heart," the stranger preached. The playwright looks back in front of him, the stranger is gone. He continued walking down the street. A lady of the evening approached him.

"Would you like a date," the woman asked?

"No, thanks," the playwright replied.

He continued to walk down the street. Again, the stranger appeared standing directly in his path. The playwright walked right up to him and stopped about two inches in front of his face. "I put my name on your play, like you asked, Gabriel," the playwright scolded. "And I said what you wanted me to say, too."

Gabriel is calm to the point of being sarcastic. He envies the body of man for their mortality. He sees all the pain in the world but still has hope for humanity. Gabriel smiled and moved his finger in a circle back toward the lady of the evening. "Are you one of us," Gabriel asked?

"Really," the playwright pleaded. "I didn't ask for any of this."

"I know, my children did," Gabriel sympathized.

The playwright turned to walk toward the woman. He glanced over his shoulder at Gabriel and stopped. "The United States of America owed more money than any country in the history of the world. Nobel prize laureates and academic professors around the world warn of the impending Financial Armageddon," the playwright seethed. "The unfortunate concept of moral hazard is any situation in which one person made the decision about how much risk to take, while someone else bears the cost, if things go badly. The President and Congress of this country make decisions about our risk of Financial Armageddon, while the people of America bear the cost, when things go badly. There is more poverty stricken Americans; now, than in the last fifty years. Things have gone badly."

"The combination of stalling growth in the U.S., debt troubles in Europe, a slowdown in emerging markets, particularly China, and military conflict in Iran would come together in to create a perfect storm for the global economy in 2013," the playwright fumed. "If we fail to heed your warnings, Western democracies will face 'the fiscal death spiral' that begins with a loss of credibility, continued with a rise in borrowing costs, and ends as governments are forced to impose spending cuts and higher taxes at the worst possible moment."

"In 2050, just the three entitlement program's Social Security, Medicare, Medicaid, will surpass the total revenue of the entire country, not even counting Education, Defense, Obama care, and all other government funded programs combined. Those things, our future, you so eloquently speak about, will get dramatically worse," the playwright sneered with a mounting anger in every word.

"We have no money for this. We have hit the iceberg and you know it," the playwright thundered. "The stock market will crash. The forces are too great against it. It's not a matter of if, but rather when. What do we do, where do we turn for guidance, how do we cope with the godless bloody aftermath."

Gabriel, once again, looked at him and pointed his finger at the lady of the evening. "You are, without a doubt, the worst guardian angel ever," the playwright said.

"Don't tell me how big the storm is, tell the storm how big God is," Gabriel demanded. "I am here to protect my children, not to stop something bad happening." The playwright sighed with defeat, turned and walked up to her.

"I was supposed to go to a party, but, right now, I don't feel much like going. I would very much like...to buy you breakfast? Are you hungry," the playwright asked? She looked at him with a strange curious stare.

"That would be nice," the girl said.

Gabriel watched over them as they walked off into the night.

The End of Chapter One

PART II

The Answer

Whoever said, "thank God for unanswered prayers" never prayed for the heart of a child. This childhood innocence reminds us what is pure in life. Every president was once a child, yet not every child becomes president. A mother or father once told their child, "Someday you could become president." That phrase was seldom appropriate in a world filled with kings and tyrants. Thrust upon a child, this special gift makes us great. His intentions may not have started out admirable. His road may not have been innocent, but his destiny may have already befallen this world.

You understand, I would know. Of the thousands of angels in Heaven, I was chosen to tell Mary her baby would be the one to save the world. Once more, I have been summoned to bring you hope.

Our child is a forty-five year old President of the United States. He stands concluding a historic speech to the nation, his voice rings loud and clear. The Senate chamber is a two story room with a hundred individual desks, one per Senator, on a multi-tiered semicircular platform facing a central rostrum in the front of the room. The Senate floor itself is overlooked on all four sides by a gallery on the second floor. John spoke from the podium with great zeal and confidence. He's a strong good looking man, quick-witted with a silver tongue, and intensely charismatic. John Henry spoke against all oppression as if he is speaking directly into your soul. It was a noble speech in defiance of tyranny. Your President Dwight Eisenhower said it, as well. "Every step we take towards making the State our Caretaker of our lives, by that much we move toward making the State our Master."

I am Gabriel and I have the special task of coming to Earth and making important announcements and telling of special events. This child is the answer to your prayers, like it or not, this is his story. As always, I am proud to have a ringside seat to the fate of humanity.

The Speech

"Once again, our courage has been tested, perhaps for the last time, perhaps for all time. On this day, surging gas prices have drained the life out of our economy. The stock market crash crippled our financial leverage. The unemployment rate, the means to our existence, is at an all-time high; but, America will not go quietly into the night," John proclaimed with a commanding tone to lead a nation. "We are ready for battle."

"I believe the immortal words of Abraham Lincoln still command the truth we hold so dear in our lives today. He said it so eloquently on December 20, 1839. Many free countries have lost their liberty, and ours may lose hers; but if she shall, be it my proudest plume, not that I was the last to desert, but that I never deserted her. I know that the great volcano at Washington, aroused and directed by the evil spirit that reigns there, is belching forth the lava of political corruption in a current broad and deep, which is sweeping with frightful velocity over the whole length and breadth of the land, bidding fair to leave unscathed no green spot or living thing; while on its bosom are riding, like demons on the waves of death, the imps of that evil spirit, and fiendishly taunting all those who dare resist its destroying course with the hopelessness of their effort; and, knowing this, I cannot deny that all may be swept away. Broken by it I, too, may be; bow to it I never will."

"The probability that we may fall in the struggle ought not to deter us from the support of a cause we believe to be just; it shall not deter me. If ever I feel the soul within me elevate and expand to those dimensions not wholly unworthy of its almighty Architect, it is when I contemplate the cause of my country deserted by the entire world; standing up boldly and alone hurling defiance at her victorious oppressors. Here, without contemplating consequences, before high Heaven and in the face of the world, I swear eternal fidelity to the just cause, as I deem it, of the land of my life, my liberty, and my love."

"And who that thinks with me will not fearlessly adopt the oath that I take? Let none falter who thinks he is right, and we may succeed. But if, after all, we shall fail, be it so. We still shall have the proud consolation of saying to our consciences, and to the departed shade of our country's freedom, that the cause approved of our judgment, and adored of our hearts, in disaster, in chains, in torture, in death, we never faltered in defending."

"What words will we be remembered about us? What deeds will we do? Will we be as timeless as the unforgettable words of Mr. Lincoln?

'It's rather for us to be here dedicated to the great task remaining before us that from these honored dead we take increased devotion to that cause for which they gave the last full measure of devotion that we here highly resolve that these dead shall not have died in vain. This Nation, under God, shall have a new birth of freedom and that government of the people, by the people, and for the people, shall not perish from the Earth.' This is who we are." The audience of Senators and Congressman stand to their feet and roar with approval.

"Therefore, our direction is clear and our cause just. Make no mistake, my friends, the future of America is once again at risk. The debt of this nation is a dangerous matter of national security. Therefore, let us strive in all ways to finish our work for we will not place profit over people, self-interest over justice and oppression over equality," John announced with conviction. "In this country, every man is guaranteed a chance for a better life, and no one will ever take that away. We will face our enemies, as we always have. The United States of America will never succumb to any threat, not now, not ever. God Bless America!" The audience loved him, John waved as in a presidential victory. He walks among the crowd, shaking hands. The people are reaching out to him. Brian, Tom, and several Secret Service agents are on all sides as he moved toward the exit.

"Do you think the world will listen?" John asked outside the chamber.

"John, you're in danger," Tom said nervously.

"I'm always in danger," John reminded. Tom saw a young man off in the distance walking toward John. He recognized him as John's driver. He is young with dark slick backed hair and lean for being a few inches short of six feet. He is always polite and eager to please when John is around. As a rule, he does not speak unless spoken too. He is not secret service, but has a history of military service, probably the marines. He appears to be of foreign birth, definitely not Caucasian American. He saw the young driver reach into his jacket. For a moment, Tom glanced away pretending to be distracted. The young driver walked out of shadows by the limousine, pulled a small handgun, and fired several shots. Brian jumped in front of the President. He has taken a bullet for the President and falls. Tom quickly received a wound in his left arm. John froze and slowly fell to his knees with blood hemorrhaging from his neck. The young assassin raced from the scene.

"Down, man down," Tom yelled! He pulls his gun and fire toward the assassin as he fled. The young man falls face first to the ground. Secret Service agents surround him. "John, are you...," Tom sputtered.

"Please God, not now," John begged. Blood shoots from John's neck as Tom tried to stop the bleeding with his hands. The red liquid oozed through his fingers. He screamed into his microphone clipped to his bloody shirt.

"Advice, we have shots fired. Shots fired. The president is down," Tom shouted in a panic. "We need the ambulance, now! John, the ambulance is coming."

"Michael," John groaned softly.

"Where's Michael, get Michael," Tom yelled. Michael is dressed as a Lutheran priest, arrived quickly and saw John hemorrhaging from the neck. He can't believe his eyes as he bends over the President.

"We failed," John trembled. He can barely speak.

"Good men will never abandon the truth," Michael advised. "You have set us free." John's eyes began to close. The fear and pain left his face and replaced by the fear now in Michael's face.

"Go, now!" Michael orders. John is carried by the secret service to the ambulance and speeds away to a hospital. In the darkness, Michael's silhouette stands to watch the ambulance disappear into the night.

The Early Days

Every president leads two lives. The one he lives as the leader of the free world and the one that got him there. John Henry's run to become President of the United States began in a small country house in the deep woods of southeast Texas; a grown man sits on the porch with his five-year-old son. This country house is rectangular in shape and the walls are constructed of log, the foundation and chimneys are stone and the gable roof is covered with asphalt shingles. The deliberately rustic look continues in the interior with wide board floors, exposed wooden beams, and a massive stone fireplace. The old porch is open air so the children can be seen from the front of the house.

From a car, two men approach in business suits with legal papers and a briefcase in hand. They are cautious to a fault. "Stand next to me," Richard said. Richard is a mountain of a man. Strong chin, barrel chest, legs like tree trunks standing like a statue on top of a mountain. His hair is brown and wavy but his face is clean cut. There is no confusion in his voice; he is a man's man. As the two men approach the porch, John raised the rifle at them. His charismatic smile is deceptive for a five year old. His eyes are clear and his stance is focused. He knows how to hold a rifle like a man. He is unafraid.

"Does he have to do that," one man asked?

"It's not a real gun," the second man answered.

"John Henry," Richard barked. With a stone cold glance of a hardened veteran, John fired a shot and hit one man squarely in the foot. Richard roars with laughter while the man grabs his foot in pain.

"He shot my foot," the first man screamed.

"You're lucky it wasn't me," Richard proclaimed sharply.

"Okay, okay," the second man accepted. "As you requested, Mr. Henry, I have the new agreement."

"That's my money in that case," Richard demanded?

"You'll get it, after you sign," the second man trembled while cautiously handing over the contract. Richard glanced toward his son with approval as he signed the contract.

"Gentlemen, the way I see it, the rich have been doing it to the poor since the beginning of time, but not this day, not here. I'm not a lawyer by accident," Richard announced. John pointed his gun at the second man and grinned. Richard handed a second signed copy back to him and took the briefcase. He opened the briefcase and nodded to John. "Now, get off my land, you carpet bagging crooks. You never change," Richard bellowed.

"Old man, there's no place for you in heaven," the first man fumed.

"Sir, I doubt there is a heaven," Richard professed in disgust. "But if there is, I'm sure I'll never see you there." John Henry steps forward to point the gun at the men as they slowly back away. Richard just sits on the porch laughing at the top of his lungs as the car left the property.

"Is mom going to tuck me in?" John said that evening in John's bedroom.

"She's still not feeling well, maybe tomorrow," Richard replied. "You did well today, I am proud of you."

"Can you tell me a story, please," John asked? "Mom tells me a story before I go to bed."

"Sure, when the world was young, great kings ruled the land. All the power and riches of the Earth flowed through their kingdoms. When they conquer their enemies, the king would decide what was fair and just. He was the law. He had the power," Richard explained. "Power is what's most important in life."

"Is he brave," John asked?

"The bravest man of all," Richard agreed.

"I'm not afraid of anything, father," John boasted. "I'll be the bravest king in the world."

"Yes, you will. But today, great kings are called Presidents. They bring freedom and hope to their people and that is what made them great," Richard exclaimed. "Hope can be the most powerful weapon of all. It's what we dream about, when we're awake. It is our reward for a life well lived."

"I will, father," John promised. Young John is getting sleepy. Richard puts his hand over young John's eyes.

"Someday, I'm sure you will," Richard replied.

"Can you be king with me, daddy," John asked?

"Of course," Richard agreed. "Now get some sleep, King John."

Just after sunrise, John and Richard are cutting wood to prepare for the day. John is watching closely his father swing an axe. "Son, go see what your mother wants for breakfast," Richard requested. John gladly runs into the house.

"Mom, Mom," John shouted like he did a thousand times before. He enters the bedroom where his mother is sleeping. He quietly stopped to look at his mother. She is gray haired with a weathered face. She was beautiful in her earlier days. The frontier has taken its toll on her. She is not breathing. She is cold and motionless and her face is without pain. John stared at her, for a moment, with a blank look of disbelief on his face. His shoulders drop, head droops and eyes sadden but do not cry. He slowly turns and walks out of the room. His mother has passed away.

The next day, Richard and John put flowers on the grave of his wife. John does not cry. The grave is located on a hill next to the house in a small fenced area under a large oak tree. "Is mommy in Heaven," John asked?

"I've never been partial to that line of questioning, counselor. I can't give you that answer. I've never prayed for anything in my life and never apologized for my actions," Richard preached. "We're in this world for a brief time. The only thing we can count on is ourselves, son. I promise, no one else will."

"Why did God take her away," John asked? "Did she do something bad?" Richard kneels to speak with John, man to man.

"She did nothing bad and God still took her from us. She lives in our hearts, now," Richard explained. "If that's Heaven, then I suppose so."

The oil company trucks come onto the property and begin the process of drilling a well. Richard and John walk through the woods with their guns and come upon the oil well. "Father, what did those men want," John asked?

"You ask a lot of questions," Richard said. "I suppose the same thing all men want, money."

"Why did they give it to you," John asked again?

"Because they had no choice, that's how you do business in America," Richard expressed.

An explosion blows the rig and oil shoots in the air. Father and son fall to the ground. Black oil is flying everywhere. "What is this," John cried?

"Black gold, son, black gold," Richard replied. "We will be kings. You can have anything you wish. What do you want most?"

"I wish we had mommy back," John stated.

"Me too, son, me too," Richard consoled.

Thirteen years later, John is with some of his baseball teammates in the back of a truck. John is one good looking kid with a boyish face and the body of a man. The team stopped off at a huge house to let him out. The mansion stands where the old house once stood. It is white with two stories, twelve rooms, and six columns in the front. The porch is twice and large as the old house. The front lawn extends forty yards from the house into the street. The grass is as green as a golf course with trees fifty feet tall on all sides. John jumps out of the back of the truck and walks up to the house. Richard is on the long porch, in the cool shade, drinking a beer. He throws a cold one to John.

"How was the game," Richard said?

"Snatched victory from the jaws of defeat," John said in an arrogant tone.

"Congratulations," Richard asked.

"I swear father, this game builds such great character in men," John replied.

"Sport, for all its trials and glory, it does not build character in a man it merely reveals it," Richard professed.

"Someday, I will be a governor of great character," John boasts.

"Politics, the second oldest profession, and bears a remarkable resemblance to the first," Richard laughed.

"Father, I will be the Governor of Texas," John said proudly.

"Are you willing to do the right thing when everyone thinks you the fool," Richard advised?

"Of course," John said.

"Lincoln, Kennedy, both honest man in politics, you know what happened to them," Richard said. He points his finger at John like a gun and pulls the trigger.

"Funny, how's your heart," John asked.

"It's a Christmas miracle," Richard replied with excitement.

"The doctor told you to give up drinking, didn't he," John snapped.

"What's the point of having vices if you can't enjoy them," Richard explained with disappointment.

"Let me know how that works out for you," John grinned.

"Tonight's your last night before you leave for college," Richard said. "What are you going to do?"

"The Dorsey twins," John boasted as he tossed the game ball to Richard.

"I mean, what are your plans at college," Richard repeated?

"Father, I'm going to be the Governor of the Great State of Texas, that's all that really matters," John bragged.

"You're going to need allies. Choose your friends wisely," Richard warned. "Trust me, your enemies will find you on their own."

"And take no prisoners, right," John said.

"Wise beyond your years, you must be studying the law," Richard approved. John stared his father in the eye with disapproval.

"I shall free the world, amass a great fortune, and marry my queen," John promised.

"At least you're honest," Richard laughed. "Let me know how that works out for you."

"Father, Political Science is the study of kings. I will study Business and the Law," John proclaimed. "But, Yale is the best Political Science school in the nation, second to none."

"Champion of the people, perhaps you'll make a fine king, after all," Richard said. A car horn honks in the distance. John and Richard turn to see two blonde cheerleaders in a convertible pull up to the house. They are waving enthusiastically toward John.

"What do you think," John asked?

"What's not to like," Richard laughed.

"And it's not even my birthday," John joked. He walks confidently to the car and kissed both girls, wave's goodbye to Richard and jumps into the back of the car.

Yale

New Haven, a moderate-sized port city, is about ninety minutes away from New York. That's far enough away to make New Haven part of New England, and not a New York offshoot. To call it a port city is perhaps misleading, since its days as a prosperous center of shipping and industry are long past. New Haven is recognized as the cultural capital of Connecticut, the campus is a few miles from Long Island Sound, and refreshing sea breezes can still be felt, even if you have to climb one of the towers on campus to see the water. It is Heaven on Earth for beach towns along the Connecticut coast. In short, far from hiding in their dorm rooms in the walled-in courtyards of green lawns and shady trees, students are aware and caring of their surroundings in New Haven. John walks toward the dormitory areas surrounded by the other freshman classmates. His head turns to see a beautiful girl on the lawn. "I like this place," he thought.

In the dorm, he finds his room number and his roommate already inside. "Room 201," John said.

"What brings you to New Haven," Brian asked.

"Superior intellect and the hottest girls on the planet," John expressed.

"Nice, I'm Brian Runey from LA."

John throws his bag onto a bed without a care. "John Henry, I'm from Sixth Street, Austin, Texas," John announced. "Want to get a beer."

"I thought you'd never ask," Brian said. He pulls two beers out of a hidden refrigerator under his bed.

"Nice," John acknowledged.

"Really, why Yale," Brian said?

"Someday, I'm going to be the Governor of Texas," John proclaimed with confidence.

"Sounds expensive," Brian questioned.

"Not a problem," John said.

"Nice, you might want to check out Phi Delta Beta," Brian explained. "They've produced more governors and presidents than any other house on campus."

"How about you, why Yale," John asked?

"My father's the head of the Economic Advisory Council for the State of California," Brian added. "I got as far away as I possibly could." Brian is a blue blood capitalist with an eye for money and the finer things it can buy. He is daring, competitive, and bold in the world and never backs down from an opportunity to win. He is handsome but more importantly confident. A blue eyed blonde haired surfer boy from California. He never met a rule he couldn't break. He is the first guy you want when going out on the town and the last guy you want in a bar fight. With all his faults, deep down he is a great guy. You just have to pull away the layers to find him.

"Nice," John said.

That evening at the Phi house, John and Brian walk up from the street. They stop to look at the rush party going on with the music playing and the beer flowing. The house looks much like his house in Texas.

"This is the place where legends are made," Brian explained.

"Then legends, we shall be," John said arrogantly.

"They're going to like you," Brian laughed.

"What's not to like," John laughed. Michael walks up behind them and puts his arms around their shoulders. He escorts them into the house.

"Into the house, boys," Michael demanded. "Phi Delta Beta was established in 1849. We've been throwing outrageous parties ever since. What are you studying?"

"Business and Economics," Brian said.

"The money man," Michael laughed.

"Political Science," John said.

"This is your lucky day," Michael said. "Phi's has forty Captains of Industry, Twenty five Leaders of the Free World, and one mighty theologian. Did I mention the smoking hot ladies?"

"I should probably avoid the mighty theologian," John emphasized quietly.

"Too late, how about a beer," Michael laughs. Brian gave John the idiot look as they follow Michael to the bar.

"Hi, Michael," said two of the most beautiful women they had ever seen.

"Did I mention the smoking hot ladies," Michael repeated? "Bartender, two beers for my friends, so what do you think?"

"Doesn't get any better than this," John smiled.

"Awesome," Brian said.

"Seriously, pledging Phi Delta Beta is one of the best things that have ever happened to me. If you have any questions, just ask anyone. They'll be happy to answer any and all questions you have," Michael grinned as he walks off to talk with the two girls that just said hello by the bar.

"Thanks, I think this is it," John expressed.

"I'm in, too," Brian confirmed.

After the rush week is over, Brian and John find themselves pledging Phis. At the Phi house, the Big Brother award ceremony matched the big brother to their pledge little brothers. The pledge master is overseeing the ceremony. "Phi's is and has always been, a

Fraternity for Life," the pledge master preached. "Only by living these principles, year after year, does one gain a true understanding of what it means to be in a Fraternity. Brother Michael White, at the end of this life laid the grave. Therefore, with the teachings of God, we do what ought to be done for our fellow man. We charge you with the honor and education of one, John Henry, to perform the duties as big brother, now and forever. Do you accept the privilege?"

"With the spirit of brotherhood and the faith of my brothers, I accept this privilege," Michael answered trying not to laugh. He is a one of a kind individual, smart and seasoned. He understands his role in the universe. He is cool and under control with a certain sense of right and wrong that keeps him sane in the crazy old world around him. He insists on honesty to a fault. He will forever see the moral correctness of mankind while loving a double cheeseburger with an unmistakable passion. He looks wholesome from the outside, the boy next door. Not particularly tall or handsome, but with a glow from the inside that woman are inescapably drawn too. He is the last guy you want to go out with on the town or with to a party and the last guy you want in a bar fight, but he is the most important person in the world when deciding your fate. Yet, he is one of a kind.

"Booyah!" the active class yelled. Michael puts a pin on John as his little brother during the ceremony. The beer flows and the actives and pledges drink well into the night.

"Congratulations," Michael said.

"Thanks," John said.

"Don't thank me yet," Michael warned. "The Audie Murphy mud rally is coming up later in the backyard of the fraternity house. It is a rite of passage. You might say it's a chance to distinguish yourself from the others."

The Pledges, in white thermals, are huddled up in a group in the backyard of the house. The actives are at the very back of the yard in a group, drinking beer, smoking cigars, and chanting. A single member active addresses the pledges.

"This is the worst pledge class I've ever seen in all my years in this Fraternity. Can't you do anything right," the pledge master shouted?

"Sir, yes sir," the pledges yelled together.

"How many fraternities are there at this University," the pledge master bellows?

"One sir," the pledges respond together.

"What are the rest of them," the pledge master scolded?

"Boy's Clubs Sir," the pledges yelled together.

"Your mothers would be so proud, pond scum, listen up," the pledge master approved. "Tonight's the Audie Murphy. Audie was the most decorated American soldier of World War II and a celebrated movie star for over two decades. Audie, with just a tank mounted machine gun, single handed, held off an entire enemy regiment, so his wounded brothers could get back to safety. He was a true American hero."

"Booyah," the active class shouted.

"Tonight, you must show the same courage and patriotism. Your test, if you choose to accept it, is to survive the gauntlet of shame. If you succeed, pledge ship is over and you'll become members of Phi Delta Beta for the rest of your miserable lives. Fail and you will bring dishonor to your pledge class. We'll begin Brotherhood Week, right here, right now," the pledge master warned. "And remember, it's all or nothing. If one pledge fails to complete the challenge, everyone fails. Is that clear?"

"Sir, yes sir," the pledges yelled together.

"May the spirit of Audie Murphy be with you," the pledge master proclaimed. As the pledge class approached the gauntlet, they see it is full of mud, beer, trash, and other such disgusting items. The actives are chanting, "Audie, Audie!"

"Prepare your honor for Audie Murphy, pond scum," the pledge master ordered. The pledge class backs away from the gauntlet into a huddle.

"We don't have to do it, if we stick together. It's just a test," Tom proclaimed cautiously. Tom is an old dog, comfortable and loyal to the end. He is not the smartest guy in the room but trustworthiness can be an admirable quality. He is a gentle giant unless you upset him, then run for cover and don't look back. He is six foot six inches tall but not overweight or unattractive. He grew up in a small town where people trust one another until proven otherwise. He is the last one to go out with for a night on the town, but the first one you want on your side in a bar fight. "Stick together boys."

"This is crazy. Let's get out of here," Brian advised.

Across the street at the Alpha Sigma house, a few Alpha Sig sisters are on the roof with binoculars watching the entire event. Elizabeth's one of them on the roof. "I love Brotherhood Week. It's so ridiculously manly," one of the sisters shrieked.

"They won't do it. They never do. It's just a weird test of male testosterone," another sister added.

"Who is Audie Murphy any way," the first sister laughed. The girls giggle and continue to watch closely.

In the back yard, tension is building toward the Audie Murphy. "Are we going to do it," Brian questioned?

"Not me, I'm not getting in that," one pledge brother warned. John is standing impatiently at the back of the group.

"Go big or go home boys," John yelled. He darts in a full sprint into the gauntlet and slid the entire length. "Take no prisoners!" He rose to his knees and began throwing handfuls of mud at the active class.

"You're dead meat, John Henry," an active shouted in anger. Mud hits this active in the face.

"Come on," Tom ordered.

"Let's go," Brian snapped. The pledge class rushed the edge of the gauntlet and dove in headfirst. The class began throwing handfuls of mud at the actives. They panicked and scattered in all directions.

"Booyah," John shouted.

"Booyah," the pledges yelled together. The muddy pledges attack the abandoned beer kegs and proclaim their victory.

"What were you thinking," Tom said.

"Necessity, my brothers, makes brave men of us all," John admitted. "How's that beer taste?"

"Like victory," Tom shouted.

At the Alpha Sigma rooftop, Elizabeth is looking through her binoculars. She slowly pulls them down. "I haven't seen that before," she acknowledged. She looks interested while the other girls laugh.

After the evening festivities are over, Elizabeth, in a red corvette convertible with another sister, pulled up next to John, Brian, Tom and a few other pledges covered in mud, drunk, singing and walking in the middle of the street.

"You boys fall in the mud," Elizabeth laughed.

"What mud? I don't see any mud. How about you guys," John said.

"No, this is a hundred dollar Swedish body massage. I'll need help cleaning up, how about it," Brian asked.

"The last thing I want to do is hurt you. But wounding you is still on my list," Elizabeth grinned.

"You're hot, can I get your number," Brian asked.

"I wouldn't give you my zip code," Elizabeth laughed.

"Oh," the pledges laughed. Elizabeth laughs again, looks at John and speeds away. The guys recognize that look. The pledges push John and laugh at him while drinking beer.

The next night, Michael and John go out to celebrate the end of pledge ship. They see two girls sitting at a table. Unknowing to John, one of them is waiting for Michael. They each have a pitcher of beer. John recognized Elizabeth. He has the devil in his eyes as Michael introduced him. "John Henry, I would like you to meet Lisa Manchester and Elizabeth Roth." Michael announced. "They're Alpha Sigs."

"Are you stalking me," Elizabeth inquired to John. She is beautiful in every feature. Her hair is golden blonde with tan bronze skin. Her teeth are perfectly white. She is lean and hard from working out all her life. She is the kind of girl that walks into a room and turns every head. She is the perfect definition of eye candy, but that is not her best quality. She is wicked smart and sophisticated as a woman can possibly be. Not book smart, street smart. The kind of smart that drives men crazy and she knows how to turn it on and off with a glance. She definitely knows what she wants and how to get it. She has more testosterone than most men her age. She is not one to be pursued, she is a predator.

"Always," John grins as Elizabeth accepts his advance.

"We've already met," Elizabeth giggled.

"Really," Michael said. "Elizabeth is from New York. Her family has been in politics for years, as well as the oil business, among others. Lisa is my girlfriend. We met at Cox Chapel when we were freshman. She thinks I'll make a fine Pope someday or perhaps a gangster."

"Stop talking and let's dance," Lisa ordered.

"Of course," Michael said. Michael and Lisa leave to dance and let John and Elizabeth get to know each other. She looks suspicious of John.

"John Henry, didn't he die in a legendary contest of man versus machine," Elizabeth expressed.

"He tried to save his job and the jobs of his men," John explained. "He beat the industrial machine, but exhausted, he collapsed and died."

"Is that your fate John Henry," Elizabeth said. John is uncomfortable with that statement and a bit annoyed as he pours a beer for Elizabeth.

"Not to change the subject, but, why would Michael want to become a priest," John asked? "He's not exactly pope material".

"Perhaps because his father is a Bishop in the Lutheran church," Elizabeth said sarcastically.

"Good point. But, why would Phi's give me a Big Brother like that," John questioned.

"Because, I suppose, they're smart," Elizabeth suggested sarcastically.

"True, but he's not even Catholic," John stated.

"How about you, Mr. Henry, what's in your future," Elizabeth inquired?

"Political Science the art of letting other people think they're getting their own way," John proclaimed.

"Really," Elizabeth said.

"Hey, I will be a great king, conqueror, visionary, men of power and riches, like the kings of old, rulers of all they perceive," John announced.

"Interesting," Elizabeth said.

"And how about you, what do you like," John inquired.

"All the really fun things I enjoy are either illegal immoral, or fattening," Elizabeth grinned.

"Imagine that," John smiled.

"Actually, my father's a former Senator from the state of New York," Elizabeth said. "My family has lived in New York for generations. Our political affiliations date back to the revolution. You might say I come from old money."

"I'll bet you're quite the debutante," John responded.

"You might say that," Elizabeth acknowledged.

"My father is a self-made attorney. He passed the bar in Texas without ever going to college," John said. "When I was five, we found oil on our land."

"Well, imagine that," Elizabeth smiled.

"Today, he owns the largest law firm in Texas. Dozens of well-educated lawyers work for him," John grinned. "You might say I come from new money."

"I'll bet you're quite the sugar daddy," Elizabeth responded.

"You might say that." John acknowledged. Elizabeth and John smile as if they have been friends all their lives. They dance and talk for hours as the bar closed.

"Last call," the waiter said.

"No, thanks, I've an English test in six hours," John announced.

"You'll definitely need a priest for a big brother," Elizabeth consoled.

"I suppose. It's been nice meeting you, Elizabeth," John said.

"Well, Mr. Nouveau Riche, talking with you has been the conversational equivalent of a multiple orgasm," Elizabeth grinned.

"You're welcome," John accepted.

"You should take me home now," Elizabeth said.

"That's exactly what every man wants to hear," John grinned with the devil in his smile.

The next afternoon, John is asleep in his dorm room. Michael enters the room looking for him. "Get up, we have places to be," Michael shouts. "I hear you and Elizabeth hit it off pretty well last night."

"What makes you say that," John said?

"She dumped the last guy I introduced her to after twenty minutes," Michael announced. "Have you been sleeping all day?"

"My head hurts," John said.

"We have vespers at six o'clock," Michael shouted. "That's in ten minutes."

"Stop," John pleaded?

"Are you one of us," Michael asked?

"I hate to disappoint you, but I don't believe in God," John said. "Now, go away."

"No you're not," Michael demanded.

"What do you mean, no I'm not," John said.

"It doesn't bother me for you to say there are fifty gods or no God," Michael said. "The fact is eighty five percent of the registered voters in the State of Texas are Christians. You'll never even win a justice of the peace election without their vote."

"How do you know that," John exclaimed? Michael is annoyed with the lack of John's attention.

"Well, little brother, tell me this," Michael questioned. "Are you for capital punishment?"

"Yes," John said.

"Most Christians are not," Michael preached. "Are you for abortion?"

"If a woman wants it, sure," John said.

"Again, Christians are not," Michael preached. "Would you support segregation if it were the law, again?"

"If it were the law, yes," John said.

"Well then, Mr. Henry, the Christian voters are going to kick your ass," Michael predicted.

"The law supersedes matters of faith," John argued. Michael is now completely disgusted and gets in John's face.

"Without faith, there is no courage for life," Michael said impatiently. "For the last time, pledge, get up! I'll not be late, for you." Michael throws dirty clothes and hits John in the face.

At vespers, the pledges are sitting quietly in a single row in a pew. John's sitting at the end of the pew sleeping.

"Is that John sleeping?" the active said. John began to snore loudly.

"God hates me," Michael admitted.

It is a beautiful fall afternoon on the campus of Yale, the trees are golden, the air is cool and a lecture room is packed with forty eager students. The professor entered the room and prepared for the class. He is an astute individual with a tweed coat and longer than normal hair. Articulate and laid back for a professor. His glasses are round with the educated nerd look, yet they look surprisingly good on him. His wit and sarcasm are due to his formal power over the class. He decides your grade and doesn't want you to forget it. He is not so much into the details of life, but rather the big picture is important to him. I suppose tenure does that for a man. John, Brian, Tom, and Elizabeth are in the class waiting quietly. "As human beings, we're endowed with the freedom of choice, the right to succeed or fail, and we can't pass off our responsibility upon the shoulders of God or nature," the professor instructed. "We must carry this burden ourselves. It's entirely up to us. This is written by A. J. Toynbee. He was a British historian who wrote of the rise and fall of civilizations and the 'false gods' of modern nationalism. Welcome to the History of Political Science. I'm encouraged by the prospect of creative minds in my class. If you see any, be sure to let me know."

"I am Professor Argyris and this semester we'll endeavor to discover a few cutting-edge concepts. First, my class is hard. Second, you're not the first person in the world to arrive at new thoughts and ideas. And finally, with a considerable amount of stress, you will conceive the birth of an original thought, and it will be painful." The class grumbled in discomfort.

"In your life, you'll attempt to achieve great things and fail, and ignore the little things that truly matter; however, the real danger is that we shall attempt nothing with our lives. That's why you're here," the professor reminded. He turned from the front and moved to the chalkboard. He picked up the chalk and wrote two words, 'Famous Quotes'.

"These words are gifts from men, long since cold in the grave. They are meant to help us prepare our minds for the world that lies before us," the professor advised. The class looked concerned while Brian raised his hand.

"What's classified as an original thought," Brian questioned.

"It's a journey or adventure for you to discover. To experience life, good or bad, right or wrong, doesn't matter, just attempt something and learn from it. If it helps, I'll tell you what it's not," the professor instructed. "The young girl in the fifth row is quite beautiful." The professor points to Elizabeth as John looks at her. "That's not an original thought. I'm sure most every male student on this campus has had this exact same thought, among others," he claimed. Elizabeth blushed and looked down. "Miss, you've something you'd like to add."

"Great minds discuss ideas; average minds discuss events; and small minds discuss people. Quote the greatest first lady of our time, Eleanor Roosevelt," Elizabeth said proudly.

"Beautiful and smart, quite a deadly combination," the professor agreed. John's showing a jealous disposition. "You, young man, what's on your mind?"

"Hope is what we dream about when we're awake; yet it is the worst of all evils because it prolongs man's torments," John assured. "Even reality is irrelevant. The only thing that really matters is the perception of it."

"Is that the reality you speak of," the professor questioned.

"The only reality is the one we create for ourselves," John replied.

"Well said," the professor acknowledged. "Words, like the dew that falls on the morning grass, cause millions of people to…think. So who among you has the courage to command them, to respectfully lead a nation with them? It's not what happened in history that we remember, rather how we remember it, in a word, Politics. Perhaps this semester has promise, after all."

That Saturday afternoon, John is a senior living at the fraternity house. Some of the brothers are playing basketball in the backyard. John and Brian are on the balcony drinking beer and getting a little afternoon sun.

"The boys will miss you after you graduate," Brian stated.

"I'm afraid the real world's not like life here," John said. "It's guns and limo's out there, brother. Who can you trust?

"There's no brotherhood out there," Brian admitted. "We have to be our own mafia. You know there's nothing we can't do or get with a little help from our brothers."

"I know. Most people look for a job after graduation," John noted. "I'll create my own future."

"I'm all about the money," Brian admitted. "What's your plan?"

"Dare to be great, to defy authority, everything for one purpose, to be a king among men," John pledged. "Do you have the courage?"

"Guns and Limo's," Brian repeated.

"Mr. Henry, UPS is here. There's a letter for you. You have to sign for it," a pledge said. "Sir, can I get you another beer."

"That would be wise, young man. You'll go far," John approved as he began to read the letter. Quiet sadness, then anger overcame his face.

"What is it," Brian said?

"It's my father, he's been taken from me, too," John groaned. "So be it, we will take what we want from this world, whenever we want."

"And you're the only child," Brian already knew the answer.

"The attorneys want to meet. I'm the executor," John announced.

"Where there's a will, I want to be in it," Brian grinned. "You mean of your estate."

"The funeral is Wednesday," John said.

"I'm sorry to hear about your dad, but your future just got a lot closer," Brian pointed out. "When are you heading home?"

"In the morning, tonight, we drink to my father," John said.

"Take no prisoners," Brian repeated.

"You're the only brother I have," John claimed.

"I'm not going anywhere," Brian affirmed.

"I need to book a flight," John said.

"Are you taking Elizabeth with you," Brian responded?

"I suppose, I should," John admitted.

The Funeral is underway at a church in Austin, Texas. Inside the church, a priest spoke from a pulpit. "At this time, Richard's only son, John, would like to say a few words," the priest said. In the church, Elizabeth is sitting in the audience with John. The Dorsey twins are there, too. They both sneer at Elizabeth, she grins. John is dressed in black, handsome as ever he stumbled up to the pulpit.

"I'd like to thank you all for coming," John began. "Father would be ever so proud to see you here today. Few men will have the greatness to bend history itself. Each time a man stands up for an ideal or strike out against injustice, he sends forth a tiny ripple of hope. Those ripples build a current that can sweep down the mightiest walls of oppression. That was my father. As a lawyer, he had the courage to enter the moral conflict. He believed the future doesn't belong to those who are content with today, timid and fearful in the face of bold endeavors. Rather, it belongs to those who can blend vision, reason, and courage in a personal commitment to the ideals and great enterprises of American Society. It is the only way he could live. He was a true king among men. I hope to be such a man, as he. Thank you, Father, for being there for me." John walks out of the church with Elizabeth by his side. A rather serious looking attorney walks up to John with a letter.

"John, your father asked me to give you this note after his funeral. He was my friend. He wanted you to have those two, over there," the attorney grinned as he points to two Great Danes tied to a tree.

"Good one Dad," John admitted. "Can you do something with them until I return from school?"

"It would be my pleasure sir," the attorney said.

"They're adorable. I love them," Elizabeth laughed. The attorney walks towards the dogs and both dogs jump on him. John is shaking his head in amazement while Elizabeth is thoroughly enjoying the moment.

"And it's not even my birthday," John joked.

"Read it John," Elizabeth pleaded. "What does it say?"

John stopped as he realized he was about to read the last words of his father. Richard's voice was in his head. He gently read the letter to Elizabeth while trying to fight back the emotions. *Every morning you are handed twenty-four golden hours. They are one of the few things in this world that you get free of charge. If you had all the money in the world, you couldn't buy an extra one. What will you do with this priceless gift? Remember, you must use it, as it's given only once. Once wasted, you cannot get it back. Son, my death means nothing to me. When we are living, death's but a faraway dream, and when it's finally here, it's too late to really care. Please, don't regret growing older, it's a privilege denied to so many. So what will you do with the time you are given? Always remember what happened to the man who suddenly got everything he ever wanted. He lived happily ever after. I love you, son.* John folded the letter and walked away.

With this Ring…

John sits in an airplane with Elizabeth flying back to New Haven. He looks concerned as he orders a drink from the flight attendant. "That was quite a speech. I wish I had known your father," Elizabeth admitted.

"A flood of memories rushed over me like a tidal wave. As a child, he raised me after mother passed," John recalled. "We put flowers on her grave, together."

"How did your mother die," Elizabeth asked?

"God took her from us," John stated. "When I found her in bed, she was gone. The doctors told us it was cancer."

"I'm sorry," Elizabeth consoled.

"What kind of God would take away a mother from a five year old boy," John seethed in disgust. "I was angry for many years. The light was gone from my life." John stopped as hope left his face; Elizabeth reached out to hold his hand.

"What are you saying," Elizabeth asked?

"I lost my father, today. I barely had a mother. I have no brothers or sisters, no family. I'm an orphan in this world," John proclaimed. "I want you with me."

"You have me John," Elizabeth assured.

"Remember what happened to the man who suddenly got everything he ever wanted. He lived happily ever after," John reminded. "I want to grow old with you Elizabeth Roth; will you marry me?" She kissed John lightly.

"Of course, I'll marry you," she agreed with small tears of joy streaming down her face.

"When we land, perhaps we should shop for a ring," John admitted.

"Not necessary, my family has friends in the diamond business," Elizabeth grinned. John has a naive look on his face while Elizabeth is quite content.

"Really," John said. She reached over and kissed him the way a happy new wife would kiss her husband for the first time.

Governor Henry

In a corporate suite at the University of Texas gymnasium, a basketball game between the Texas Longhorns and the University of Connecticut is being played. It is time for the family to meet John. Elizabeth, her father and mother, and a few close friends are drinking and eating Texas T-bones. "Can I get you a drink," John offered.

"Of course, I understand my future son-in-law will be running for Governor of Texas," William acknowledged. "When do you plan to run?"

"The next election's in two years away," John said.

"Texas needs to grow its industrial base, revive its economy, and balance its deficit," William advised. "Any ideas on how that might happen?"

"Keep it simple. There's no such thing as a Win-Lose proposition," John expressed. "Successful business and economies rely on both sides winning. If one side loses, then ultimately, both sides lose because no further business will continue between the two, it's self-fulfilling."

"Interesting," William replied. He is an elder statesman in the most honorable sense of the word. His silver hair is always in perfect order, every hair in place. He is comfortable with an air of confidence that makes an older man attractive. He plays golf, tennis, and swims three times a week and it shows. He liked the finer bourbons but single malt scotch is always acceptable. You won't find a beer in his hand, ever. His wife is his same age, beautiful and refined with an air of New York aristocracy. He is charismatic to a fault and never gets angry because it is important for him to always be in control. He is a dominating man in every sense of the word.

"It's the same with the economy, state politics, and even national politics. You raise taxes, create austerity, raise interest rates, somebody loses," John advised. "Grow the economy and everybody profits, business, taxpayers, and even the government wins. But, inevitably it breaks down and lawyers like me get paid, and we get paid a lot."

"So there's no such thing as a Win-Lose proposition," William acknowledged.

"I swear I don't know why it's so hard to understand," John said.

"Easy to understand but difficult to turn it all around," William assured.

"Cut costs and increase revenues," John said. "You're right, it sounds simple, but it's not. You have to change the game so everybody wins." William looks impressed. He spoke slowly in a fatherly tone as he puts his hand on Johns shoulder.

"Convictions are a wonderful thing," William reassured. "I like you, son, so here's a tip. Texas is giving away six points. They will win the game by eight."

"But, we're losing by nine with seven minutes to go," John said.

"Doesn't matter, everything has their price John," William advised. "I'll see you back at the house. I need to say hello to a few friends." He shook John's hand and walked away. John began talking and making drinks with his friends in the suite. Eventually, the final buzzer sounds.

"Are you ready, darling," Elizabeth asked.

"We actually won by eight," John uttered strangely.

"That's good John," Elizabeth said sarcastically. "Where's my father?"

"He said he would meet us at home," John replied. "He wanted to see a few friends while he was here."

John prepared for his Governors speech in downtown Austin on the steps of the capital. Media coverage was there. "Our destiny lies in our own hands," John began. "In man's long, upward march from savagery to slavery and throughout the two hundred years of our history, there have been many deep, terrifying valleys, but also many bright and towering peaks. One peak stands highest in the ranges of human history. One union holds out the promise of justice and opportunity for every citizen: That union is the United States of America. I'm proud of

America, I'm proud to be from Texas, and I am proud to announce my candidacy for the Governor of the Great State of Texas." A small crowd cheered with approval, but with not too much enthusiasm.

"Texas is the embodiment of hope for progress and America is the world's greatest democracy," John proclaimed. "Together, we remain the symbol of man's aspiration for liberty and well-being. We are Texans." Several banners in the background are not to John's taste.

As the weeks go by and the campaign slowed, John calls Michael from his downtown campaign office. A crowd of Occupy Wall Street, Tea Party and Christian protesters are outside the building, John looked out the window at them. He called Michael using the speakerphone. "Michael, how are you," John asked?

"John, it's good to hear from you," Michael replied. "I understand you're running for the Governor. How's it going?"

"Someone told me once, I needed the Christian vote in Texas," John grunted. "Well, there's a Tea Party outside my office, with tents and picket signs calling me a racist, baby killer, and Go Occupy Yourself."

"We've had this conversation before, haven't we," Michael reminded? "You're not exactly Christian material."

"Yeah, I get it, but I'm not breaking any laws, they are," John protested. "I've had the chief of police throw them in jail twice, and the next day they're back, preaching again."

"You bring out the best in people," Michael laughed.

"I've done nothing wrong," John expressed, "what is happening Michael."

"Christians don't like killing innocent people, homosexuality isn't God's way, and capital punishment is just legalized murder," Michael advised.

"I haven't killed anybody, yet, I'm a lawyer. I've forgotten more about the law than most people will ever know. Seriously, I am the law," John snapped. "Why are they demanding I break it?"

"The Christian faith is based on God's law, not your laws," Michael affirmed.

"It's criminal and they're costing me the election," John complained.

"This isn't something where you can ride both sides of the fence. They've come to your front door." Michael stated. "These people are serious. They believe God's on their side."

"So I can kiss my political career goodbye and for what," John sneered.

"Christ's a forgiving God," Michael assured. "But, I'm afraid those people are not so willing to forgive."

"Sorry hypocrites, I have a crushing need to make an example of somebody," John fumed. "What is wrong with these people?"

"Christians have one foot in this world and one foot in the next.

That's what makes them misunderstood," Michael admitted. "The rules of this world do not apply to them."

"So it's them or me," John declared.

"Lighten up little brother, it's just politics. You play the game or the game plays you" Michael said. "You know that."

"Okay, Michael. It's been good talking to you," John agreed.

"Try not to burn any crosses, okay," Michael laughed.

"My father dedicated his entire life to the law," John expressed with conviction. "These Christians are completely defiant of it."

"Yeah, we're funny like that. Look John, I'm on your side. Call me, if you need me, little brother," Michael reassured. "I'm always on your side."

John meets up with Elizabeth on the campaign trail. Frustration is all over John's face. "I've been in sixteen cities in the last ten days," John explained. "I'm not really sure what town I'm in."

"The election's three weeks away," Elizabeth reminded. "The polls show us falling further behind Governor Jackson."

"No kidding, my career is over before it has begun," John complained as he witnessed his lifelong dream fading before his very eyes.

"Can I help," Elizabeth said?

"Not unless you have a magic wand," John implored.

"My father has experience in these matters," Elizabeth said. "Can I call him?"

"Sure, okay, I love you," John said.

"I love you, too," Elizabeth said.

In John's campaign office, he is alone. He reluctantly reads the latest voting margins on his computer. He is losing by a significant margin. William confidently walks into John's dark office.

"Good morning John" William exclaimed.

"What's good about it," John muttered. "Haven't you read the papers?"

"You know the race isn't always won by the fastest,' William proclaimed. "How do you think the race is going?"

"Not quite like I planned," John stammered trying to find his voice.

"That's too bad. You'd have made a fine Governor. The State of Texas needs you. Have you prayed about it," William grinned.

"It's not funny; prayers are for the weak, William. I've never prayed for anything in my life and never apologized for my actions," John seethed. "We're only in this world for a brief time. The only thing we can count on is ourselves. No one else will."

"John, I have friends that can answer prayers. But, they're going to want something in return. It has to be a win-win for everyone, understand," William demanded.

"What do I have to do," John asked?

"Well, as Governor of Texas someday, they're going to want you to run for the Presidency of the United States," William admitted.

"Oh, is that all," John laughed. "I'm not even the Governor of Texas, yet."

"Let's just say we share the same interests. You wouldn't be the first President they've elected," William assured. "What do you think?"

"I think it's crazy," John snapped. "The President of the United States, I wouldn't know...,"

"You'd be king. Isn't that what you really want, to rule the common man," William reminded. "But, perhaps, it might not ever happen. You would actually have to get elected and that might be a long shot."

"What if I say, no," John replied.

"You could spend the rest of your days, here in Austin, running your father's law firm," William explained. John looks defeated, followed by a glimmer of hope.

"What if I accepted your offer," John pointed out.

"A great adventure, Elizabeth's head would be spinning for years. But, it's all or nothing," William warned. "There's no middle ground, no turning back."

"I'll bet you were quite the politician in your day. Okay, William, I'm all in," John announced. "When do we start?"

"We just did, sport," William said.

At campaign headquarters, Martha, his secretary, walked into

John's office. She looked like everyone's mother. Sweet, plump, and a long arm of kindness for everyone that came into contact with her; she brought John cookies at least once a week. She was thrilled to bring him the local morning newspaper. The headline read, "Scandal: Governor Jackson accused of Tax Evasion". She can't help herself from smiling at John. "Sir, have you seen this," Martha exclaimed.

"Oh my God, turn on the Television please," John shouted.

"The Governor's race has taken a dramatic turn," the CNN newsman said. "With the latest tax evasion scandal, the polls are showing the incumbent Governor's popularity falling dramatically. With two weeks remaining for the election, challenger John Henry has taken a three percent lead in the current polls."

"Incredible," John shouted as his cell phone rings.

"I just watched the news," Elizabeth said with excitement.

"It's incredible," John laughed.

"My father called earlier to say congratulations," Elizabeth said.

"What else did he say," John asked?

"He said, his prayers had been answered," Elizabeth admitted.

"Really, that's great," John replied as he recalls his deal with William.

"John, there's only two more weeks till the election," Elizabeth screamed. "You can win."

"It's incredible, isn't it,' John replied quietly. "I'll see you tonight."

"I love you, too," Elizabeth shouted.

The press is waiting outside the Governor's Mansion. It is the most historic house in Texas. It sat on a beautifully landscaped city block in Austin near the Capitol building. Built in 1856, it is the oldest continuously occupied executive residence west of the Mississippi. The press has surrounded the front gate as John and Elizabeth finally arrive. "Governor Henry, how did you first get involved in politics," the reporter shouted?

"Why, he married into it, of course," Elizabeth laughed. The reporters followed them as they continued up the lawn.

"You'll make a fine first lady of Texas," John assured.

"Yes, I believe I will," Elizabeth boasted.

"Come on, Tinker bell, Captain Hook, to the castle" John shouted to the two Great Danes. "Welcome to Camelot." Elizabeth blushed while the two Great Danes run free on the lawn of the Texas mansion.

The first four years flew by like the blink of an eye. John and Elizabeth have two young daughters to occupy their spare time. Lisa Ann and Kimberly are pretty, sophisticated, and well behaved. They behavior is focused and give the impression to be well beyond their years. They are perfect little ladies. John liked to say, "They are fortunate; they have Elizabeth's looks and Elizabeth's brains." In the office of Governor, John was at his political best. He was born to do this job.

Inside the Texas mansion, newspaper headlines showed John Henry re-elected Governor of Texas for a second term. Brian, the Director of Economic Development, sat privately in John's office waiting to conduct business with John. "Congratulation on the second term," Brian acknowledged.

"So what's the latest on the new State Highway project," John asked.

"I know the contractor on this one," Brian said. "They've promised us land along the route. A million dollar commercial property at the intersections, all we have to do is say yes."

"So we're in the mafia, after all," John expressed.

"Guns and Limo's, baby," Brian said.

"How do we cover our tracks," John commanded?

"It's the standard offshore deal," Brian replied. "No names, no principles, no trails and no taxes."

"So nobody gets hurt," John questioned?

"Trust me, it's a done deal," Brian said. "You don't have to do anything but stay out of the way."

"That's economic development," John pointed out.

"If you see a blind man selling pencils, steal his pencils, steal his nickels, and his dog," Brian laughed. "We're just white collar mafia in a modern world, and we don't take prisoners."

"You know what the trouble with the rat race is," John said.

"You're still just a rat," Brian grinned.

"If you're not on the inside, then you're nobody," John proclaimed.

"Why do you think insider trading is illegal," Brian acknowledged? "It's so unbelievably profitable."

The group is gathered around John at the West Texas cabin retreat. It is a beautiful rustic house with beamed ceilings, wood paneled walls. There is a sense of liberation at the cabin, not found in Austin. Because the perimeter was guarded, we could do whatever we pleased and we did. That's a freedom, incidentally, that you don't fully appreciate until you've lost it. "We are here to celebrate the achievements of the past eight years, but more importantly, to make our mark upon the future," John announced. Tom got a Champagne bottle and handed it to John. "As of next week, I'm declaring my candidacy for the Presidency of the United States. Would you like to go to Washington?"

The group roared as the champagne popped, girls came out of the back room, and the party began. "Are you serious? How did you do it," Brian rejoiced?

"I made a deal with the devil and some very influential people, too," John stated. "Are you ready to be rich beyond your wildest dreams?"

"Oh yeah," Brian shouted. John strolled into a bedroom with two girls.

"You sure are pretty," John grinned. "What's your name?"

The next week, John appeared on the local news for a statement. Michael stood in the wings watching. "To this great state, and the kindness of the people of Texas, I owe everything," John said emotionally. "Here, I've lived most of my life, and have passed from a young man to become your Governor. I now leave, with a task before me, greater than any before. Without the assistance of God Almighty, I cannot succeed. With that assistance, I cannot fail. To God's care, I leave you, as I hope in your prayers you'll go with me, I bid the great state of Texas a fond and affectionate farewell. We are going to Washington, DC." John's sarcasm is visibly upsetting to Michael as John walked off the stage. "How was that?"

"You're hypocrisy knows no bounds," Michael sneered.

"Thanks for coming," John answered.

"Oh, you've come a long way since your fraternity days, little brother," Michael assured.

"It's been good," John grinned. "I called you here for a reason. Michael, I need you to join us. I want you to consult on religious matters of the State, as a member of my cabinet in this race for the presidency."

"The trouble with fighting for the human spirit is most of one's time is spent defending the undesirable," Michael snapped. "You know anyone like that?"

"You said play the game. Tom is the secretary of security. Brian is the secretary of economic affairs. The brothers are all together, even you," John said arrogantly.

"Who knew you'd be so good at it," Michael suggested.

"Michael, Texas is a great state," John assured. "Seriously, a good friend's supposed to side with you, even when you're wrong. After all, everybody sides with you, when you're rich." John smirked and walked past a disgusted Michael.

"But you're always wrong," Michael reminded.

"I heard that. Pack up, we're going to Gettysburg," John ordered. "We've a Presidency to win."

"God help us all," Michael feared.

I Solemnly Swear...

After eight years as Governor of Texas, a seasoned John Henry made his announcement speech on the battlefield of Gettysburg. The media was in full coverage.

"On this hallowed ground, Former President Woodrow Wilson once spoke if it. He said, 'Upon these famous fields and hillsides their comrades died about them. In their presence it was an impertinence to discourse upon how the battle went, how it ended, what it signified!' Do we deem the Nation complete and finished? They were willing to die that the people might live free. But their task is done and their day's turned into evening. They look to us to perfect what they established and make it secure. There's no enemy within its borders, no power among the nations of the Earth to make it afraid," John began. The larger crowd is responding enthusiastically to John's speech.

"This American nation, when it made that first noble, naive appeal to the moral judgment of mankind to take notice, at last, has been established to serve men, not masters," John proclaimed with passion. Elizabeth proudly looks on from her seat with the two children.

"It's with this devotion that I am proud to announce my candidacy for the Presidency of the United States of America," John announced with conviction. "Whom do I command? The ghostly hosts who fought upon these battlefields long ago and are now departed, their glory won? I have in my mind another host whom these set free of civil strife in order that they might work out in days of peace. That host is the people of this nation, the great and the small; and undivided in interest, if we've but the vision to guide and direct them and order their lives aright in what we do. God Bless us all. God Bless America."

At campaign headquarters in Washington, John waited to meet his national campaign manager. "John, I want you to meet Frank," William advised. "He's your new campaign manager." Frank is middle aged man with unimpressive features. There is nothing particularly unique about him. He is remarkably average to look at. If you pasted him on the street, you probably wouldn't even notice him. Yet, his demeanor is cold and calculating. He is thorough and meticulous in ever endeavor; nothing is left to chance with him and that is what made him dangerous. He flaunts his wealth and considers himself an elitist and proud of it. If you peel away the layers, you might even find a psychopath. "He'll serve as your political advisor and chief strategist on the campaign. Do you understand?"

"Sure, what do we do first," John requested.

"I like him, already," Frank joked. "I've some speaking engagements for you in Florida and fund-raising in Tennessee."

"Other people's money," John assumed.

"Absolutely, and if it doesn't work out, too bad for someone else," Frank said.

"Heads we win, tails they lose," John grinned. "So, how do we get there?"

"I've got a jet," Frank said arrogantly.

"I like him, already," John laughed.

While flying to Florida, John and Frank are planning strategy on the first class jet. Champagne is flowing all around them. "We have to get you polished," Frank advised.

"What do you want me to say," John said.

"It's not what you say. It's how you say it," Frank stated. "Deliver the lines with conviction and passion. This is America. The people want a strong leader. Later, when you're President, what you say matters. Until then, we promise everything to everybody."

"Won't they remember," John objected.

"Not a chance, whoever slanders the most wins," Frank assured. "The American people are bombarded with media. A thousand messages a day get conveyed to the public through television, radio, newspaper, and now internet. It's everywhere."

"Media overload," John said.

"If the American people like you, you're in. It is charisma and television. Think Ronald Reagan," Frank reassured. "Look good, sound good, and be strong."

"How can you be sure," John questioned.

"You'd be surprised who we've worked with," Frank bragged.

"It used to be about what I can do," William indicated. "Now, America is about, what I can become. You will win, John, I promise."

"It's all taken care of," Frank added. "Elizabeth's going to make a fine First Lady." John sits comfortably back in his private jet seat. A beautiful young flight attendant brings him a drink and a cigar.

At campaign headquarters in Washington, John is patiently waiting for the results to come in. "With sixty percent of the popular vote in, John Henry's taking a commanding lead for the Presidency of the United States," the CNN newsman announced. "He needs only twenty four electoral votes to ensure victory. We predict that will come sometime in the next two hours."

"You did it, you did it again, the White House," Elizabeth screamed. "I can't believe it. It's so surreal."

"My exploits have become legendary," John admitted. They take the stage for the victory announcement. They raise their hands in victory as the balloons come down around them.

John's Inaugural Address is being held on a fine fall day. At the podium with his right hand raised, he took the oath of office. Elizabeth grinned the entire time. He makes his address, "We have every right to dream heroic dreams. Those who say that we're in a time when there are no heroes; they just don't know where to look. You can see heroes every day going in and out of factory gates. Others, a handful in number, produce enough food to feed all of us and then the world beyond. Their patriotism's quiet, but deep. Now, I've used the words 'they' and 'their' in speaking of these heroes. I could say 'you' and 'your' because I'm addressing the heroes of whom I speak you, the citizens of this blessed land. Your dreams, your hopes, your goals are going to be the dreams, the hopes, and the goals of this administration. In the days ahead, I will propose removing the roadblocks that have slowed our economy and reduced productivity," John explained with confidence. "It's time to reawaken this industrial giant. And these will be our first priorities, and on these principles there will be no compromise." The historic crowd applauded with significant approval.

"This is the second time in our history that this ceremony has been held on this West Front of the Capitol. At the end of this open mall are those shrines to the giants on whose shoulders we stand. Directly in front of me is the monument to a monumental man, George Washington, father of our country. He led America out of revolutionary victory into infant nationhood. Off to one side is the stately memorial to Thomas Jefferson. The Declaration of Independence flames with his eloquence. And then, beyond the Reflecting Pool, are the dignified columns of the Lincoln Memorial. Whoever would understand in his heart the meaning of America will find it in the life of Abraham Lincoln. We each must pay the price of freedom to be heroes. Our duty's entirely up to us. We are the American people. We are the heroes of the world. Thank you very much." John, Elizabeth, and the children waved to the crowd.

"That was magnificent," Elizabeth observed.

"Is this the center of the universe," John boasted.

"I believe it is my king," Elizabeth agreed, "let us retire to the White House."

The White House is situated in the western part of the city. It has a southern and a northern front with the southern sloping towards the Potomac and commanding a view of it. A semi-circular balcony extended out from the Parlor on this side and overlooked the private garden. The high basement gives the house a third story on this side. On both fronts, the grounds are laid out with tastefully planted forest-trees and shrubbery. The walks are gravel, broad and delightful. The mansion is two stories and the northern front is ornamented with a lofty portico of four Ionic columns in front and three on either side. Beneath this portico drive the carriages of visitors; immediately opposite the front door, across the open vestibule or hall, is the Reception Room. The East Room has four mantels of marble with Italian black, and gold fronts, and very handsome grates; each mantel is surmounted with a

French mirror, the plates of which measure one hundred and fifty-eight inches, framed in splendid style. Four other large mirrors, two at each end of the room, reflect the rays from three large chandeliers, from which descend glass pendants, which glitter in the light like diamonds. John sits in the Oval Office like a fish out of water on his first official day as President of the United States. William walks through the door. Inside the Oval Office, three large windows behind the President's desk face south, as well as four doors leading into different parts of the West Wing. It is positioned to provide easy access to his staff in the West Wing and to allow him to retire easily to the White House residence at the end of the day. The ceiling is adorned with an elaborate molding around the edge and features elements of the Seal of the President.

"Congratulations," William said. "How's it going?"

"Not quite like I expected. We're actually here," John grinned. "It's amazing."

"Good. You realize I'm going to ask a few favors along the way," William reminded. "You are prepared for that."

"Sure, I get it, I'm not that naïve," John said. "Do I have to kill anyone?"

"The tree of Liberty needs to be watered from time to time with the blood of patriots and tyrants," William responded.

"That's Thomas Jefferson," John recalled.

"Not to worry," William assured. "America will be behind you."

"Seriously, does it really matter," John replied.

"No, but it's always been a good idea," William reassured. "I'll be in touch, Mr. President. Enjoy the day."

"What's not to like," John laughed? William is leaving the Oval Office when Tom walked in. William stopped and shook Tom's hand.

"Hello, William," Tom greeted. "John, I've a matter of national security." William looked over his shoulder to John as he walked out the door.

"Security is your profession, talk to me," John said.

"The CIA has discovered evidence of nuclear weapons being transported over the Afghanistan-Iranian border," Tom warned. "Satellite images and intelligence confirm the weaponry to be nuclear in nature."

"How did we get this," John exclaimed.

"CIA covert operations in the region," Tom said. "I was advised where and when to make observations."

"Did we attempt to confront these terrorists," John asked?

"I sent a small group of local marines into the area. I had to act quickly," Tom explained. "There was a confrontation."

"And…," John asked.

"It's like they knew we were coming," Tom revealed. "There were no survivors. The bodies were desecrated."

"These men deserve our highest honor, they're heroes," John

commanded. "Break the story through the normal White House channels."

"What's your message," Tom asked?

"I'll not be threatened by nuclear assault from anyone, anywhere," John scolded. "Iran will open themselves up to UN inspectors immediately. Any hesitation will be considered an act of war."

"They'll refuse," Tom advised.

"I hope they will," John snapped. At that moment, John realized his first act as President would be monumental.

On the White House television, CNN news reporters are presenting the story to the world. "In an act of heroic bravery, a small group of marines stationed at the Afghanistan-Iranian border took on a terrorist group smuggling nuclear weapons into Iran. Satellite photos produced detailed weaponry being transported across border when marines encountered the terrorist regime. A US medical team on the scene discovered no survivors from the US led marines," the CNN newsman explained. "The President of the United States is demanding immediate inspection of the area by UN investigators. There has been no response from the Iranian government at this time."

"We can never allow ourselves to support evil," John demanded. "The long-term price is almost always disastrous."

"With the declaration of war against the oil-rich middle east, the price of a barrel of crude oil has surged in futures trading. Oil traders in the pits are franticly trading Oil stocks on the floor of the stock exchange" the CNN Newsman reported. "The price seems to have come to the pump. With five dollar per gallon gasoline, America faced a severe drain on the national economy and seems destined for another economic recession, if not already. The stock market's down another seven hundred points today on heavy trading as the war continued."

William walks into the Oval office.

"Good morning, William, I trust all's well in your world," John snapped.

"As always, Mr. President," William replied.

"The war is going well, but that's about the only thing I can say," John expressed.

"That's to be expected, but you've done well," William said. "Your first one hundred days have been very impressive."

"Sure," John replied. "Elizabeth wants you and mother to spend time with us at Camp David. Relax and enjoy your granddaughters."

"I appreciate that, but we have work to do," William revealed.

"Like what? The economy's stalling and your oil war is escalating," John pointed out. "Seriously, I'm beginning to understand how Herbert Hoover created a world-wide depression, all by himself."

"It'll be fine," William reassured. "You did the right thing. You'll be remembered as one of the most respected Presidents in American history."

"Enough, what else does the devil want from the American people," John snapped.

"They want to wear them down with taxes, perpetual debt, and in the end, break their will to resist until they're completely dependent and helpless," William explained.

"Imagine that, and how do they profit from that," John sneered.

"Create economic bubbles and let them burst," William admitted. "They profit on both sides of the market because they control it and so do you, John. You'll have anything you wish."

"I'm the President of the United States," John barked. "Why do I feel like I've fallen down the proverbial rabbit hole?"

"Business is booming and we've made millions. Success and audacity go hand in hand," William insisted. "Embrace it, John, and you'll be unstoppable."

"Audacity," John roared. William hands John a piece of paper.

"There's a Swiss bank account with twenty million in it," William stated. "Only you can sign for it. Call and check the balance, whenever you want."

"Seriously," John paused.

"Have one of your friends do it," William asked. "Brian's trustworthy, isn't he?"

"And what in the world am I to do with this," John insisted.

"Spoil my granddaughters," William said. "You did well." William opens his jacket and gets two cigars, hands one to John. John smells it and puts it in his jacket.

"Okay William, thanks, I'll enjoy this later," John approved. William gets the scotch from the cabinet.

"I haven't seen Michael around much lately," William asked. "How is he?"

"He's fine," John said.

"You know your popularity among Christian voters is at a record low," William stated. "You lost their votes in the election, but it really didn't matter, after all. Did it?"

"I'll speak with him, soon," John reassured.

"If the Christian voters had their way, you'd never have become President," William expressed. John looks out the window at protesters in the street.

"I know, just like Texas," John said.

"I'm sorry to say, but a group of Christian right-wing Senators is conspiring against you, as we speak," William explained. "They call themselves Tea Party Senators."

"Why do Christians believe they're not of this world," John said? "And now, they attack me. Where's my forgiveness."

"These Senators believe they're chosen by God to lead this country," William declared.

"Yeah right, do we know their agenda," John asked?

"Impeachment for the atrocities of an unjust war, profiteering from an economic collapse and a complete lack of Judeo-Christian morality that borders on anti-Semitic," William quoted.

"And I thought they didn't like me," John grinned.

"They're calling you an atheist, John," William warned.

"Well, that's just bad for business," John admitted. "What would you do, if you were in my shoes?"

"Eliminate the problem," William said.

"Do it," John ordered.

As weeks go by, the power and corruption of the Presidency have begun to affect John. His demeanor has changed for the worse. At noon, John and Brian are having several drinks and a cigar. They both have bags under their eyes. "It requires a great deal of boldness and caution to make a great fortune," John explained. "But once you have it, it's ten times as hard to keep it."

"Yeah, speaking of that, I called that bank account you told me,' Brian said. "It has a twenty million dollar balance. There's something you're not telling me."

"A day of reckoning is coming," John revealed. "Money is the most important thing in the world and I'll need a war chest to win."

"So re-election's job one," Brian said.

"Always, go big or go home," John commanded.

A voice on the intercom announced Michael is due for his meeting in the office. "Michael to see you sir," the secretary replied.

"Send him in," John said.

"Good afternoon," Michael said. "Hello, Brian."

"Hey, buddy. I'll get right on that, John." Brian left with a glance back at John.

"Michael, I've a question," John said. "Do you believe that absolute power corrupts absolutely?"

"History dictates that to be true," Michael stated. "Why do you ask? Are you feeling guilty or just drunk in the afternoon?"

"A clear conscious is the sign of an ambiguous memory. I've never really been innocent," John replied. "But, are we actually using our power to make America free, to benefit the registered voters, of course."

"Freedom and stewardship are two different things," Michael explained.

"So, do you think you're free," John asked.

"I expect nothing from anyone," Michael declared. "I fear no man. Therefore, yes, I'm free. However, freedom belongs with God; it's his gift to humanity. However, when government fears the people, there is liberty."

"Touché, old friend," John approved. "It's the Christian voters that

I'd like to discuss. It seems we lost their vote in the past election and yet, we're still able to win. Perhaps I don't need their votes, after all."

"What are you hiding," Michael asked.

"I hope that no American will throw away his vote by voting either for me or against me solely on account of my religious affiliation," John said. "It's just not relevant."

"You think Kennedy believed the Christian vote wasn't relevant," Michael exclaimed.

"Catholics love thy neighbor as you would yourself, but with all sincerity, choose the finest neighborhood," John grinned.

"I see. You've lost your moral compass in this presidential charade," Michael snapped? "What's really bothering you."

"Perhaps, it's just the hypocrisy of the church. The centuries of extortion and crusades in the name of God that offends me. What kind of God wished death upon his enemies and builds massive cathedrals in his name," John questioned? "I know money can't buy happiness, but it sure makes grief a whole lot more fun. I mean, what real power does the church have when only money rules."

"So, this is your original thought," Michael taunted.

"Do not mock me," John scolded.

"But it's so easy when you've been drinking," John answered. "You mock everything you've ever known, the fraternity, Yale, America, Elizabeth, even your father. What's next, John."

166

"Your Christian elite have stood in my way ever since Texas," John protested. "I'm done with them."

"Oh right, perhaps you should meet them," Michael added. "I know a few esteemed colleagues from the Christian Cooperation. Perhaps, they can convince you of a higher calling."

"I know my calling, but for you Michael, I suppose, in principle, we should meet," John said sarcastically. "Of course, when a man says he approves of something in principle, it means he hasn't the slightest intention of going through with it.'

"Your insecurities bore me," Michael stated. "But, I'll arrange it."

"You sure you wouldn't like a drink," John grinned.

Jogging outside the White House perimeter with William, John is breathing very heavily. It's an overcast day in Washington with a light rain.

Two Secret Service agents are behind and in front of them. "I've been running for three miles," John gasped. "Can we walk for a while?"

"You really should be in better shape. Here try this, it is called Evolv. It's cellular level oxygen regeneration super water," William explained as he hands a bottle to John. "It is amazing."

"Will it help me live longer," John begged.

"Only if you want to," William said. "We need to talk."

"Every time you say we need to talk, people die or worse," John acknowledged. "Give us some room boys." The secret service agents back off slowly from them. "What's bothering you, now?"

"Checked your bank account, lately," William stated.

"Why do you ask," John said?

"It has a hundred million dollars," William announced. John stopped walking and looked William in the eye.

"It's not going to end well, is it William? We're not talking war or insider trading, are we? This is about need," John predicted. "What does the devil need now?"

"The same thing influential men have desired since the beginning of time," William assured. "Worship from the masses as an act of patriotism to the United States."

"You mean Caesar worship," John acknowledged. "I'm familiar with it. He established law and order from the chaos. He brought peace, safety, and prosperity to the conquered land, and the masses were grateful."

"Today, just as then, the establishment demands the same thing, a deified ruling class," William explained.

"Secular humanism," John asked.

"Don't be ridiculous," William said. "These people are aristocracy, John. It's always been about money and power."

"Aristocracy, explain it to me," John snapped. "I am the President of the United States."

"Oil is the cash cow that feeds Wall Street. Wall Street washed the money with insider trading. We know the end result, before anyone even knows it's even begun," William admitted. "Politicians, like you, make sure nobody goes to jail, ever."

"You have it all figured out, but what happens to America," John questioned.

"You're an educated man. You know that no civilization, no culture, no country has ever ruled forever. The Romans were conquered by the barbarians. China, Japan, and Germany were all great countries that once dominated the world. All have fallen from power," William explained. "In the first economic war of the twenty first century, Ronald Reagan bankrupt Russia without even a single shot."

"We're not in danger William," John expressed.

"Denial doesn't become you," William replied. "It's a capitalist country with no capital. Your America owes sixteen trillion dollars and you're too old to ever pay it back. Every single day, ten thousand people turn sixty-five. This will continue for the next nineteen years. It's never good to be old and broken. Without the ability to print money, we'd have been dead long ago."

"The deficit is big enough to take care of itself," John demanded. "I'm not worried; we can print money."

"Like some third world country, the Fed props up the market like a façade," William laughed. "Your deficits are slowly killing you,

169

your dollars are worthless, and every day the Government is digging the hole deeper and deeper, until one day you can't pay it back, any of it." John can't take much more of this. His frustration with the lack of hope is devastating. He looks like he's having a nervous breakdown.

"Why are you telling me this," John yelled?

"Democracies never last very long," William whispered. "It's bloody, exhaustive, and in the end, there has never been a democracy that didn't commit suicide. Now, it's on you."

"It's not my fault," John barked. "I didn't create this."

"I'm not saying it's your fault, I said I was blaming you. See the difference. Politicians have been lying for decades," William said. "There are people who think the government should give them more just because they are alive, and you did."

"What's your point," John replied?

"Facts are stubborn things, John. Governments are broke everywhere, they're all up for sale. The IMF just bought Greece and they'll not be the last. Do you understand what's happening, John? America murdered itself, but they are not alone. The crash of 2008 was just the beginning. You see, when the music stops, and it will, do you want to have a seat at the new table? That's my point," William demanded. "Patriotism died when people started only caring about themselves." John realized he is in over his head and cannot win.

"You've a meeting with the Christian Cooperation, right. We've something planned for them. Frank will give you the details."

"You want to take on the Christian church in America," John stammered.

"It has begun, John, and it's going to get worse," William dictated.

"You seriously want me to deliver a death blow to Christianity," John groaned. "I can't do it, I won't."

"It's for the money," William commanded.

"What could this possibly have to do with making money," John said?

"That's not your concern," William ordered.

"Not my concern," John laughed. "I'm the President of the United States."

"The world changes, whether we want it to or not," William stated.

"Am I ever going to meet this aristocracy," John asked?

"They've been watching you since Texas," William announced. "I will tell you this, if you did meet, you wouldn't like it."

"Why did you stop at Senator, why not President," John inquired.

"Influence, it's what I do best," William said.

"So back in Texas, when I won the Governor's job, how did you know the Governor was guilty of tax fraud," John questioned.

"Who said he was guilty," William replied.

"It's in your blood, isn't it," John sneered.

"Don't be afraid to see what you see," William said. "Remember, you called me. What should I tell them?"

"A hundred million dollars, plus a seat at the table," John acknowledged. "Alright, William, I'm all in." John is completely defeated, his soul is gone.

"Trust me. It's good to be a wolf, in a world full of sheep," William assured as he realized he has won the day.

"Go away," John, scolded as he glared at him.

In the White House, a private meeting room with a great table and several large chairs sat the ten Christian political leaders. Michael sat anxiously at one end of the table waiting. John's late, of course. A chair at the head of the table sits empty as everyone waited for him to arrive. Finally, with his arrival announced, everyone stood and waited until John sat down. "Pardon my tardiness, gentlemen," John said. "The country has needs."

"John, I would like to introduce you to the Christian Cooperation," Michael said. "Religious leaders here represent all the Major denominations and factions in America."

"Welcome to the White House," John grinned. "What can I do for you, gentlemen?"

"We have spoken with Michael at great length and we are concerned," the cooperation council member said. "Mr. President, faith means being convinced God exists, just like this table exists. If you don't believe in God's existence, faith might seem impossible, but that's not true. In fact, the greater your doubt in God, the more heroic your faith can become."

"Do you actually see me as heroic," John questioned?

"The Christian Cooperation is a political organization that cares deeply about the role the government serves in protecting, rather than threatening, our civil liberties," Michael explained.

"We work to identify, educate, and organize Christians to promote effective political action when needed," the cooperation member declared.

"I see, to serve the Lord or perhaps your own agenda," John suggested. "I recall during the crusades, men fought in the name of God killing millions of their enemies because they didn't believe in our God. No wonder our enemies attack us. They call us the Great Satan. Yet, our democracy endures."

"God's not on the side of any nation, yet we know he's on the side of justice," another cooperation council member assured. "The voice of the Lord is the voice of reason."

"I believe hypocrisy is the voice of today's church," John exclaimed. "Perhaps, it is those evangelical ministers, making millions from their TV ministries, living in mansions and yachts. They take money from widows and promise salvation which they can't deliver. They've been getting away with it since Roman times when you could buy your way out of perdition for just few gold coins. Now that was religion. How are you so different?"

"We're driven by the belief that people of faith have a God-given right to be involved in the world around them," the cooperation council member said. "That involvement includes social and political change as a stewardship."

"It's imperative that people of faith become committed to doing what Ronald Reagan called the hard work of freedom," an elite member of the council proclaimed.

"Yet, you let your world slip away. When Christians needed you most, you weren't there," John pointed out. "So, listen closely gentlemen. The country is broke. We need the money, so, this is the new law of the land. Secular states and agencies will take the Separation of Church and State to the next level."

"John, the Presidential stance is to be the defender of religious faith," Michael instructed.

"Before I refuse to take any more of your questions, I have a statement," John dictated. "This government's official religious stance is one of religious freedom or tolerance, with "Darwin's 'Origin of Species' as the only scientific truth.""

"People of faith will still believe. How do you intend to achieve such an ungodly ambition," the cooperation council member questioned?

"The war between Secular Humanism and Christianity has been building for centuries," John indicated. "It's beyond my control."

"What," Michael said?

"An extensive education and propaganda campaign's undertaken to convince people, especially the children and youth, to abandon religious beliefs. Thousands of church properties will be confiscated for public use. If they resist, your clergy will be imprisoned for any unlawful anti-government activities. And ultimately, all faith-based funding will cease. The tax-exempt status that you covet most has been revoked," John ordered. "We owe more money than any country in the history of the world, ever! It's time to pay!" John shouts with his fists on the table.

"This is an outrage," the elite council member shouted.

"I'm not finished sir," John commanded! "The state will outlaw monastic religious orders and take away basic civil rights of members of the clergy who violate the law."

"You'll never get away with this," Michael demanded.

"Congress will never stand for it," another cooperation council member added.

"Under the doctrine of separation of powers, thanks to Richard Nixon, the manner in which the President personally exercises powers is not subject to questioning by another branch of government," John scolded. "You're too late."

"Christians have been persecuted for centuries and survived because of their faith in God," the cooperation council member expressed.

"The Christian who talks the talk but has no spine to walk the walk," John insulted. "You mean, that Christian."

"John, please reconsider your position," Michael advised. "Think of the consequences."

"Muslim countries hate us and want to wage a holy war against us," John taunted. "Why should I reconsider?"

"The Declaration of Independence is very clear, "whenever any forms of government becomes destructive of these ends, Life, Liberty, and the Pursuit of Happiness, it's the right of the people to abolish it, and to institute a new government," the leader of the council membership finally spoke. "Patriotism means to stand by the country. It does NOT mean to stand by the President or any other public official save exactly to the degree in which he himself stands by the country. It is patriotic to support him insofar as he efficiently serves the country. It is unpatriotic not to oppose him to the exact extent that by inefficiency or otherwise he fails in his duty to stand by the country. Theodore Roosevelt said that and, thanks to him, we're not too late."

"When you see a rattlesnake poised to strike, do not wait until he does to crush him. There is nothing I love as much as a good fight. Your petty threats may have meant something in the past," John warned.

"But now, you're weak. Countries around the world fear us. They fear me. I can drop bombs on anyone I please. That's why there's peace."

"Fear is not peace," Michael argued. "Is this your resolution, sir?"

"Christianity and Secular Humanism can't coexist," John said. "Your defiance will not help you in this war."

"You think you can win such a war," the Cooperation Council member stated.

"Bring it on, I can do this all day," John's sarcasm is out of control. "A little rebellion, now and then, is good for the soul."

"So, the soul of man lives to serve himself, no God, no Heaven, just the grave," Michael sneered.

"You put your fist in the face of God and demanded the right to do as you want, not me," John stormed. "Now, you're reaping the consequences of your own rebellion."

"The kingdom of Christ lies within man," Michael shouted.

"To bad this country rejected Christ," John responded. "What we see, here today, is definitely a result of corrupt minds."

"You'll burn for this," the Cooperation Council member snapped.

"Sir, I doubt there is a heaven. But if there is, I'm sure I'll never see you there!" John grabbed his papers and walked out in disgust.

The next morning in the White House, the television is on, "In an effort to balance the federal budget, a series of legislation enacted by the

President directs the IRS to revoke the tax-exempt status of all religious organizations and disallow any tax deductible contributions made to any religious church or non-state run religious organizations," the CNN newsman declared. In a statement from the White House press, "It's imperative that America balance the national budget through cost cutting initiatives and revenue enhancements. Most initiatives will be painful, but necessary, to achieve the sound fiscal goals of the nation. The tax-exempt status of religious organizations will be revoked, effective immediately, faith based funding will be withdrawn."

"In a local interview, Pastor Stephen Reed has vowed never to give up his church to the government seizure of property." During the interview, "Pastor Stephen, how will your parish survive," the local CNN reporter asked?

"I don't see how we'll be able to continue without the contributions from our members and the funding received from the government," Pastor Stephen Reed explained.

"What do you plan to do about this," the local CNN reporter said?

"We must pray for the soul of our President," Pastor Stephen added. "Dear Lord, do not hold this sin against him."

Outside the White House, Police are escorting three Senators in handcuffs out of the building. As one is about to get in the police car, he looked back at John. John paused to laugh before getting into his limousine. This particular limousine belonged to Bill Clinton. Every inch of the limo's metal skin is backed by military grade armor, which offered the highest level of protection with the least weight and bulk penalty. The cars windows, which do not open, are actually transparent armor. The cars armor is at least five inches thick. The interior is also environmentally sealed to protect the occupants from chemical and airborne germ warfare terrorism. Two call girls, dressed in next to nothing, are waiting for him. "Ladies," John grinned.

"Where to sir," the young driver asked?

"Augustina Lutheran Church, please," John ordered.

"Yes sir," the young driver said.

"Take your time son," John directed. The limousine pulled up beside the church. Augustana is located between the busy, trendy DuPont Circle district and the eclectic Adams Morgan. The main entrance is up a fairly inaccessible number of steps if you're not young and fit. It is a warm and welcoming place. There are two call girls undressed lying back in their chairs. John buttoned his shirt and slowly exited the limousine. He entered Michael's church from the side entrance, without secret service. The church is empty in the afternoon. "Michael, you need to understand the truth," John stated.

"You don't have any idea of the truth," Michael warned. "I know the truth. You worship a golden calf. You walk through this world, blind to everything meaningful."

"Come on, expecting the world to treat you fairly because you're a Christian is like expecting a bull not to attack you because you're a vegetarian," John taunted.

"Going to church doesn't make you a Christian any more than standing in a garage makes you a car," Michael retorted. "Your words grow tiresome, old friend. Your soul is wicked to the core."

"I'm a god now, Michael," John declared.

"Why would anyone ever worship you," Michael insisted?

"Greed is good, Michael. He who has money has friends," John stated.

"The wicked have only accomplices," Michael said.

"It's that voice in my head that says, *this is the real me*. I can't help it," John said. "It makes me feel alive."

"That's not your voice you hear," Michael assured.

"Don't be naive? One percent of the people in this country control half of all the wealth. They control the future for everyone. They make the rules, not us," John admitted. "America may have been a democracy once, but that was long ago."

"We are never defeated unless we give up on God," Michael stated. "He created the universe and Christ died to forgive your sins."

"Then how dare we make his death meaningless by not committing more," John mocked.

"Blasphemy is that why you've come," Michael sneered.

"Michael, it has begun. It's the government of the few, by the few, and for the few," John pointed out. "Everything's for sale. Even you pass the collection plate."

"My god, forty million Americans need food stamps just to survive and you worship money," Michael groaned. "Materialism is easily repaired, but the poverty of the soul is irreparable."

"No one cares about America, the economy, the national debt or anything that doesn't involve their right to watch Oprah," John expressed.

"We must recognize the fundamental rights of man," Michael scolded. "There can be no true national life in our democracy unless we give unqualified recognition to freedom. You don't care about anyone but yourself."

"Why should I care," John argued. "No one wins. Which side are you on?"

"It is no accident that the age of capitalism also became the age of government by the people," Michael said. "What happened to you?"

"Don't you see the Christian and Political worlds are the same? They're dominated by fools, charlatans, and bureaucrats," John feared. "Whoever possesses a voice that opposed the established order is going to be a victim."

"Victims, you should know," Michael taunted. "Great is the guilt of an unjust war."

"I'm sorry, Michael. I can't change the past. Being Phi's is one of the best things that have ever happened to us," John reminded. "You introduced me to Elizabeth, you're my best man."

"What's your point," Michael snapped.

"You're my friend, Michael. Don't you understand there are no more patriots? Nobody puts the country first. The Government's bankrupt, we cannot sustain this level of debt, anymore. It's over," John warned. "We are on a path of destruction that no man can undo. It's just evolution, Capitalism to socialism to fascism. Are you one of us? I promise I can save you."

"But, I can't save you," Michael answered. "This nation was founded not by men of religion, but by the Gospel of Christ. That is the reason people of other faiths can come here seeking asylum, prosperity, and sanctuary. America is where you come to be saved, John. Without God, democracy will not and cannot endure. You're right, it does corrupt absolutely."

"Are you one of us," John scolded. "I will not ask again."

"If greed is good, then what in the world is bad? Consider me no longer your friend, John Henry," Michael demanded. "You're dead to me."

"I guess if you want a friend, get a dog," John replied as he realized he has lost the day and turned toward the exit.

"Before God, we're all equally wise and equally foolish," Michael preached. "I can't make you see the truth that you so deny…"

"Save it for your flock, padre," John left before Michael can finish his sentence.

"You want to make God laugh, tell him your plans," Michael whispered.

Michael walked down the city street and into a restaurant in downtown Washington. He sits at the bar, discouraged and beaten. Overhead, CNN is on the television. "In the past year, the economic recession has shown no sign of letting up. Inflation's rising due to skyrocketing gas prices driven up by the War in the Middle East, real unemployment has risen to seventeen percent with twenty million Americans unable to find work at all. Religious organizations have closed in record numbers as dwindling contributions have failed to save these sacred institutions," the CNN newsman declared.

"They begin the evening news with 'Good Evening' and then go on to tell you why it isn't. Is it just me or is everything going crazy," the old man at the bar complained as he turned to Michael? "Oh sorry, Father."

"It seems that way," Michael groaned.

"In a local story reported recently, Pastor Stephen Reed of the Church of St. Marks was arrested for illegal violations against the government," the CNN reporter said. "While in prison, his body was discovered by a prison guard, beaten to death. There are no suspects in the murder at this time. It's another local tragedy resulting from these difficult times. The funeral will take place tomorrow at Basilica of the Shrine of the Immaculate Conception. A large crowd is expected to be in attendance to honor the fallen minister."

"Jesus Christ," Michael whispered.

The Intervention

The White House press reports the president and his cabinet will go to Camp David to work on the economic budget. Camp David is the presidential retreat in Catoctin Mountain Park in Frederick County, Maryland. It is about as secure a sealed-off location as exists in this country. No one gets near it who is not supposed to get near it. Concrete barriers, war wagons filled with security personnel with automatic weapons at the ready, human ring after human ring of law enforcement assigned to keep all unauthorized persons away. The helicopter lands at Camp David pad. John, Tom, and Brian have already been drinking heavily. "We are gods," John proclaimed. "No one can stand against us. The world is ours."

"What's on the agenda for the evening," Brian said.

"Whatever you like," John grinned.

"You really should be more concerned about all the women," Tom insisted. "What if Elizabeth or your daughters found out."

"I'd just write a book," John laughed. "A hundred years ago, a man could have as many wives as he could afford."

185

"Hey, one picture is worth a thousand denials, so don't get caught," Brian advised. "The only thing missing is Marilyn Monroe."

"That's what I mean," John laughed. "Real men want just two things from life; danger and play. Women are the most dangerous playthings in the woods."

"You sure about this," Tom said.

"Reality only exists in fairy tales. Relax, these girls are the most wholesome toys that money can buy," John assured.

"You're the Terminator," Brian laughed as they enter the cabin full of women.

"Oh my," John thought. "I wonder how much fun I can have before I rot in my grave."

"Champagne sir," the young driver asked.

"Yes, thank you, young man," John agreed. "You'll go far."

"Yes sir," the young driver opens the bottle of Champagne for John.

"Is this to your liking," Brian suggested as the party with girls, drugs and sex began.

"What's not to like," John laughed?

At two o'clock in the morning, while everyone is asleep, John still drunk with a dry mouth, gets up to get a drink of water. Through a window, he saw a light in the woods off in the distance. It's a strange light that seems to glow and fade away. He goes outside the door to get a better look. Two secret service guards are seated on the front porch. "What do you think that is," John asked?

"Camp David is secure sir, the secret service agent stated. "You want us to check it out?"

"I want to check it out. A lot of little scary things go bump in the night," John suggested as they walk slowly towards the light. "Stay here, that's an order." John cautiously walks closer to the light. Suddenly the glowing light focused directly on him, John falls to his knees. The two secret service men rush to him.

"Are you alright, sir," the secret service agent pleaded.

"I can't see. I can't see," John stammered.

"I've got you sir," the secret service agent said. The Secret Service men assist the President to his feet. John staggers back towards the cabin with the agents. People in the camp come out to see what has happened. "Get everyone out," the secret service agent demanded. "Take them all to the helicopter and get them out of here."

"Why," John screamed at the top of his lungs.

"What is this," Brian shouted. "What are you doing?"

"He can't see," the secret service agent repeated.

"Can't see what," Brian snapped.

"Anything," the secret service agent said. "There was a bright light and then he fell to the ground."

"What do you mean he can't see," Tom pleaded as he grabs John and looks into his eyes. John tried to speak but can only ramble a few words.

"This is crazy," Brian panicked. "What do we do?"

"I've cleared the inhabitants and secured the perimeter," the secret service agent ordered. "We need a doctor, as soon as possible."

"It's three o'clock in the morning," Brian screamed.

"Kill me now," John shrieked again.

"Oh my God, lock this down," Tom commanded. "Get the White House physician."

"Yes sir," the secret service agent replied.

At dawn, the White House doctor and specialist rush inside the cabin at Camp David. "What happened," the doctor asked.

"For the past three hours the President hasn't been able to see. We're told it was by a bright light," Tom insisted. "He continued screaming and we don't have any sedation."

"With all those drugs around, are you kidding," the doctor exclaimed. He examined John's vital signs. "His blood pressure's dangerously high, heartbeat is very erratic. The pupils are still reacting to light normally."

"Tom, what is going on, this can't happen," Brian shuddered.

"There's no detachment of the retina, cornea is clear, the retina pigment's not depicting any flash blindness," the specialist explained as he began his examination. "There could be nerve damage but that's rare resulting from a bright light."

"He's not in circulatory shock," the doctor added. "But he seems to be in excruciating pain."

"Flash blindness is not usually accompanied by reports of pain," the specialist declared.

"So what do you think it is," the doctor said?

"I've never seen anything like it," the specialist guessed.

"Lucifer," John screamed.

Inside John's dream, Gabriel in his black trench coat stood side by side with John atop a mountain range. As they looked upon the world, flashes of death are visible below them. Millions of souls cried out in desperation. John could only watch as battles rage in front of him. This stranger stood beside him, emotionless, cold, and undaunted. John saw the bloody history of the world played out with Mongols attacking Rome, Hitler's destruction of Europe, and Vietnam's Saigon falling right before his eyes. Then, he saw a different assault. He had not seen this before. Bombs going off around him with bodies mangled in the destruction. He was merely a spectator. Poverty and sickness engulfed the world with millions of helpless people begging for life.

"Do these dreams foretell the end of this world," John begged. Gabriel said nothing. They watched until he slowly placed his hand upon John's shoulder. Suddenly, they stood upon a hill overlooking three wooden crosses with men nailed upon them. It was the crucifixion. The mob of people raised their arms in celebration. A soldier with a spear thrusts it into one of the men. John cried out but could only watch. "Why do you torture me," John screamed. Gabriel appeared next to Jesus and whispered in his ear. The agony left his face as Gabriel turned to look at John.

"Who would stand and fight against the tyranny of man that would bring darkness down upon the world," Gabriel proclaimed. "What if he never lived for us? What if the One Nation under God never existed?" Gabriel pointed off into the distance. Atomic blasts cover the world as far as John could see. He fell to his knees as the world diminished into fire. Gabriel put his hand over John's eyes. "If you do not wish to see this befall your world, I can help you," Gabriel offered.

It is raining heavily at Camp David as night falls on the cabin. Thunder and lightning roll over the cabin like a tidal wave. "Sedate him again," Tom begged.

"It will kill him," the doctor said.

"He's had no food or water for three days," Tom exclaimed.

"I can't keep a needle in his arm long enough to provide any help," the doctor said as a crack of thunder rolls throughout the cabin.

"He's completely mad," Tom replied.

"He can't leave Camp David like this," the secret service said.

"We're expected at a conference in New York, first thing in the morning on the state of the economic recession," Brian added. "He can't do it."

"Why do you torture me," John cried out.

With a knock at the cabin door, there stands a silhouette of a man slowly walking in from the rain. Michael is dressed in his clerical garments and collar. His hair and coat are dripping wet as he makes his way into the cabin. "John, it is Michael," Brian announced.

"Hypocrite," John screamed.

"I know who the hypocrite was," Michael said calmly.

"Have you come to betray me again," John scolded.

"Because of you, I'm no longer blessed," Michael preached. "After Jesus rose from the dead, he appeared before Thomas and showed the scars on his hands." And Jesus said, 'Blessed are those who have not seen a miracle, yet still believed.' "Now, I'm no longer blessed and neither are you."

"You've come to murder me," John seethed.

"You have nothing to fear from me," Michael admitted. "God has already saved your soul from the other side."

"I've seen the other side," John revealed.

"I have, as well, old friend," Michael acknowledged. "An angel of God called me in the night. He told me to find you."

"I can't see," John cried.

I said to him, "I know this man. I know all the evil he has done to your people in this world."

But he told me, "You've been chosen to proclaim his name. He would show you how much you must suffer for him." Michael placed his hands upon John's eyes. "Christ, who appeared to you in the night, sent me to heal you."

"Let me burn," John begged.

"The Holy Spirit now dwells within you, forever," Michael whispered. "John, receive your new sight."

Michael slowly removed the hand that covered John's eyes. His eyes blinked and watered as Michael removed his hand; John is able to see. He looked around the room and began to cry, then suddenly stopped. He realized what had happened in his life. All the damage he brought upon the world rushed back into his mind. He cried out, but no sound heard. He reached for a breath of air, and let out a blood-curtailing scream as he fell to the floor.

"What are you waiting for," Michael proclaimed. "Stand and be baptized and wash away your sins." Michael brought water from the kitchen and baptized John on that very spot.

"Me too, Michael," Tom asked. Michael baptized several of the secret service agents, as well, but Brian remained in the background and kept his distance.

The next morning, John was sitting up eating soup and a sandwich in bed while Michael examined him. Michael sat on the bed watching him eat. John stopped eating for a moment and hung his head in shame. "Michael, can you forgive me," John pleaded.

"Of course, it's my job," Michael grinned.

"I had a life of greed, nothing was ever good enough," John admitted. "What happened to me? I don't understand."

"It's the Holy Spirit," Michael assured.

"What am I supposed to do," John said.

"What you do for God's people, you do for God," Michael reassured. "What you do for America, you do for the world."

"I've never felt anything like it," John stammered. "It's like checkmate, but where do I go from here?"

"People came to America to escape persecution and injustice," Michael said. "They've been waiting and hoping for someone like you."

"But...," John sputtered.

"John, you're blind for three days," Michael revealed.

"It felt like a lifetime," John answered. "If felt like minutes."

"Your redemption has been a long time coming," Michael said. "What did you see in your dream?"

"A world without Jesus, without America," John replied, "what if it never happened? The world was cold, empty, and full of hate. Life and death knew no differnce in this world."

"What did he say to you," Michael asked.

"Why do you persecute me," he said as I fell to my knees. "Who are you, Lord," I said? "Michael, I knew exactly who it was."

"I know," Michael said.

And then he said, "I'm Christ, whom you are persecuting!"

"Then what," Michael pleaded.

"At that point, the voice began talking very slowly," John stated. He spoke, "I've appeared to you to appoint you as a servant and as a witness of what you've seen."

"What did you see," Michael exclaimed?

"I saw the crucifixion, the spear penetrating his side," John replied fighting back his tears. "I was helpless to save him. I witnessed everything, all of it, even the end of the world."

"Did he ask you to do anything," Michael questioned?

"I'm sending you to them to open their eyes and turn them from darkness to the light," John proclaimed.

"You must bear witness," Michael said.

"To what, the end of the world," John snapped.

"Truth for its own sake, John," Michael advised.

"What truth," John said.

"He didn't come to make life easy, but to make men great," Michael preached.

"This is crazy," John stammered. "They're going to put me in a padded room."

"Why do you care," Michael expressed? "When you live for the next world, you can do great things in this one. What exactly happened to cause the end of the world?"

"It was bordering on blitzkrieg. Our planes on the ground destroyed, ships torpedoed in ports, tanks that did not move, lay to waste. Thousands of abandoned cars on the highways, nothing was moving," John admitted breaking down in tears. "I could hear enemy planes dropping bombs on everything."

"What's the last thing you remember," Michael said?

"Hundreds of atomic blasts, they were everywhere, as far as I could see," John revealed. "The night sky became day and the world was consumed by fire."

"Revelations," Michael stated.

"I felt the torment of millions of souls cry out, then suddenly stilled," John feared. "Why is this happening to me?"

"It's your redemption," Michael suggested.

"My redemption," John questioned. "I have no voice for this."

"The Christian's always listening for the voice of God above all others in the world" Michael preached. "Perhaps it was your zealous persecution that will make them listen."

"I don't deserve this," John said. "I can't even describe this."

"You've been give an amazing gift of sight," Michael claimed. "What the world might look like without hope."

"Hope is what we dream about, when we're awake," John recalled from his youth.

As the cabinet members moved to the helicopter, John was wrapped tightly in a blanket and looked completely exhausted. "Absolute secrecy is demanded here," Michael ordered. "This must never leave the Camp. John's life would be in danger. Is that clear? The world will know the truth, all in good time." Brian stepped away from the group and secretly sent a text to Frank. Frank received the text message and trembled.

On the way to New York, John and Brian looked out the window of the limousine at the homeless people in the city. "We're almost to the conference," Brian announced.

"Take us by Wall Street," John ordered the driver. "I want to see the occupation before we arrive."

"Occupy Wall Street," Brian asked. "I heard it is packed down there."

"In the past, we've taken full advantage of the business presented before us, but it's different now," John said. "Certain special interest groups are not going to like what I've got to do. It's going to be dangerous."

"Dangerous," Brian replied.

"Yes, our economy produced sixteen trillion in debt and we will never pay it back," John stated. "America now stands at the edge of the abyss."

"We can raise our debt ceiling," Brian said. "Congress will approve it."

"We're here sir," the young driver announced as they turn onto Wall Street.

"How does that help anything," John snapped as he got out of the limousine. "Those people are broke, just like America."

"I don't think it can ever be paid," Brian advised while looking at hundreds of people living in tents.

"Raising taxes won't help; cutting spending just makes it worse," John added. "We're talking about years of neglect and abuse. Where did it go so wrong?"

"When you take away incentives from those who are willing to work and give to those who are not, democracy dies." Brian stated. John covered his head with a disguise and began walking toward the people in tents.

"Adam Smith in the Wealth of Nations told us, 'it is political corruption that prevents prosperity,'" John explained.

"The government has been bought and paid for, long ago," Brian argued.

"The Tea Party tried to tell us, didn't they? We think we're the only country to ever lead the world, we're invincible," John insisted. "Every country felt the exact same way and they all ended up just like this. People came here for the opportunity of a better life. Now, they come for food stamps."

"The Fed printed two trillion dollars on top of seven hundred billion in bailouts, TARP funding, and eight hundred billion more in stimulus," Brian advised. "Each year, we bring in a trillion dollars in tax revenue and we still spend two."

"Just because you throw five trillion dollars at a problem, doesn't mean you fixed it," John snapped. "Someone always loses, that's why it doesn't work."

"I've managed to create an entire economic system built on welfare," Brian said.

"Politicians could never solve this problem, so we pushed it off on the next generation and proclaim our righteous success," John groaned. "It's worse than hypocrisy, it's treason." John walked up to a middle-aged homeless man and kneeled in front of him. "Sir, do you know why you're here?"

"Because the power of corruption and greed are stronger than the collective human spirit," the middle aged homeless man mourned.

"What do you hope to gain from all this," John asked?

"A better world," the homeless man pleaded.

"But, what do you want," John said.

"Just to have a chance to succeed," the homeless man replied.

"No one is guaranteed success in America, but everyone is guaranteed a chance," John said.

"A chance, where have you been," the homeless man snapped. "Our last chance is over."

"How do you feel about that," John asked?

"I thought I wanted a job; turned out I just wanted a paycheck. I'm sorry, I'm just sick and tired of being sick and tired," the homeless man shouted. "I've got no place else to go."

"What can I do to help," John consoled.

"A job, that would give me respect," the homeless man responded. "What is it you want, Mr. President? Yes, I know who you are."

"A second chance," John said. "Everyone deserves that."

"If you ever get a first chance, you'd better make the most of it," the homeless man replied.

"Don't lose hope," John begged.

"If I do, you won't find me here," the homeless man beseeched with fear in his eyes. John touched the man's head as he walks away.

"Are we so far gone that we don't recognize a patriot, when we see one," John expressed. "Is that who we've become?"

"Look, we've laundered billions through Wall Street in order to manipulate an artificial improvement in the stock market," Brian admitted. "Unfortunately, this bull market came with a price. Sixteen trillion is a relentless death spiral this country has never seen. We solved the short run problem, but the long run for America is hopeless. You just can't keep printing money forever."

"It's not real, is it," John questioned.

"It never was," Brian replied.

"Our silence has made cowards of us all," John feared.

"What are we supposed to do," Brian said.

"Turn it around, in every corporate turnaround, you must do two things," John expressed, "cut costs and increase revenues."

"You want to cut government spending and raise taxes," Brian said.

"That's never worked," John pointed out. "We have to increase revenue and cut expenses for the American people, the middle class. Increase their incomes and reduce their cost of living."

"Turnaround the middle class," Brian questioned.

"It has to be energy. How else can we ever grow the economy with this albatross around our neck," John pleaded? "The government won't do it. What would a fifty cent drop in gas prices do?"

"Add seventy billion to the economy, leaving more money for clothes, restaurants, and business," Brian stated. "It's a real world manufactured stimulus to the economy."

"Business would improve, incomes would rise," John advised. "But what about a four dollar drop in prices, and not just a year, forever."

"That changes everything," Brian said. "But it's not realistic."

"I've known oil all my life. It made me who I am," John added. "Wall Street and OPEC manipulate us like a puppet, we give them our wealth, and they send us a car bomb wrapped up like a jet."

"Not exactly the American Dream," Brian said.

"The dream is dead unless we do something," John admitted. "Look around, if we don't do it, who else will."

"OPEC could do more to prevent a global recession than anything the Fed could ever do," Brian said. "Printing money is all we have left."

"We're no better than a third world country. Broke, dependent on oil, and in complete denial, top to bottom, it's unsustainable," John complained. "What were we thinking?"

"We weren't, we're too busy taking," Brian said as they return to the limousine. "The government doesn't solve problems, they subsidize them."

"Give us another credit card to buy more Oil," John snapped. "What a joke, two-bit junkies, strung out until our next fix."

"It's every man for himself," Brian said.

"So we wait and hope," John said, "for something or somebody who never comes."

"It's a corporate state now and welfare state," Brian claimed. "I don't know anymore."

"We have forgotten God with the vainly imagined wisdom and virtue of our own mind, too proud to pray to the God that made us,"

John complained. His patience is running thin. "What would happen if the Middle East stopped shipping us crude oil? What if our supply lines were cut?"

"We have seven hundred million barrels in the US Strategic Reserves," Brian replied.

"How long would that last," John questioned in frustration?

"At current level of consumption, about 38 days," Brian predicted.

"Are you crazy," John scolded? "So everything's fine, until it's not fine."

"Our allies would sell us oil but only until it became vital to their own interests and security," Brian said. "There would be rationing, then it would just stop."

"Just like the great Roman Empire, they thought their government would thrive for centuries," John sneered. "It was invincible, just like us."

"Not exactly like us," Brian disagreed.

"Really, when Rome fell it wasn't because they were defeated," John said. "It was because barbarians surrounded the city of Rome. They cut off all supplies into the city. They literally starved themselves to death. The barbarians entered the gates of Rome without even a fight. They defeated themselves and the world was thrown into the dark ages. Is that how it will end for us? Without America, we might as well be in the Dark Ages."

"What do you mean," Brian said.

"Oppression and tyranny ruled the Earth for centuries. Then, a new world was discovered, America. Freedom has slowly defeated oppression in every part of the world," John preached. "But without us, tyranny will come back and America will be but just an experiment long forgotten."

"America will never fall into the hands of a foreign power," Brian stated. "We'd rather die than live without freedom."

"Give me liberty or give me death," John snapped in anger as he pushed Brian back against the limousine. "It's when people forget God that tyrants forge their chains. Is that true?"

"Yes," Brian said in defense.

"Then its nuclear winter," John vowed. "If we can't survive, no one will."

"We all die," Brian pleaded? "Have you lost your mind?"

"You think I won't push the button to save America," John warned with his left hand on Brian's throat. "Freedom dies with us. Then, you really would understand the living death spread upon this Earth."

"You wouldn't," Brian sputtered pushing away John's hand.

"Wouldn't I? Nobody wins, everybody loses. I've seen it," John warned again. "How else could it possibly end? We're just whistling past the graveyard." John released Brian as a crowd began to form.

"You think you have some miracle antidote for the emptiness of despair in this country," Brian argued.

"Get in the limousine," John ordered. "Remember Professor Argyris's theory? When you're in a situation you can't control, you have three choices, fight, and escape or adapt. Well, here we are. We've no chance to escape, we've been adapting for years and it's made us crazy. I've no choice left but to fight."

"How do you intend to fight," Brian asked?

"Lincoln freed millions of slaves with the Emancipation Proclamation," John declared. "That was an Executive Order. It's my last chance."

"John, understand something, everything is for sale, especially the government. It goes to the highest bidder and that bidder is Oil," Brian admitted. "It is Washington's dirty little secret that everyone knows and no one talks about. You want to take them on? Start a revolution. Who do you think you are? Oil donated two billion dollars to both US campaign budgets and it's nothing to them. They back both parties, so they always win."

"For years, the tobacco companies bought politicians so they could put carcinogens in cigarettes, just to increase sales. Their cancer killed millions and we beat them back," John pointed out. "It's no different with the oil companies."

"This will end badly John," Brian promised. "How do you think this is going to end?"

"If we eliminate OPEC costs for the American people, that money will go into American business. With their revenues improving, they will be able to hire the unemployed. These same businesses will pay more in taxes. That's how we increase our revenues," John professed. "That's how we turn this country around, everybody wins."

"You want to commit political suicide, go ahead, but, like it or not, they own us. That's our fate," Brian argued. "We need to talk with Frank."

"We are not prisoners of fate, just of our own minds," John said. "How many sons of Americans have died in foreign wars over oil? This slavery has to end."

"I agree, in principle, but we still need help," Brian insisted. "You want to fight, we'll lose everything."

John realized Brian would betray him; he moved to the side seat and motioned the driver to drive. "I'll do what I have to do and that's our dirty little secret," John revealed. "I will speak to Frank, not you, understand."

"Why do you always sit there," Brian questioned.

"If someone was trying to kill me," John grinned, "where would you think, I might be sitting?"

"That's not funny," Brian grunted looking at his seat compared to John.

"How much is Frank paying you," John whispered?

"Driver, stop the car." Brian shouted looking John in the eye. He gets out and slams the door. John sits back in disgust as he feels the painful sting of betrayal.

Late that evening in the White House bedroom, John and Elizabeth prepare for bed. This bedroom was the favorite of Jackie Kennedy as a first lady's suite and other first ladies, the room is traditionally the Master Bedroom of the White House and part of the master suite. A small dressing room and bathroom adjoin to the west. "I spent the day with the Daughters of the American Revolution," Elizabeth stated. "They are really quite nice."

"I walked through Occupy Wall Street, today," John groaned. "It wasn't nice at all. Elizabeth, I need to apologize."

"Are you alright," Elizabeth asked.

"No," John uttered.

"What is it," Elizabeth said?

"I've been wrong about far too many things," John admitted. "I've taken so much and given nothing in return."

"It's not true," Elizabeth said. "I know it's been difficult, but you've done well for yourself, your family and the American people."

"You don't understand. Something happened to me," John emphasized. "I had a vision of the future at Camp David."

"What, you're at Camp David for three days and I never heard a word from you," Elizabeth replied.

"I need to do something," John revealed.

"What," Elizabeth said?

"Take a stand," John informed. "Take a stand against the people who would harm America."

"Terrorists," Elizabeth asked.

"Not quite," John said.

"Do I know them," Elizabeth said?

"Friends of your father," John stated.

"Friends of my father," Elizabeth scolded. "What idiot told you turn against my father?"

"God spoke to me," John exclaimed.

"God, are you crazy, have you lost your mind? Listen to yourself. You'll be impeached then locked away," Elizabeth screamed. "What about your daughters?"

"I was blind, but now I see," John answered.

"What is wrong with you," Elizabeth snapped? "Why would God ever speak to you?"

"To free America from the shackles that bind her," John stated.

"What are you saying, John," Elizabeth expressed with great concern.

"It's just a game. Our economy improves, then gas prices rise and it kills the economy. And when we're down, gas prices fell which improved the economy, it never ends," John pleaded. "OPEC is the puppet master who pulls our stings and we dance whenever they please."

"What does this have to do with my father," Elizabeth questioned?

"He controls it. His vision of America is one of oppression and tyranny, for his own gain," John urged. "Until now, I've stood with him. I can't preside over the dissolution of the greatest country in the world, I won't."

"Don't force me to choose between you and my father," Elizabeth warned. "You might not like the result."

"This is my life," John snapped.

"And you expect me to stay with you," Elizabeth scolded.

"What about the children," John said? "What are they supposed to do?"

"Our children will be fine," Elizabeth insisted.

"I wasn't talking about our children," John whispered.

"My father will crush you," Elizabeth realized she could win this argument with John.

"I don't care. Cowardice does not promote peace. America's barely two hundred years old, we're still making history, but this will not be the history I'm making," John vowed. "We're just an experiment nobody thought would make it, much less lead the world. There's never been a country like it. I won't do it."

"What do you think you're going to do, John Henry, defeat the political establishment and die like some kind of a martyr," Elizabeth shouted in frustration. "I can't stand to look at you," She grabbed her purse and ran out of the bedroom crying.

"Yeah, I'm having a bad day, too," John thought as he sat on the bed completely exhausted.

The next morning, John is signing legislation at his desk with a mountain of paperwork surrounding him. He was a beaten man. "John, do you have a minute," Tom asked.

"That may be all I have," John responded.

"You know loyalty means everything to me," Tom admitted. "We've been through a lot over the years. But...,"

"But what," John said.

"We seem to be at war, but not a military war, some kind of an economic war," Tom said.

"We live in an atomic age, military wars are a thing of the past," John assured. "If we were ever attacked, the sky would rain fire upon our enemies, no one wins because there are no survivors. As a result, we're left with the only war of the twenty first century, an economic war."

"I don't understand," Tom asked.

"Reagan defeated the Soviet Union without a single casualty. They went bankrupt," John informed. "If we declared an economic war on China, we would stop buying all Chinese goods. Their economy would fall into a depression, unlike the world has ever seen. They wouldn't be able to feed their one billion people. Remember, China was a third world country of farmers before we started buying from them."

"Yeah, but that's China," Tom questioned.

"The Middle East was a desert full of camels before we started buying their oil," John explained. "Stop and you'll see a mass exodus of power and capital from the Middle East."

"How do you fight such a war," Tom said?

"Sun Tzu, the art of war, made your enemy surrender without a fight," John instructed. "First, become the lender of last resort; assume their debts so they're obligated to you. Second, drive them into bankruptcy and force their default. Third, create hyperinflation to kill any and all hope of recovery. They'll surrender to you when their stock market crashes, government fails, and blood runs in the streets. The new government seizes control without a fight. That's how communism got its start."

"You didn't answer my question," Tom pointed out.

"Honestly, defeat the middle class. Cut the supply line of credit to their economy and everything crashes," John professed. "Public debt is, by far, the greatest danger to be feared."

"God bless MasterCard," Tom said. "But where's this war fought."

"Innovation or inflation, reinvent the game or throw yourself on your sword with hyper-inflation, the atomic bomb of an economic war," John advised.

"What is hyperinflation," Tom asked?

"When a country borrows forty cents of every dollar they spend, it opens Pandora's box to a massive devaluation of their currency," John instructed. "A loaf of bread cost a hundred dollars."

"When Pandora's Box is open," Tom warned, "all the evil in the world is free."

"And the only thing left in it is hope," John assured.

"Why do we let it happen," Tom asked?

"To pay off debt, politicians view it as the path of least resistance, it's easy. Unfortunately, today America borrows forty-two cents on every dollar, but don't worry, the world doesn't end from hyper-inflation," John reassured. "It's just a slow painful death we seek."

"Speaking of death, we've received several threats on your life," Tom advised. "I believe there will be an attack on Air Force One by smaller biplanes filled with explosives."

"Of course, they are," John said sarcastically.

"I've arranged a flight to London. You'll be seen entering the plane. I'll smuggle you out before it took off," Tom instructed. "This will draw them out."

"You don't get old by being stupid," John said.

"I'll try to take them alive," Tom promised. "I need to find out who's behind it, the assassins are just pawns."

"These people are more powerful than you know," John

proclaimed. "In a world full of lies, it seems telling the truth will get you killed."

"I'll do everything I can to protect you," Tom urged.

"Can I ask you something," John said?

"Of course," Tom replied.

"If Columbus never discovered the new world," John questioned. "What would the world look like to you?"

"I never thought about it," Tom replied.

"Do we take it for granted? What we have, who we are," John asked. "All the wars we fought for freedom, was it worth it."

"I believe so," Tom assured.

"I wonder if, in a thousand years, we'll still be fighting for our freedom against oppression. Will there, finally, come a day when there is no more tyranny left in the world. Is that what we dream about," John said. "Have I changed that much to you or am I just crazy?"

"John, you're blind for three days. You didn't eat or drink anything," Tom recalled. "I'll never forget it, I thought you'd gone completely insane, but you're not."

"Perhaps it was more like temporary insanity, at least I hope so," John grinned.

Redemption

Before John is to address the nation, he rehearsed his speech with Michael in a secure room. "It's twenty minutes until your speech," Michael said. "Are you ready?"

"Michael, how can anyone possibly believe a word I say," John groaned?

"I believe in the American people," Michael assured. "If given the truth, they can be depended upon to meet any national crisis. The great point is to bring them the real facts and let them decide. John, Abraham Lincoln said that. Just deliver the speech as it is written and let it come from your heart."

"That's what I'm afraid of," John moaned.

"The question you have to ask yourself is," Michael advised. "Am I willing to make history?"

"I've done so many horrific things. I have ordered the murder of innocent men, profited willingly from the death of others. I have violently persecuted the church beyond measure," John groaned louder. "For what, to be the king of nothing, what do I say to that?"

"Are you one of us," Michael asked?

"I am," John said.

"Then tell them, he reigns above," Michael reassured. "John, most people believe they're human beings going through some kind of spiritual experience, you and I know better."

"We are spiritual beings going through the human experience," John admitted.

"And now, you've been charged to save the church, you once persecuted," Michael pointed out.

"Persecuted, I've done everything I could to destroy what's good in this world," John admitted.

"Trust me, you've been given something most men never get," Michael said, "a second chance."

"Why me," John questioned?

"Your history defines you, John," Michael acknowledged. "You were what is worst in men. It's not easy to abandon the darkness you once knew."

"Michael, the whole world is afraid of me, it's too late," John feared.

"Do you not see the irony? If John Henry can be saved, anyone can," Michael joked. "You're trying desperately to save a nation that can do nothing for you in return."

"What if I fail," John moaned.

"You mean who will raise their voices when yours is carried away on the wind. John, a child born today will see a world population grow beyond its water supply, oil supply, and food shortages that will starve millions," Michael declared. "You are the one God chose, but you are not alone."

"All this will be my fault," John responded.

"Christians have been fighting this battle for centuries. It's who we are," Michael assured. "We will either remain silent or finally say enough. We will either lie down or fight the good fight. We either take back America or lose it forever. It's up to all of us."

"If I give this speech, they'll never let me live," John assured.

"Then you must be on to something," Michael grinned.

"They'll not sit by and let me destroy everything they've built," John snapped. "I still don't understand any of this. What am I supposed to do?"

"Teach them to number their days that we may apply our hearts unto wisdom," Michael preached.

"Days, I doubt I'll see the sun rise," John insisted.

"Days roll into years and years to decades. Life goes by so fast, then in a blink, it's over. And the world goes on without you," Michael advised. "Now, make your peace, before it's too late." A Secret Service agent approached John and hands him a note from Tom.

"Please, bring me my daughters," John asked.

"Yes sir," The secret service agent said.

John read the note to Michael. *The attack on Air Force One at zero eight hundred this morning was unsuccessful. We shot down the terrorist plane over the Atlantic, no survivors.*

"It just keeps getting better, doesn't it," John moaned.

"A life without the courage for death is slavery," Michael responded.

"Will he save me, again," John asked.

"I don't know," Michael said.

"When I'm gone, promise me you'll brush away the leaves from my grave," John implored.

"This war will not be won by the meek," Michael vowed. "Promise me, you won't give up."

"Necessity makes brave men of us all," John agreed. "Alright Michael, I'll not go quietly into the night."

Behind the curtain, Michael and John stood together just a few feet away from the podium. A Secret Service agent walked up. "As you requested sir," the agent said. Lisa and Kimberly walked up to John. Elizabeth stood off in the shadows listening.

"Yes sir," Lisa said.

"I want you to know, that I'm sorry," John apologized. "All the things I told you were important in life, money, power, possessions. It's not true."

"What's wrong Father," Kim asked?

"I was never there for you," John stated. "It's my job to protect you, nurture you, and help you to grow into women. I've failed you and I'm sorry. But, I will not let you be stained by this world."

"I don't understand," Lisa said.

"Money is important. It's like blood and water for the body. Without it there is no life, but it is not the point of life. The point of life is to swim your own races, follow your own dreams no matter where the journey may take you, and believe in yourself when no one else will," John advised. "I love you more than anything in the world. It's what's in your heart that matters to me most." John looks around for something to show them.

"See this chair. It's not real. In a hundred years, it will no longer exist. It'll be at the bottom of a landfill somewhere. But things like love, hate, courage and freedom have been around for thousands of years. You can't see or touch them, but they're the only thing that's real in this world," he consoled as the girls try not to cry. "My life has been blessed because you're in it. It's the love in your heart that means everything to me. That's what's important."

"I love you father," they sniveled as they hug his neck and began to cry."

"I want you to know, if something happens to me. God would never take me away from you," John reassured. "Do you understand?"

"Father," Lisa cried trying to hold back the tears.

"Do you understand," John pleaded? "I'll always be with you, in your heart."

"Yes father, I understand," Kim cried.

"I need to do something, now. It's just for you. I want you to understand the world you will inherit," John promised. "From this moment on, I will do everything in my power to protect you."

"Father," Lisa wept.

"Can you do one thing for me," John pleaded?

"Yes father," Kim said.

"Remember me," John begged.

"Oh, Daddy," Lisa cried out completely forthright. The girls hug his neck with love. In the distance, the secret service passed by Elizabeth on their way to see the President. She has tears coming down her face, as well.

"Sir, you're on in sixty seconds," the secret service urged.

"Thanks, now, to your seats girls. I love you so much," John replied. The girls leave with the secret service. John paused silently to gather himself.

"You love them very much," Michael affirmed.

"I didn't know who my grandfather was," John explained. "But I'm much more concerned to know what my grandson will be."

"You're a good father," Michael reassured.

"Has our situation ever happened to anyone you know," John questioned.

"Two thousand years ago, a man named Paul," Michael said.

"What happened to him," John asked?

"They cut off his head," Michael grinned trying to hold back the laughter.

"If you thought about saying a prayer for me, now might be a good time." John expressed giving Michael a long cold look of attitude.

"Bow your head," Michael grinned with sarcasm. "Yea, though I walk through the valley of the shadow of death, I will fear no evil," John looks at Michael and rolls his eyes. "For thou art with me; thy rod and thy staff they comfort me. Thou preparest a table before me in the presence of mine enemies; my cup runneth over. Surely goodness and mercy shall follow me all the days of my life: and I will dwell in the house of the Lord forever."

"Now, I know why I hate you," John acknowledged. Michael fixes John's tie and lightly slaps his face.

"Audie Murphy would be so proud," Michael joked.

"Almost ready for you, sir," the secret service said.

"John, some people wonder all their lives if they've ever made a difference. You'll never have that problem," Michael advised. "This is your destiny, John Henry."

"And it's not even my birthday," John grinned.

Outside the White House, a CNN Newscaster spoke with the White House in the background. "In an unanticipated broadcast, the President of the United States will be addressing the nation this evening in a live proclamation from the Senate floor in just a few moments. We're not exactly sure of the reason for this Presidential address, but our insiders believe the President's trying to gain support for a new freedom Energy Supply Bill Initiative currently being sent before Congress as an Executive Order. With current fuel prices at an all-time high, this legislation would be a welcome relief to many Americans struggling to make it through this severe economic recession."

As Tom's entering the building, he's pulled aside by a short stumpy stranger in a hood. The stranger hands him a letter. He opens the letter and it reads 'Assassination, I am your negotiator.' "What's the meaning of this," Tom snapped?

"Relax, Tom," the negotiator ordered. "After the attempt, you're going to shoot and kill the gunman."

"What, who are you? We don't shoot to kill, that's not protocol," Tom commented. "You're under arrest for threatening the President of the United States."

"No, I'm not Tom, I have your family," the negotiator replied. He handed an iPhone to Tom. Tom looked at the screen. He saw his wife tied to a chair crying for help.

"Lisa Ann? You hurt her and I'll kill you," Tom warned.

"I've no need to hurt her or your family if you follow instructions. She's seen nothing," the negotiator assured. "They will be released at Washington Monument, as soon as you successfully complete your task."

"How do I explain the failure of protocol to take the gunman alive," Tom blurted.

"You felt your life was in danger. It was an act of self-defense. You'll be a hero," the negotiator reassured.

"I doubt it," Tom snapped.

"If anything goes wrong, you'll never see your family again," the negotiator vowed. He took the letter away from Tom. "No doubt about it." As he quickly left, he turned to speak to Tom. "He didn't speak to God."

The stranger jumps into a black van that speeds away. Tom walks inside the building for the speech. Tom pulls up his hand microphone. "Is the President wearing the bullet proof vest," Tom suggested.

"Affirmative sir," the agents replied.

"Take us to Code Red," Tom ordered, "and put security and medical resources on full alert."

"Yes sir," the agents replied.

The President enters the Senate to begin his historic speech to the nation, his voice rings loud and clear. It is to be a noble speech in defiance of tyranny. Everyone rose and clapped as he entered the

Senate. He moved to the podium to begin his speech. A note was resting on the podium. *Hope is what we dream about, when we are awake. I love you, Elizabeth.* He looked up at Elizabeth with renewed inspiration.

"Ladies and Gentleman of the United States of America, I would like to welcome you on this most important of days," John began. "For over two hundred years, freedom has been the right of every person and the future of every nation. It is the very nature of man to yearn to live free. But on this July 4th, freedom belongs with God. It's his gift to humanity and America's great responsibility to protect it. This is who we are in our world." John paused to search the room. He points to a man in the balcony.

"Sven Haugen, would you stand, please, for everyone to see you," John asked. "Show your arms and let them see what the scars of oppression really look like." Sven stands and pulls up his sleeves. He is not a young man. His face is weathered from living a hard life. His hands have scars from years of manual labor. Yet, there seems to be an inner peace about him that transcends his outward appearance. He smiled a particularly warm smile that exuded happiness rarely found in most men. You might say he is happy or content with his world. That is more than most men can say.

"Sven's life began in Romania," John announced. "When he was sixteen years old, a science teacher in his school told him about the creation of the world. Sven believed that God created the world and he said so. He read that in the Bible. Later that day, the secret police showed up and escorted him out of school. His parents were told he would be leaving them for a while. Sven spent the next eighteen months in a Romanian prison. He slept on a concrete floor, had an open window with bars that could not stop the freezing winds, and was routinely tortured with electric shock and cigarette burns to his hands and arms." Sven standing, nods his head in approval.

"After eighteen months, he was released. He fled his homeland to Italy where he was hunted. He escaped to Germany, but they didn't want him, either. With no place to turn, only America would accept him. Today, he's home." Tom walks into the room and cautiously stands watch. His eyes are fixed on every move.

"Sven lived the words from the Statue of Liberty," he said. 'Give us your poor; you're tired, your huddled masses yearning to breathe free. Send these, the homeless, tempest-toss to me; I lift my lamp beside the golden door!' He's a free man in America because we allow people to escape a heartless world of tyranny and oppression. This is who we are, our destiny in this world. I thank God for the opportunity to let us help you. Your life, your suffering makes us a stronger nation, for what we have to do." The entire room stands and applauds with the camera focused on Sven.

"Personally, I ask your forgiveness for my past deeds, my cowardice, and my greed," John explained. "The truth has escaped me all my life, until now. God, grant me the courage to apply your wisdom. Please forgive me. Therefore, let every nation know, whether it wishes us well or ill, that we shall pay any price, bear any burden, meet any hardship, support any friend, oppose any foe to assure the survival and the success of liberty. With his blessing, we know that here on Earth; God's work must truly be our own." William looks unimpressively at John.

"Yet, regrettably, the death-knell of this nation had rung, as soon as the established order became lodged in the hands of those who sought, not to do justice to all citizens, rich and poor alike, but to stand for one special class and for its interests, as opposed to the interests of all." John looks directly at William while Congressmen in the room look at each other with confusion.

"Was it greed, corruption, or just envy that lead us to our debt crisis? In simplest terms, we're drowning in an ocean of credit card debt and we can no longer make our minimum payments. Much like many Americans, this too is our enemy. Of course, we can get more credit or print more money to prolong the end. But either way, nothing's fixed, nothing's changed. We have mortgaged our future for the greed of today. We must think and act anew, then stand firm. We must reinvent our system, economy, and our lives because this established order isn't working." John slams a fist on the podium.

"We let this happen, but it is not our destiny to be imprisoned, not this day. It's every captured soldier's duty to try to escape. If we value the freedom of our mind and soul, then it's our duty to escape this economic oppression and to take as many people with us as we can," John affirmed looking at Sven. "Thank you, Sven, you are a true hero."

"In this moment, our hope lies with innovation. It was once the driving force of our country, innovation to build the best, to be the best. But, when American innovation is withheld from the people, it enslaved us all. Ladies and gentlemen, we have come to understand that finally, this treason is exactly what has occurred. The internal combustion engine required us to be vitally dependent upon foreign oil suppliers and their special interests. OPEC would lead you to believe, they're helping us. I promise they are not. Our dependence on them is no secret. However, my secret is, today is our independence day." William looks at Elizabeth; she looks back at him with remorse.

"The American oil companies have been a great champion for the people. History will note, they served this country well in the past, but their time, just as the dinosaur, has long come and gone. The internal combustion engine monopolized our lives, took our capital, and oppressed our children's future. Every time we fill our tank, OPEC's grip around our throat, gets a little bit tighter. With this cross to bear, we will never be the free country God intended us to be." Brian puts his hands on his face in amazement, the room is silent.

"The truth has been driven from this country with lies. The

technology for the electric automobile engine has been in existence for decades. Our enemies have withheld and suppressed it for their own gain. It is no accident. The entire world cried out for this injustice. We will not be ruled by tyrants. Truth be told, we were warned. President Roosevelt declared in an address to Congress in 1938, 'The liberty of a democracy is not safe if the people tolerate the growth of private power to a point where it becomes stronger than their democratic state. That, in its essence, is fascism. The ownership of government by an individual, by a group, or by any other controlling private power,' he said. "But we will not be sheep, lead to slaughter," John promised looking directly at William.

"With great respect, I call upon our history. Patrick Henry, Alexander Hamilton, Thomas Jefferson, George Washington, Theodore Roosevelt, and Abraham Lincoln to give us the wisdom of a nation founded by God," John took a moment to regroup.

"Lincoln once said, 'my dream is of a place and a time where America will once again, be seen as the last best hope of Earth.' His Emancipation Proclamation was an Executive Order that set free millions of American slaves from a life of oppression and with great courage, we did it. This Freedom Energy Bill is my Executive Order, which taxes all foreign energy imports related to the internal combustion engine," John declared. "Those dollars, in turn, will go to subsidize companies that design and mass produce electric automobile engines, not tomorrow, today. I know, there are those who will say, it's wrong and it can't be done; but, they have their own agenda. There are no constraints on the human mind, no walls around the human spirit, and no barriers to our progress except those we ourselves erect. Today is the day after Pearl Harbor, once again, and we have awakened a sleeping giant. We, like Henry Ford, will make the electric car affordable for every family in America. Therefore, with great conviction, let this be our last declaration of independence." Elizabeth looks at William. He was frozen in time.

"In America, electricity is cheap, abundant, and we have it. The sheer magnitude of dollars saved on gasoline expense for the American people, in just a single year, is one trillion dollars," John announced. "But not just for a single year, for generations going forward. We will break loose our chains, OPEC knows this and they are afraid." William looked at Elizabeth, but this time, she does not look back.

"Business will flourish in the new economy like never before. This energy savings for America will create over fifty million jobs throughout every sector of our economy. For the elderly and sick, it will fund health care reform and medical innovation for all. For the children, the war on poverty will be won and no child will ever go hungry again. Families will be able to send their children to colleges all over this great nation. Our children will have it better than any generation before it. And most importantly, the tax exempt status of religious organizations will be restored. Mankind must put an end to oil oppression before it puts an end to us because our political freedom without economic freedom is simply an illusion. We must be free. We cannot escape the responsibility of tomorrow by cowering from our duties today," John instructed. "I will not shrink from the fight ahead, I welcome it." The entire room of Congressmen rose in approval and John waited in silence.

"Therefore, by the grace of God, I humbly beseech Congress to grant me this Executive Order, so that whatever we do, in word or deed, we shall do all in his name. For this is once and for all, who we are," John admitted in a softer, calmer tone. Elizabeth holds her daughter's hand. John stands tall to scan the room for his daughters.

"I promise to my children, from the rising of the sun, until the end of the world, America will stand against oppression and we will win. We shall provide the light when nothing but darkness and tyranny reigned down upon us and we will win. We shall champion the cause of freedom for every man, woman, and child in this world and we will win. This is who we are and with my last breath, there will be no compromise." John shouted with passion as the crowd roars with approval, and then spoke softly and slowly. "In my heart, I know it to be true, that this, One Nation under God, is the *Last Hero* in a heartless world of tyranny and oppression." The crowd stands and roars the loudest of all.

"Once again, our courage has been tested, perhaps for the last time, perhaps for all time. On this day, surging gas prices have drained the life out of our economy. The stock market crash crippled our financial leverage. The unemployment rate, the means to our existence, is at an all-time high; but, America will not go quietly into the night," John proclaimed with a commanding tone to lead a nation. "We are ready for battle."

"I believe the immortal words of Abraham Lincoln still command the truth we hold so dear in our lives today. He said it so eloquently on December 20th, 1839. 'Many free countries have lost their liberty, and ours may lose hers; but if she shall, be it my proudest plume, not that I was the last to desert, but that I never deserted her. I know that the great volcano at Washington, aroused and directed by the evil spirit that reigns there, is belching forth the lava of political corruption in a current broad and deep, which is sweeping with frightful velocity over the whole length and breadth of the land, bidding fair to leave unscathed no green spot or living thing; while on its bosom are riding, like demons on the waves of fear, the imps of that evil spirit, and fiendishly taunting all those who dare resist its destroying course with the hopelessness of their effort; and, knowing this, I cannot deny that all may be swept away. Broken by it I, too, may be; bow to it I never will."

"The probability that we may fall in the struggle ought not to deter us from the support of a cause we believe to be just; it shall not deter me. If ever I feel the soul within me elevate and expand to those dimensions not wholly unworthy of its almighty Architect, it is when I contemplate the cause of my country deserted by the entire world, and I standing up boldly and alone, and hurling defiance at her victorious oppressors. Here, without contemplating consequences, before high Heaven and in the face of the world, I swear eternal fidelity to the just cause, as I deem it, of the land of my life, my liberty, and my love."

"And who that thinks with me will not fearlessly adopt the oath that I take? Let none falter who thinks he is right, and we may succeed. But if, after all, we shall fail, be it so. We still shall have the proud consolation of saying to our consciences, and to the departed shade of our country's freedom, that the cause approved of our judgment, and adored of our hearts, in disaster, in chains, in torture, in death, we never faltered in defending."

"What words will we be remembered about us? What deeds will we do? Will we be as timeless as the unforgettable words of Mr. Lincoln? 'It's rather for us to be here dedicated to the great task remaining before us that from these honored dead we take increased devotion to that cause for which they gave the last full measure of devotion that we here highly resolve that these dead shall not have died in vain. This Nation, under God, shall have a new birth of freedom and that government of the people, by the people, and for the people, shall not perish from the Earth.' This is who we are." The audience of Senators and Congressman stand to their feet and roar with approval.

"Therefore, our direction is clear and our cause just. Make no mistake, my friends, the future of America is once again at risk. The debt of this nation is a dangerous matter of national security. Therefore, let us strive in all ways to finish our work for we will not place profit over people, self-interest over justice and oppression over equality," John announced with conviction. "In this country, every man is guaranteed a chance for a better life, and no one will ever take that away. We will face our enemies, as we always have. The United States of America will never succumb to any threat, not now, not ever. God Bless America!" The audience loved him, John waved as in a presidential victory. He walks among the crowd, shaking hands. The people are reaching out to him. Brian, Tom, and several Secret Service agents are on all sides as he moves toward the exit.

"Do you think the world will listen?" John asked outside the chamber.

"John, you're in danger," Tom said nervously.

"I'm always in danger," John reminded. Tom saw a young man off in the distance walking towards John. He recognized him as John's driver. He is young with dark slick backed hair and lean for being a few inches short of six feet. He is always polite and eager to please when John is around. As a rule, he does not speak unless spoken too. He is not secret service, but has a history of military service, probably the marines. He appears to be of foreign birth, definitely not Caucasian American. He saw the young driver reach into his jacket. For a moment, Tom glanced away pretending to be distracted. The young driver walks out of shadows by the limousine, pulls a small handgun, and fired several shots. Brian jumps in front of the President. He has taken a bullet for the President and falls. Tom quickly received a wound in his left arm. John froze and slowly fell to his knees with blood hemorrhaging from his neck. The young assassin raced from the scene.

"Down, man down," Tom yelled! He pulls his gun and fires toward the assassin as he fled. The young man falls face first to the ground. Secret Service agents surround him. "John, are you...," Tom sputtered.

"Please God, not now," John begged. Blood shoots from John's neck as Tom tried to stop the bleeding with his hands. The red liquid oozed through his fingers. He screamed into his microphone clipped to his bloody shirt.

"Advice, we have shots fired. Shots fired. The president is down," Tom shouted in a panic. "We need the ambulance, now! John, the ambulance is coming."

"Michael," John groaned softly.

"Where's Michael, get Michael," Tom yelled. Michael is dressed as a Lutheran priest; he arrived quickly to see John hemorrhaging from the neck. He can't believe his eyes as he bends over the President.

"We failed," John trembled. He could barely speak.

"Good men will never abandon the truth," Michael advised. "You have set us free." John's eyes begin to close. The fear and pain leave his face and is replaced by the fear now in Michael's face.

"Go, now!" Michael orders. John is carried by the secret service to the ambulance and speeds away to a hospital. In the darkness, Michael's silhouette stands to watch the ambulance disappear into the night.

In route to the hospital, John passed out again. "He's falling into a coma," the paramedic warned. "Grade three bleeding with a thirty percent blood loss and climbing." Paramedics remove John's shirt to find a bullet proof vest with bullets on it, but blood's coming from his neck. "A vest, smart," another paramedic said.

"You don't get old by being stupid," Tom said.

"Not smart enough. He's lost a lot of blood," the paramedic warned. "The vertebral artery's completely gone. If we don't stop the bleeding, he'll die."

"Sir, can you hear me? Stay with me John," Tom begged. "What have I done?"

"I need more plasma. He's at a forty percent blood loss grade," the paramedic urged. "How far is it to the hospital?"

"Three miles," the ambulance driver shouted.

"Let's hustle, boys," the paramedic shouted. The ambulance is pulling violently into the ER driveway.

"Ballistic trauma," the doctor advised. "Get him into the operating room, now!"

"His vital signs are fading quickly. He's bleeding to death," the paramedic snapped. Rushing into the hospital, the operating room, and the President flat lined as the monitor sounded a long beep. Gabriel in his long black trench coat stands in the back of the operating room unnoticed.

"He's not responding. Apply electroshock. Go," the doctor shouted. Nothing happened. The heartbeat is still flat. Elizabeth arrived at the operating room; she was able to observe from behind a glass window. She is crying desperately. "Again go," the doctor yelled.

"No response," the nurse said nervously.

"This is the President of the United States, again," the doctor shouted. They pause as the sound of the long steady beep continued. Everyone stopped. The room was silent. "I've done all I could. The President is pronounced dead on arrival, as of 8:55 p.m.," the doctor ordered. He turned, took off his gloves, and walked away. The room is filled with silence except for the heart monitor steady flat tone. John lay dead on the operating table.

Gabriel walked over to John, still unnoticed by the medical staff and gently touched his shoulder. John's eyes open, but the heart monitor continued to flat line. John recognized Gabriel from his dream. He sighed in relief.

"Are you one of us," Gabriel asked?

"I am," John said.

"The prize will have to wait. Your journey has just begun," Gabriel instructed with a gentle and soft voice.

"But, I want to go with you," John begged.

"Why," Gabriel said?

"That's all that really matters," John informed.

"But, this is your time," Gabriel grinned.

"What then shall I do, with the time I'm given," John asked?

"Do not be afraid any longer," Gabriel assured, "speak your mind. I will be with you, always." Gabriel removed his hand from Johns shoulder. John's eyes close again.

As Gabriel disappeared, the flat heart monitor tone continued for several seconds. Suddenly a single faint heartbeat began and then a second. John grasped for air, his eyes opened, and the doctors rushed back into the operating room and began to revive him.

THE END OF PART TWO

PART III

The Journey or The Prize

A hundred years ago, powerful men and women built a world that you call present-day. In their journey, some men sacrificed their life so the cause of freedom would live for their children. Today, no man is left alive to tell of their sacrifice. Yet, I know the people of the day; I witnessed them face their judgment with conviction and undying faith.

Your President Samuel Adams was there, as well. This is the way he told it, "If ye love wealth greater than liberty, the tranquility of servitude greater than the animating contest for freedom, go home from us in peace. We seek not your counsel, nor your arms. Crouch down and lick the hand that feeds you; and may posterity forget that ye were our countrymen." Be grateful for the world left specifically for you. It is fragile, to say the least.

It is with sincere regard that I pose these last questions to you. Is it the journey or the prize you seek? What do your children mean to you? Are you one of us? I have answered your prayers, but your destiny is still in play. There are more sacrifices to be made, more deeds to be done. The world is far from safe. Therefore, never forget the words Mr. Kennedy challenged you with, "Ask not what your country can do for you, ask what you can do for your country."

Consequently, the last adventure is yours. You are alone upon this stage. Will you leave this world a better place than when you found it? In the end, I hope your conviction and undying faith are enough. This story is yours. You will face the same judgment as all those who came before you. I wish you all the luck in the world. Life consists not of holding good cards, but in playing those cards you hold well. May God be with you," Gabriel said. "And I will, as always, enjoy my ringside seat at your fate."

Lystra

John Henry is sixty something years old. His hair is turning gray with a solid gray goatee. He still looked in shape. He seemed to have a calm exterior about him while others are trying to cope. He is direct, focused, and daring as ever. He is a man on a mission. Tom is driving an electric Hummer thru the desert towards a small town in the distance. Michael is in the very back with two secret service agents, along for the ride. The Hummer moved quickly through a dirt road slicing through poverty on all sides. "Why does it always look like death?" Tom asked.

"In the past ten odd years, we've done a lot of unusual things," Michael replied. "But, this doesn't feel like one of them. Remind me again, why are we here?"

"Redemption, it is always redemption," John advised. "What exactly are you afraid of."

"Oh, dying I suppose," Michael whispered.

"Go big or go home," John reminded. "There are worse things than dying in this world. All these people know is fear, poverty, and tyranny. If we don't help them, what will they do?"

"Lystra is a town run by warlords," Tom warned. In the distance are ancient ruins such as a church with a big cross-marked on the wall, a winery house like building and ruins of a city located over the top of a hill which is locally called *Alyssums* where another church ruin stands. According to superstition, the hidden city was constructed over the hill to hide from enemies of ancient Anatolia. Lystra is located on the ancient Persian Royal Road in what is now modern Turkey.

"I doubt they really want us here, look at them," Michael warned. "There is no law, here."

"We've nothing to fear from men or their hatred. Our only battle is with the devil himself," John acknowledged. "He's surely waiting for us."

"He lives here, alright," Michael agreed.

"And how will we recognize him," Tom asked.

"Oh, you'll know him, when you see him," Michael guaranteed.

"Don't worry, he'll find us," John assured. They stop at the center of a town square while a little boy knocks on the window.

"Mister, can I've a dollar," a little boy said?

"Sure, what's the name of this village," John asked.

"Lystra," a little boy stated.

"We're here," John grinned.

"What are you thinking," Michael asked?

"Let's get out and introduce ourselves," John suggested.

"That's what I'm afraid of," Michael groaned as they slowly exit the car. Tom keeps his hand on this pistol.

"Stick together, folks," Tom advised. A crowd began to gather around them. John stands up on a large round stone water fountain in the center of the square. "My name is John Henry. Ten years ago, I was the President of the United States. I've come halfway around the world to speak with you." Tom, Michael and the two secret service agents form half circles around John.

"If we stay calm, they'll stay calm," Tom assured.

"The day of oppression and fear is over. I've come to set you free. Free from the bondage of fear and tyranny. There's only one way to achieve salvation in this world and that's through your faith in God," John preached. "He gave men this gift of salvation, free of charge. You need not fear the wrath of men. Faith in God is all you need, to set you free, forever." A military truck full of soldiers drove up behind John.

"Heads up," Tom said nervously.

"Courage," John ordered. "Who among you has the courage to face down your enemies? How strong is your faith in Christ?"

"I do," a crippled old man remarked as he moved to the front.

"Come forward," John answered.

"I've been poor and crippled all my life," a crippled old man begged. "I wish for just one day, to walk among the people. I still believe that day will come." The soldiers jump off the military truck with machine guns.

"Faith is all you need. Come forth, be baptized, and you will be set free from your bondage," John promised. The leader of the soldiers is last to step out of the truck. He has the devil in his eyes. He stared at John. "Then come, fear not the devil that tempts you."

"Christ, set me free," a crippled old man pleaded.

"The Lord loves you. His love can overcome all things," John prayed. "You've only to accept his love and your soul will live forever." John placed his hand on the man's head and he stands, dropped his crutches and walks without aid. The crowd is shocked then amazed.

"It's a miracle," a crippled old man cried.

"Free me, heal me, save me from the devil," voices from the crowd could be heard.

"Stop," the Major ordered. The soldiers surround the crowd and move in towards John. They point their guns toward Tom and Michael. Everyone reached for their guns at the same time.

"Don't," John snapped.

"Don't what," the Major barked. He fired a shot into the crippled man. He falls to the ground. "How dare you come into my town and preach your lies. There is no Heaven, only blood here. What do you know?"

"I know the devil, when I see him," John acknowledged. "It's been a long time."

"Their souls belong to me, padre," the Major demanded. "They do my bidding."

"These people belong to God," John argued. "They've seen the glory and their souls will never belong to you, again."

"I doubt that," the Major scolded. "Take them." The soldiers quickly disarm Tom, Michael and the secret service and hold them hostage.

"He was the President of the United States," Michael announced.

"Do you hear me," the Major ordered to the crowd. "Kill him or die yourself." The people of Lystra throw stones at John and take him to the ground. John defends himself for a few moments but there are too many. They kick and hit him as he lays motionless on the ground.

"John," Tom shouted.

"You've something to say," the Major laughed.

"No," Michael sneered.

"Take them to the jail," the Major ordered. "Dispose of the bodies. I don't wish to see them again."

"God help us," Michael whispered.

"Back to work or die in the sun," the Major commanded. The soldiers get into the military truck and drive away. A few of the townspeople drag the two bodies down the street. They disappear in the distance.

The sun is setting while Michael, Tom, and the two agents are sitting inside the jail. Michael awaits the Major's response.

"Do you plan to kill us, too," Michael asked.

"Perhaps, in the morning," the Major suggested, "that's enough for one day, but tomorrow is another. Sleep well."

"You just murdered the President of the United States," Tom stated. "He saved America."

"Oh, he's more than just that. His death has been long overdue," the Major taunted. "Ask your friend, he knows." The Major looked at Michael.

"Knows what," Tom asked.

"He doesn't know, does he," the Major laughed.

"Tell me what Michael," Tom said.

"Don't listen to him," Michael whispered.

"Michael," Tom snapped. The Major laughed and walked away.

"Shut up Tom," Michael scolded.

The next morning, the Major entered the jail. "Here he comes," Tom warned.

"I've decided to spare your lives. Go and tell the world their hero is dead," the Major advised. "But, I'll take your electric car and guns. You can walk out of town, if you wish. But, if I ever see you here again, I'll kill you, I promise. You're nothing to me. Do we understand each other?"

"I understand," Michael agreed.

"Yes, you do," the Major grinned. The guard opened the jail door and the men walked out into the street.

"We have to find John," Tom vowed.

"He's dead," Michael said.

"I don't care. Someone must know something," Tom insisted. "We should ask around."

"That would just get us killed," Michael warned.

"It's John," Tom snapped. "We need to find him."

The little boy walks up to Michael. "I know where he is, follow me," the little boy said. They quickly walk behind a building.

"We must be careful," Tom whispered. The group walks down several allies until they reach the outskirts of town.

"Are we close," Michael asked?

"Almost," the little boy said.

In a grove of fruit trees off the road, Gabriel and the crippled man stand over two bodies. They both crouch down to examine John's body. Gabriel reached out to touch John's shoulder.

"Does that hurt?" Gabriel said softly.

"Not anymore," John replied as he looks up from the dirt.

"Thank you for what you did," the crippled man grinned at John.

"It didn't turn out quite like I planned," John said.

"Yes, it did. I'm free now," the crippled man smiled in appreciation.

"Is there anything else I can do for you," Gabriel added?

"Ice pack," John laughed. Gabriel removed his hand from John. He lay back down on the ground and the two men faded away.

The group moved closer toward John's body. The boy points to a large group of trees. "Is he in there," Tom asked?

"Both," the little boy said. The group walked up on the two men face down in a ditch. Michael rolls John over.

"Oh, that hurts," John wailed.

"He's alive," Michael grinned.

"Drink this," Tom said.

"Thank you," John moaned as he drinks the water slowly.

"It's a miracle you're alive," Tom said, "but we need to get out of here, right now."

"He needs a doctor," Michael advised.

"We don't have time," Tom warned.

"You're telling me," Michael said.

"Get me to my feet," John begged. They get John to his feet and he tried to walk. The group turns to walk out of town. John turns to walk back into town.

"What are you doing," Michael shouted.

"Going back," John replied.

"Have you lost your mind," Michael bellowed?

"Apparently, courage is worth a thousand sermons," John exclaimed.

"They said they would kill us all," Tom warned.

"I told those people to have courage and courage is what they'll get," John promised. "You should stay here."

"Are you sure about this," Michael pleaded?

"Dead sure," John confirmed.

"That's not what I wanted to hear," Michael said.

"Thank you," John grinned as they shake hands.

"In Heaven, there is rest my friend," Michael preached, "in Heaven there is rest."

Tom and the secret service hesitate as John and Michael slowly walk toward the town. "What the.....," Tom sputtered. "Alright, but we do this my way. It's my job to protect you, even from yourself."

John and Michael just laugh. Together, they all walk slowly walk back to town. He reached the square and the people see him; a few people fell to their knees and cried. "I guess they remember you," Michael admitted.

"Funny old world isn't it," John grinned.

"Can we go to the doctor, now," Tom demanded.

"You're the boss," John replied. The group enters a building with a red cross. The Major watched them from across the street.

"Where's the doctor," Tom asked?

"I saw what happened," the doctor said. "He shouldn't be here."

"He shouldn't be alive, but he is," Michael snapped. "He needs your help." They lift him to the table and begin to examine John.

"I'll tend his wounds," the doctor said, "but you must leave before night fall and never return."

"Imagine that," John uttered.

"I can't believe how you're still alive," the doctor questioned.

"By the grace of God," John preached.

"Then, it truly is a miracle," the doctor answered. "I've known that crippled man all my life. You touched him and he walked."

"Then, we've something to ask of you, in return," Michael said.

"Anything," the doctor agreed.

"You must start a church in this village," John ordered, "and bear witness to what you've seen."

"A what," the doctor stammered with fear in his voice. "Did you not see the evil out there? The people of this village almost killed you."

"That's why it's so important," John said.

"I can't. The Major will kill me just like he killed you. I've seen him kill people just for the food in their hand," the doctor feared. "A church, no way, I can't."

"There are worse things than dying in this world," Michael replied. "You've witnessed two miracles. A crippled man walked in the street and now, a dead man walked in through your door. You're no longer blessed, my friend."

"Blessed," the doctor questioned.

"You've witnessed two miracles, yet you still do nothing. Your soul can live forever in the kingdom of Heaven or dwell for all eternity in the depths of despair," Michael preached. "Is that not worse than dying?"

"I don't know." the doctor squirmed.

"You don't know the hand of God when you see it," Michael warned.

"I did see it, but I'm not worthy of such a task," the doctor said. "I'm just a doctor."

"The apostle Luke was just a doctor," Michael preached. "He witnessed miracles, just like you."

"Alright, I'll do it, but you must help me," the doctor begged. John began to pass in and out of consciousness.

"I'll help you," Michael promised. "For now, just talk to the people. They trust you. Let them talk about what they've seen. That's it."

"You're either crazy, or the bravest man I've ever met," the doctor said.

"No, he's on your table," Michael whispered.

"Michael, we failed." John wailed as he drifts off. John closed his eyes and began to dream. "The prize will have to wait," John muttered before he faded into unconsciousness.

My Second Term

It is the year 2016, the President of the United States resided in a hospital bed lucky to be alive. Outside the hospital, a CNN newsman delivers the medical state of the President. "The President's alive and in a stable condition. He'll remain in ICU for several days, but doctors say he's recovering nicely. He could be back in the White House within a month."

"I tell you, if the Congress takes action on the Presidents recommendations. This country's in for one heck of a change," the CNN anchorman advised.

"We'll have to wait and see, but this Executive Order is a massive move in the right direction for a country that's in desperate need of a shot in the arm," the CNN reporter replied.

"I spoke with Congressman Cody Atkinson, Republican from Arizona, he recommended the transfer of the current Oil company tax break of four billion dollars a year directly to companies that manufacture electric automobile engines. This legislation would jump start the President's energy program, immediately. An economy without Oil, now that's amazing," the CNN anchorman agreed.

"I can see the momentum building quickly for the President's initiative," the CNN reporter admitted.

"They're calling it, the New American Economy," the CNN anchorman announced. "The world's changing and I can't wait to see it."

John and Elizabeth are talking inside the hospital room. The room's filled with flowers. John's trying unsuccessfully to get out of bed. "There are not enough flowers in my room," John complained.

"Idiot," Elizabeth said.

"I love you, too," John grinned. "You don't suppose you could help me to the window."

"Why, so you can get shot, again," Elizabeth snapped. "Idiot, the doctor ordered you to stay in bed."

"That's not for my protection," John demanded. "Come on, the people need to know their President's alright."

"Well, he's not alright," Elizabeth barked.

"Seriously, help me here," John pleaded.

"Jerk," Elizabeth said.

"You love me. You know it," John assured. Elizabeth helps John to the window. John leans out to see the crowd.

"Are you happy, now," Elizabeth said. John waved to the crowd.

"It looks like you're stuck with me," John laughed. The crowd laughs and applauds. He gave a single thumb up.

"You're one insane man," Elizabeth said.

"See, they missed me, too" John said affectionately.

"Like a head cold," Elizabeth whispered.

"I heard that," John said. "But, is the world ready to listen to a crazy man."

"They can't possibly ignore you," Elizabeth said. "God, how can anyone ignore you anymore?"

"That's funny," John grinned.

"I watched you in the operating room. I saw you die on the table. You were dead," Elizabeth cried fighting her tears. "You left me all alone. I've never felt so empty and desperate in all my life. All the things I wanted to say to you."

"Well, I'm here now," John revealed.

"Oh, shut up you jerk," Elizabeth barked as she laughed and cried at the same time.

"I know how you feel," John assured. "There's so much to say, so much still to do." John hugs Elizabeth before they kiss.

"By the way, Brian will be fine. The bullet passed straight threw his side and came out the back," Elizabeth stated.

"What happened," John asked. "I don't remember anything."

"Brian jumped in front of the gunman. John, he took a bullet for you," Elizabeth explained. "You're alive because of him."

"I had no idea," John replied.

"Well now you do, so kiss me quick before you lose me forever," Elizabeth grinned.

"It's not even my birthday," John joked.

A month later, John is in the oval office writing at his desk. "It's your three o'clock appointment, sir. What shall I do?" the secretary asked.

"Send them in," John said. Two elderly gentlemen enter the room.

"Mr. President, the House of Representatives is prepared to back your Executive Order to subsidize the building of electric automobile engines," the congressman from the south stated.

"Mr. President, the Senate's prepared to back your Executive Order, as well," the senator added.

"Nothing is that easy, and...," John questioned.

"Well, sir. There are a few requests," the congressman from the south replied.

"Yes, sir," the senator said.

"There always is," John agreed. "What do they want?"

"The big three auto makers are asking for credit in creating hybrids engines and asking for concessions in doing so," the congressman from the south asked.

"I understand, but you can't get a little bit pregnant, gentlemen. Ford, Chrysler, and GM will still make cars but with an engine that ends the economic slavery of the American people," John demanded. "Do I make myself clear?"

"Yes sir, but they're demanding something in return," the congressman from the south responded.

"I know they'll get it because we need them," John confirmed. "Tell them they'll be compensated when a working prototype's in place for mass production. Small companies don't have the ability to mass produce electric engines immediately, but they do have innovation on their side."

"And the government will...," the congressman from the south added.

"The government will grow the economy. We'll subsidize all the electric engines you can mass produce. Not next year, now," John ordered. "Cars will cost the same or less than normal. Nothing changed, except decades of oppression and slavery."

"What if they refuse," the congressman from the south expressed.

"It's simple, everybody wins. They're businessmen and this is just a business decision. You're either with us or against us," John declared. "There's no middle ground."

"I'll pass it on, sir," the congressman from the south reassured.

"And you sir," John asked.

"The oil companies have a few concessions they're demanding," the senator said.

"Be more specific," John said. "Who's expecting concessions?"

"Exxon, Chevron, and Conoco from the United States, British Petroleum, and Royal Dutch Shell from the Netherlands and Total S. A. from France," the senator replied.

"It seems I do have the attention of the world," John admitted.

"These companies want you to understand that the mass production of electric automobiles will result in a worldwide economic depression," the senator stated. "Millions of workers will be laid off and tax revenues paid to the governments of the world will decrease dramatically."

"So they ask for ransom for kidnapping the world from hope," John wailed. "Is that it?"

"No, sir," the senator pleaded.

"Yes sir, you'll not stop this country from becoming free, again," John shouted with conviction. "This is independence day."

"It will be impossible to operate effectively in a government controlled environment such as the one you propose, its socialism," the senator stammered.

"Let me see if I understand this situation correctly. The American people are done with oil company oppression. They'll vote out of office any representative that backs big oil's continued oppression of

American freedom. You're experiencing fear for the first time. You threaten retaliation in hopes of eliminating the threat, so you can continue to rape the American public," John said convincingly. "How am I doing so far?"

"Well...," the congressman from the south sputtered.

"And let's not forget about the attempt on my life," John grinned.

"There's no proof of any connection with the oil companies," the senator denied.

"Yes, they made sure of that, didn't they," John scolded.

"What are your intentions," the senator asked.

"The will of the people is the only legitimate foundation of any government," John commanded, "to protect its free expression will be our first objective."

"Yes sir," the senator agreed.

"And you are going to help me," John added.

"We will agree to disagree on that," the senator replied.

"Of course, they will," John snapped. "How much profit did Exxon make in the last quarter? Let me tell you. Eleven billion dollars profit in just ninety days. Yeah, I said billion, it's a modern miracle."

"We...I mean they earned those profits," the senator stammered. "They need it for further exploration."

"Not anymore," John demanded. "You will subsidize every laid off worker into the new economy with education, medical coverage, and wages until they have reentered the workforce."

"Never," the senator barked.

"Consider it the cost of redemption," John ordered, "for decades of oppression and pain inflected upon the American people."

"They'll declare bankruptcy and close their doors," the senator said.

"Save the drama, my friend. The world is filled with gas driven cars and planes," John pointed out. "You'll find others to exploit, just not here."

"How am I supposed to explain this to the oil companies," the senator asked.

"Simple, it's in their best interests," John explained. "Both of you, have a good day, gentlemen."

That evening in the White House bedroom, John is in bed recovering and watching the news on television. Elizabeth is brushing her teeth. On the television is CNN, "In an historic vote by the Congress of the United States, the President's Executive Order for energy reform has passed by a resounding margin. When asked the Congressman from Alabama, Carlton Smith, he explained, "It's the will of the people. They've spoken their hearts and minds. We're here only to enforce their wishes. And today, we did just that."

"The future of America appears to be a future without oil," the

CNN reporter admitted. "A White House spokesman said the President will visit the General Motors plant in Detroit next week to personally see the first electric engines come off the assembly line."

"It seems we're seeing the effects of the new economy on Wall Street, already. Oil company shares are down two percent and GM, Ford, and Chrysler are up three percent in trading this week," the CNN anchorman acknowledged. "However, the price of crude oil remains unchanged at one hundred and twenty dollar per barrel."

"We look forward to seeing the President up and around next week," the CNN reporter said. "It should be interesting going forward."

"Do doubt about it, Bob," the CNN anchorman said.

"See, I told you they'd miss me," John laughed trying to be heard over Elizabeth brushing her teeth. She stopped and looked at him; she rolled her eyes.

At the General Motors plant in Detroit, the President's limousine arrived with John and Brian. They get out with the secret service. They walk into the plant to speak to the line workers. As John enters, the crowd began to applaud. "Ladies and gentleman, the President of the United States," the announcer said.

"Thank you for having me today," John began. "The work you do here's making a stronger America for everyone. So, let's take a walk." The President walks down to the assembly line shaking hands with the line workers.

"Mr. President, it's an honor to meet you," the assembly line worker said.

"No sir, It's an honor to meet you," John replied.

"Thank you," the assembly line worker said.

"Tell me about this electric engine I'm looking at," John asked.

"It's the state of the art electric 457 engine for the new Chevy SUV," the assembly line worker said. "As you can see, it's about the same shape and size of the old engines, but it's completely electric."

"Are you going to get one," John asked.

"Absolutely, I've a family of four and we all have cars," the assembly line worker said. "Trading in my old gas guzzlers will save my family a thousand dollars a month."

"And what is your plans for the savings," John inquired.

"My oldest daughter's starting college in the fall. This will definitely help pay for her education," the assembly line worker replied. "Hopefully, so she won't end up like her blue collar father."

"I think she has a wonderful father," John acknowledged. "You're doing the right thing. She'll be proud of you." John shook his hand again and moved down the line to speak with another line worker.

"Mr. President, I'm so glad you've come," a female assembly line worker said.

"It's incredible to be here," John assured. "What's your job?"

"Quality control," the female assembly line worker said. "We make sure each engine passed twenty three quality inspections. These electric engines are going to be the best in the world."

"Are you getting one," John asked?

"I've already ordered mine," the female assembly line worker said. "It will be delivered next week."

"Congratulations," John replied.

"I'm not paying four dollars per gallon ever again," the female assembly line worker said. "Thank you, sir." She reached over and kissed the President. The crowd applauded.

"God Bless America," John said proudly.

"John, we have a meeting with the CEO of GM," Brian reminded. "We need to go."

"Congratulations, everyone," John shouted. "The spirit of America goes with you."

Inside the office of the Chief Executive Officer, John and Brian were waiting for the CEO, when he walked in. "Gentlemen, can I get you a drink," the CEO of GM said.

"Sure, thank you," John agreed.

"Scotch and water," Brian said.

"I want to commend you on your decision to subsidize electric engines," the CEO of GM approved. "We couldn't have done it without you."

"Of course, you could," John answered.

"You could've done it twenty years ago," Brian replied.

"What do you mean," the CEO of GM questioned.

"Oil companies have been paying you not to produce electric engines for years," John argued. "They've been buying up patents and you look the other way or am I missing something?"

"Your information's correct. It's just a business decision," the CEO of GM confirmed. "We need each other. Our alliance allows us to continue our business. They provide the capital we require to compete with the Japanese and Germans. It's a big world out there."

"Why haven't you looked to Wall Street for capital," Brian asked.

"I've been in business a long time, son. Our relationship with big oil is established and mutually beneficial. It's been good business for decades," the CEO of GM replied. "One shark's as good as the other."

"It's not good business if it crippled America, promoted foreign terrorism in our country, and bankrupted our economy," John snapped. "Poor people don't buy trucks."

"Are you making me an offer I can't refuse," the CEO of GM laughed.

"Perhaps, the next CEO of GM might be more cooperative," John threatened. "We've someone in mind."

"I hope you get re-elected, too," the CEO of GM warned. "I've someone else in mind, as well."

"I'm sure you understand the gravity of the situation," John replied.

"Of course, I do. You want me to walk away from the oil companies," the CEO of GM said. "The problem is, no one walks away from them and lives."

"What do you mean," Brian said.

"You make an enemy of the Cartel and you will not win," the CEO of GM guaranteed.

"The Cartel's my problem," John assured. "Your problem's making electric engines, and if there is any problems with the quality of those engines. I'll know where to find you."

"Let's cut to the chase, shall we," the CEO of GM insisted. "I'll need five billion dollars in developmental funding. Plants will have to be modernized, dealers compensated, and rebates awarded to consumers for trade-ins."

"Yes, let's cut to the chase. If I suspect any sabotage or missing deadlines," John demanded. "You're not ever going to be able to get a job sweeping the plant floor, much less manage it. You'll get your money."

"Perfectly clear sir," the CEO of GM replied.

"Good," John grinned. "The US government will be your first customer. We're placing an order for two million postal trucks, a million military vehicles, and another million cargo vans."

"Thank you sir," the CEO of GM replied.

"Don't thank me, yet," John said. "I'll make the same deal with Ford and Chrysler. The first one to get there wins."

"You don't have to do that," the CEO of GM stammered.

"Make the deliveries," John ordered. "It's just good business."

"Thanks for the scotch," Brian grinned. He and John get up to leave the office.

"You'll provide me with a few names from the Cartel," John instructed. "I'll want to speak with them personally."

"I'll be sure to tell them it's all your idea," the CEO of GM said.

"You do that," John agreed. "We'll be in touch."

In the Oval office, John, Brian, and Michael wait for an appointment with the Cartel representative. "John, what do you expect to gain from this meeting with the Cartel," Michael said.

"I don't know, but we have two hundred million cars, trucks, and buses in this country and there's a thousand ways to screw this up," John replied.

"You think they'll try to sabotage the new economy," Brian asked.

"It's in their best interest to see the electric engine fail miserably," John added.

"Regardless of the benefit to the economy or the American people," Michael said.

"In spite of the benefit, they make the rules and have their own agenda," John reminded.

"Can we win," Michael asked?

"Just like David and Goliath," John said.

"David killed Goliath with his first blow," Michael preached. "So you had better make it good."

"Any suggestions," John said?

"Faith and courage," Michael admitted. "And if that doesn't work, let loose the fire and brimstone." The office intercom sounds, Mr. President, a Mr. Wentworth to see you.

"Send him in, please," John replied. An elderly man enters the Oval Office.

"Good afternoon, Mr. President," Mr. Wentworth said.

"Come in, Mr. Wentworth. Welcome," John stated. "Have you met Michael and Brian?"

"I haven't had the pleasure," Mr. Wentworth replied.

"Welcome to the White House," Michael said. Brian remained silent.

"Thank you," Mr. Wentworth answered. "It's larger than I imagined."

"I received your name from the CEO of General Motors," John stated. "He said you are a man with the ear of the oil companies."

"I am flattered," Mr. Wentworth said. "I've a small consulting firm with an exclusive list of clientele."

"Of course," Michael agreed.

"Well, it seems that we've come to a crossroads in history," John acknowledged. "A new economy's emerging and oil isn't going to be a part of it."

"Hmm...," Mr. Wentworth said.

"What your opinion of that," John asked.

"The pages of history are written by great men," Mr. Wentworth advised, "with vision and courage to challenge the status quo."

"Then you understand our position," John replied.

"Of course, Abraham Lincoln conquered slavery, Martin Luther King conquered civil rights, and Jesus Christ conquered death itself," Mr. Wentworth remarked.

"Jesus died for the sins we commit," Michael preached.

"So he did," Mr. Wentworth agreed.

"All those men were martyrs," John said.

"Yes, so it seems," Mr. Wentworth agreed again. "I suppose some price must be paid."

"Am I to be martyred, as well," John grinned?

"I'm too old for such games. The wars that men wage have been going on for centuries," Mr. Wentworth explained. "I doubt you or I will settle them in our days."

"There will come a day of judgment," Michael preached.

"Revelation, what a story that will be," Mr. Wentworth replied.

"And the wicked shall be punished," Michael preached.

"Yes, they will. We're just passing through this world on our way to the next," Mr. Wentworth expressed. "Unfortunately, my days are coming ever closer to the end."

"I hope we have an understanding," John professed. "It has to be this way."

"We each must do, what we feel is right," Mr. Wentworth reminded. "Yes, Mr. President, World War III is coming, the war to end all wars. I've heard it all before."

"I'm sorry to hear that," John said.

"Like two fleas arguing over who owns the dog," Mr. Wentworth grinned. "It doesn't really matter what we do. May I tour the White House? I would very much like to see it before I go."

John spoke into the intercom. "Please arrange for Mr. Wentworth, a VIP tour of the White House. Take him anywhere he wishes to go," John ordered.

"Thank you, gentlemen," Mr. Wentworth replied. "Have a nice day."

"Goodbye," John said as Mr. Wentworth exits the Oval office.

"What was that," Michael asked.

"A wake up call," Brian warned.

In the White House, John's watching the sunrise from his window in the Oval Office. A loud noise came from outside the door. The door burst open. "Victory," Michael shouted!

"Oh my God, you're drunk," John groaned. "What are you doing up so early?"

"Who said I've been to sleep," Michael shouted. "We won the re-election last night. We kicked their butt."

"Seriously," John exclaimed. "You don't even drink."

"Do you not know of the first miracle," Michael questioned. "Jesus turned water into wine. Good wine, too."

"Who've you been drinking with, soldier," John commanded.

"Tom and Brian are right behind me," Michael laughed. Tom and Brian burst into the room, "Booyah". They're still drunk from the night before.

"John, sir, Mr. President, sir, John our intelligence tells us GM, Chrysler, and Ford are mass producing electric cars, as fast as they can make them," Brian babbled. "By the end of the year, we'll have over one hundred million cars on the road. Is this a great country or what?"

"That's half of all the cars in the country," Tom advised. "We did it."

"The world has officially gone crazy," Brian laughed. "It has begun, amazing."

"Gas prices are plummeting but we can't celebrate just yet, there's still a lot of work to do," John reminded. "We only have four years."

"With God on our side, who can stand against us," Michael preached.

"That's what I'm afraid of," John whispered.

"Victory," Brian shouted. "It's four more years for everybody."

"Okay, okay. Everyone goes to bed now," John ordered.

"Oh man," Tom complained. Tom and Brian leave. Michael stopped before he goes.

"You've come so far, so fast. Audie Murphy would be so proud," Michael laughed. "I'm proud of you, too."

"Okay, thanks. Now, go to bed, please," John reminded.

The CNN news on television, the newscaster reports on the first one hundred days of the second administration. "In his second term, the president's first hundred days have been something of a career performance. With record low gasoline prices, America's Gross Domestic Product has risen to six percent this quarter, and corporate earnings are exceeding expectations in all sectors. Manufacturing, consumer confidence, and the service indexes have risen to new levels driven by a very strong American consumer."

"Consumer spending makes up seventy percent of our nation's GDP. All indicators point to new levels of consumer spending. So much so, that tax revenues are on pace to create the largest economic surplus in this nation's history," the CNN anchorman proclaimed.

"At this rate, the Federal Deficit could almost be paid off before this president leaves office."

"And that's one incredible feat. It's fair to say that this has been coming for a while," the CNN reporter advised. "However, the results of the first one hundred days are nothing short of remarkable. A new economy without oil has been created in America."

"And therein lies the mystery," the CNN anchorman explained. "How long can this new age of American liberty continue?"

"So far, it's a bull market to end all bull markets. The entire world's watching everything we do. The world has got to take notice of what's happening here," the CNN reporter said. "I can't image it will be to long before electric cars are being built all around the world."

"That would mark the beginning of a Golden Age and the end of Big Oil, forever," the CNN anchorman remarked. "Oil would become a dinosaur."

"Such a different world it would be," the CNN reporter stated.

"Well, Bob, the President's first State of the Union Address is less than six weeks away," the CNN anchorman said.

"It's going to be an historic American moment, that's for sure," the CNN reporter said.

Inside the Situation room within the White House, the President's cabinet waits for John to enter. "Business is booming, Jack," Brian announced. "The country is on fire."

"We cannot get distracted," Tom commented. "We have to maintain the status quo."

"This is a defining moment," Michael advised. "The world's watching our every move we make."

"Good morning, gentlemen," John grinned as he enters the situation room. "Today's agenda is the State of the Union Address. I'll need current data on all categories of interest, military first please."

"The world as we know is at peace," the general said. "We are bringing soldiers home, for the first time in a long time. However, we shall continue to closely monitor terrorist activity in the Middle East."

"Excellent, the economic outlook," John replied.

"Economic conditions are on pace to exceed all previous expectations," Brain said. "Tax revenues are at record levels. With a four trillion dollar surplus projected this year, the Federal deficit has been cut by thirty percent. Consumer spending, stock market, and GDP are all exceeding expectations. However, food stamps, foreclosures, and the unemployment rate have fallen to record lows. Everyone who wants a job has one."

"Government Intelligence," John grinned.

"I'm sorry to say, the CIA's reporting certain levels of frustration among the oil producing countries of the world. Their revenue is are way down and unemployment in this sector is rising," Tom said. "There's civil unrest towards their governments to convert to electric vehicles. Of course, it's being met with resistance, the threat of civil war is possible, but it's not country against country. It is locals against their own government."

"I see, domestic affairs," John asked.

"The FBI reports criminal activity also at record lows. They attribute it to a one percent unemployment rate," Tom said. "It seems if you're working, you're less likely to be breaking the law."

"Great, education and welfare," John replied.

"The graduation rate is up twenty five percent for high school students. College admission is reaching full capacity. There are more students in colleges than ever before in history of America," the cabinet member said. "Low income schools are thriving with fully funded free lunch programs. No child's going hungry. We never expected this, but technology institutions across the country are reporting forty percent admissions increase over last year. We'll soon lead the world in the high tech arena."

"Thank you, gentleman," John acknowledged. "This is truly a miracle. I promise the world will take notice. It's an honor to serve God and country with you. Michael, can you lead us in prayer."

"Dear Lord, give us the strength to do your work and bless our endeavors in your name," Michael prayed. "Help us to keep our eye on the prize, now and forever. Amen."

The State of the Union Address has John seated behind his

desk speaking to the nation. "And there's no doubt, the prosperity envisioned by our forefathers has finally become a reality. Their hopes and dreams of a country destined for greatness have come true," John proclaimed.

"But, there's more to do. There's always more to do. People around the world are suffering, children are going hungry, and the poor are in need of our help. For this reason, we will support, economically and financially, any country willing to convert to electric vehicles. Any government that chooses to cooperate will be our allies," John promised. "I will support freedom against oppression, no matter where it is. That's my pledge to the world. Hope is what we dream about, when we're awake."

"What an amazing turn of events," the CNN reporter described. "America will lead the world into a Golden Age of freedom and prosperity."

The New Economy

Maria Bartiromo is interviewing John. She is dark haired with tan skin and sharp business tongue like a whip. "The Wall Street Journal Report with Maria Bartiromo" is a nationally syndicated business, financial and economic news program, distributed by NBC Universal Domestic Television Distribution. The half-hour weekly newscast appears on over two hundred stations each week and provided the clarity, depth, and insight of *The Wall Street Journal* in a television magazine format. "Mr. President, it's an honor to meet you," Maria said.

"It's a pleasure to be here, thank you, Maria," John replied.

"It is the final year of your presidency, and a remarkable presidency it has been. Your name will sit alongside the greatest presidents in history, Washington, Lincoln, and Roosevelt," Maria proclaimed. "Can we take a moment to recap the past seven years?

"Of course," John agreed.

"It didn't start out with thunderous applause, did it," Maria said.

"No, it didn't," John replied. "It started with war, economic recession, and an America divided against itself. We reinvented ourselves; both the country and I see things differently today."

"What was it that turned it all around for you," Maria asked.

"I accepted Christ into my life," John announced. "I was shown a true direction in life. After that, everything seemed to make sense."

"What do you mean," Maria asked?

"It's the choices we make in life. People are the most important thing, especially with the American spirit," John explained. "We had fallen into a state of economic and mental oppression. It had to stop."

"You mean oil," Maria said.

"Not just that, oil was just the tool," John expressed. "Oppression and tyranny have been around for centuries. Anytime the rights of free people are being exploited by the few, the masses will suffer."

"But you almost died," Maria reminded. "Was it worth it?"

"Would I do it again? Of course, it was never about me," John explained. "It's about keeping the light of freedom alive in the world."

"That sounds almost divine," Maria said.

"God's work," John preached, "was never intended to be easy."

"Faith and courage have been a theme or your administration during your second term as president," Maria said. "It's certainly impressive but, why is that?"

"The people of America have endured a civil war, two world wars, two economic depressions, and a massive assault upon our freedoms. They've withstood those events because of our faith in God and the courage to do the right thing," John explained. "In the future, our faith and courage will be tested again."

"What do you mean, in the future," Maria asked.

"Evil's always just a moment away," John revealed. "The devil's greatest trick is to convince the world that he doesn't exist."

"I understand," Maria said. "Thank you, Mr. President."

"Thank you," John replied.

"How exactly did you turn this country around," Maria asked.

"Maria, a picture is worth a thousand words," John grinned. "This chart shows the largest fourteen industries in a country. One industry is ten times larger than the others, the oil industry. Our tax revenues are derived from industry profits. These are the previous year's profits by each industry. You can see that oil dominates all other industries."

"This represents our economy with oil," Maria said.

"Correct," John agreed. "Most of our former tax revenues came from the oil industry." John pulls out a new graph.

"And what is this graph telling us," Maria asked.

"This chart represents this year's profit by industry, big difference here," John explained. "Oil profits are way down but every other industry is booming, record profits and record tax revenues for the entire country."

"With this increase, you've been able to pay off most of the federal debt," Maria confirmed.

"Correct, but the most important thing, it's not a one-time event. This will continue for many years to come," John advised. "When you raise the water level of a lake, all the boats rise with it. Raise the income level of the middle class, all the businesses in America rise with it. That is how you grow the economy."

"Mr. Henry, I'm impressed," Maria replied.

"Pretty simple, when you think about it," John grinned. "Once money stopped going in the gas tank, it went into American business. It's the land of opportunity, again. Americans don't want handouts, they want an opportunity, and we did it."

"So what does the future hold for John Henry," Maria asked. "After your presidency ends, do you have any plans?"

"I've establish a foundation to provide spiritual assistance in the undeveloped parts of the world," John announced. "My calling is to help the oppressed people of the world find hope and salvation in their life."

"How will you find them," Maria asked.

"I'll travel the world," John replied. "Where there's hatred, I'll show love; when there's doubt, faith; when there's despair, hope; and where there's darkness, light."

"That sounds heroic," Maria said.

"I believe you must become the change, you wish to see in the world," John grinned.

"Aren't you afraid of what you might find, out there," Maria said.

"Of course not," John grinned again. "I'll go bravely in the directions of my dreams and live the life I've imagined."

"How will we find you," Maria asked?

"Facebook, of course," John laughed. "The amazing technology of today ties us all together. We're just a point and click away."

"I'd like to be your friend," Maria asked.

"You got it," John promised.

"What will the name of this foundation be," Maria asked.

"The Journey," John announced.

"Why, the Journey," Maria asked.

"It's our journey through this life that makes us, who we are, who we help, and who we save," John explained. "I plan to travel with a few friends."

"I guess the question I'm thinking is why the undeveloped world," Maria said.

"The developed world is aware of everything. News travels at light speed," John explained. "The undeveloped world's in dire need of a gift, the gift of hope."

"Hope," Maria said.

"Hope is what we dream about, when we're awake," John replied.

"I've heard that before," Maria said. "Mr. Henry, you're truly a man of integrity. I wish you the very best of luck. You're the true spirit of America."

"Thank you and God Bless America," John grinned. The interview ends as Maria faced the camera.

"That was the President of the United States, John Henry. What he did for America, he plans to do, again, for the world," Maria recapped. "Congratulations, Mr. Henry, our hearts and prayers go with you."

As John exits the interview, he's given a note from the attendant. John began reading the note. It is from Michael. *John, I have terrible news. Pancreatic cancer is about to claim Elizabeth. She was complaining of stomach pains, I had the White House doctor examine her. It is malignant and in Stage 4. The doctors are giving her days, maybe weeks to live. I am so sorry to have to deliver this news. She is in our prayers.* John is visibly moved to tears.

Inside Washington Hospital, John walked into Elizabeth's room. She has several machines attacked to her and is about to go into surgery. "They're taking me in," Elizabeth cried in tears.

"I love you," John replied trying to hold back his tears.

"I love you, too," Elizabeth said. "I'm so afraid."

"I'll not lose you, not ever. You will beat this," John assured. "You'll be stronger than ever."

"I don't want to die," Elizabeth cried.

"It's not your time," John declared fighting back the tears. "God will watch over you. He'll protect you."

"John, I'm not going to make it," Elizabeth wept. "Promise me, I'll be saved. Promise me."

"I will find you in Heaven," John promised. The doctors wheeled Elizabeth out of her room toward the operating room. He stopped to speak with John.

"Mr. President, we will do everything we possibly can," the doctor insisted. "If the surgery doesn't kill her, the chemotherapy probably will. She has a twenty-five percent chance of survival. The cancer has spread too far.

"But...," John stammered.

"I'm telling you this, so you will be prepared," the doctor advised. "Do you understand?"

"Yes, I do," John agreed. John waited outside the operation room for hours. The clock on the wall turned slowly for eight hours. Michael entered the waiting room.

"I'm sorry," Michael said.

"I'm always sorry," John scolded.

"It's not your fault," Michael assured.

"Hope is what we dream about...," John seethed. "Why am I surrounded by so much death? Mother, father, and now the love of my life, every time I love someone they die. I can't take this anymore."

"The promise of salvation's not for the body," Michael advised. "The grace we seek is for the soul."

"I don't understand," John replied.

"Death's as much a part of life as love or faith or courage," Michael admitted. "You must understand, our bodies grow old and weary from this world, but our soul gets stronger every day."

"Then why do I feel so tired," John struggled.

"You're stronger than you know, my friend," Michael replied. "Someday, you'll save me from death, too."

"Why do you say that," John asked?

"Remember, I once saved your sight, and that was for a reason," Michael assured. "We just didn't understand why, at the time."

"I still don't understand," John sneered. The doctor returns from surgery.

"Mr. President, we did all we could," the doctor claimed. "The cancer was too aggressive. We're unable to contain it. There was too much damage to the vital organs. We're too late."

"Is she gone," John whispered.

"Yes, I'm sorry sir," the doctor replied reluctantly. "In the end, she did not suffer. There was no pain."

"The suffering is only for the living," John mourned.

"The hospital will notify the coroner's office," the doctor said. "They'll need a few days to prepare the funeral."

"Rest in Peace, my love," John thought.

"In Heaven, there is rest," Michael replied.

"I'll see her again, someday," John wept.

"I'm sure you will," Michael reassured.

The funeral for Elizabeth is at the Washington cemetery. There are hundreds of people dressed in black. Amazing Grace was playing before William delivered the eulogy for Elizabeth. "It's a tragedy to bury your own child, to live beyond their years," William cried. "A piece of me died today, as well. For what does the future hold, without hope or dreams of a better life? Elizabeth is what was best in me, the best in all of us. She'll live in my heart, forever."

"There will be a wake held at the home of Mr. William Roth this afternoon. All are welcome," the priest announced as the crowd began to leave. William delivered a cold glare toward John.

At the home of William Roth, John is surrounded by secret service. John approached William. "Stay here," John asked. "I'm sorry for your loss, William. I loved her dearly. It's my loss, too."

"What do you know about life," William seethed. "You're a fool."

"Excuse me," John replied.

"You heard me," William snapped. "You've set in motion events that will forever change the world."

"The world is very different now. Man holds in his mortal hands the power to abolish all forms of human poverty and all forms of human life," John advised. "And yet the same revolutionary beliefs for which our forebears fought are still at issue around the globe, the belief that the rights of man come not from the generosity of the state, but from the hand of God."

"You're so naive. Such a young man so set on becoming a king. Well, now you are. The king of a dead world," William scolded. "Your pride has brought a great evil upon this world. And it's your fault."

"My fault," John questioned.

"Many fathers will bury their children because of you," William sneered. "You've started World War III and you have absolutely no clue."

"You want to blame me for the evil that plagued the world," John argued. "Go ahead, do your best. I'll not cower to your drunken threats."

"After tomorrow," William informed, "the world will never cower to you, ever again, King John."

"World War III starts tomorrow, really William, your imagination's getting the best of you," John snapped.

"Did you think the aristocracy you betrayed would sit quietly and do nothing while you stole their power," William revealed. "Are you that stupid?"

"William, you're ranting like an old fool," John said. "Seriously, if you know something, just say it."

"There's nothing you can do about it," William barked. "God, help us all."

"Have you gone mad," John fumed?

"Today, I buried my daughter, tonight I drink to the end of the world, and tomorrow I prepare for my eternal suffering," William admitted. "Yes, my son, I've gone mad and so will you." William took a drink, laughed, and walked away while John sttod stunned by the events.

The New World Order

John is alone inside the White House bedroom; there is a lonely knock at the bedroom door. John doesn't answer it. The second knock is louder. The door opens on its own. John could care less, he just lost his wife and nothing really matters to him at this moment. "How have you been, son," Richard's ghost said with his father's silhouette standing in the doorway.

"Who are you," John asked?

"Am I the soul from which you came," Richard's ghost replied.

"Are you mad or am I," John questioned?

"Of course, not," Richard's ghost laughed.

"Then show yourself," John ordered.

"Do you not recognize your own father?" The ghost of John's father walked into the room and sat on the bed.

"Am I dreaming," John asked?

"Am I alive," Richard's ghost replied?

"I don't think so," John assured.

"Yeah, I don't think you're dreaming either," Richard's ghost groaned.

'Then, I must be dead," John realized. "Why else would you've come?"

"Don't be ridiculous," Richard's ghost answered. "I've come to prepare you."

"Prepare me for what," John asked.

"For what's next," Richard's ghost replied.

"Why, what's next," John questioned. "What's happened?"

"I never was much of a father. I never told you how to live or what's important in life," Richard's ghost admitted. "I thought, perhaps, you'd learn from watching me. But, I wasn't much of a man."

"You're my hero," John disagreed.

"A son only sees the good in his father," Richard's ghost acknowledged.

"You were the richest man in the city," John said. "You taught me what it means to be a man."

"No, the truly rich man is one whose children run into his arms, when he has nothing," Richard's ghost proclaimed. "That's what it means to be a man."

"But, you were always there for me," John assured. "You're always so strong, never afraid of anything."

"I was weak," Richard's ghost shouted.

"What do you mean," John asked.

"There were always temptations and failings," Richard's ghost scolded. "That's what the Devil does for a living."

"The devil," John replied.

"That's why I'm here. Your children are not really yours," Richard's ghost explained. "They're the offspring of Life, longing for itself."

"You tell me this from the grave," John accepted.

"It's not our flesh and blood that made us father and son, it's our spirit," Richard's ghost revealed.

"You're my father," John reassured. "You always will be."

"As my father once told me," Richard's ghost said. "All statesmen are delinquents. I never believed it until now."

"What has happened, father," John expressed. "Why have you come?"

"You're now the father," Richard's ghost acknowledged. "You must take with you the essence of fatherhood, to care for the children of the world. Turn back from the plane of your existence, take with you the lessons of your journey and begin again. March with the children, step by step, side by side, over the road less traveled."

"I don't understand," John answered. "Why do you speak to me in riddles?"

"Sometimes the poorest man leaves his children the richest inheritance." Richard began to fade away.

"Father," John pleaded.

"I must go," Richard's ghost demanded. "It has begun."

"Don't go, I need you," John begged.

"I give you all the faith and courage, which I never had. What was silent in the father, now speaks in the son." Richard's silhouette faded away. John lay down in his bed, closed his eyes, and fell asleep.

Again, a knock on the door; he looked at the door but said nothing. His adrenaline was pumping. A second knock is louder as the door opened. He dared not speak. "Sir, I'm sorry to wake you but there has been a tragedy," the White House aide implored.

"What," John replied?

"At 3:30 am, the city of Tel Aviv, Israel has been attacked by an atomic bomb," the White House aide announced. "It has been completely destroyed, nothing survived."

"Oh my God," John whispered.

"The Israeli government's on full alert and is threatening nuclear retaliation against the Arab nations," the White House aide advised. "Al-Qaeda rebels are claiming responsibility for the attack, among others."

"William...," John feared.

"What," the White House aide said.

"Nothing, organize the military to full alert status. Call together my cabinet, right away," John ordered. "Get me the Prime Minister of Israel on the line, now."

"Yes sir," the White House aide said.

John looked at a picture of his father on the bureau. "Thank you, father," John whispered.

John is in the situation room as the other cabinet members enter. He is on the phone with the Israeli Prime Minister. Confusion and fear filled the room. The cabinet members gather. "We're just minutes away from starting World War III," the general warned. "If this happens, World War IV will be fought with sticks and stones."

"I know, but it's a trap," Brian replied.

"We're being baited," the general advised. "The Arab nations are not trying to destroy us. They want you to react, we can't let them win. It's our only hope."

"He hung up on me," John shouted.

"What's going on, John," Tom pleaded?

"Israel is widely believed to possess nuclear weapons and one of the few countries in the world to develop them. Israel maintained a policy known as nuclear ambiguity. They have never officially admitted to having nuclear weapons. Yet, repeating over the years that it would not be the first country to introduce nuclear weapons to the Middle East. Rather, leaving ambiguity as to whether it means it would not create, nor disclose, will not make first use of the weapons or possibly some other interpretation of the phrase, until now," John exclaimed. "He said he would wait twenty four hours, but if they are attacked again, he would drop a hundred atomic bombs on the Arab nations, regardless of the consequence."

"The beginning of the end," Michael feared.

"No one wins an atomic war," John stated.

"We must find out who's responsible for this and stop them, now," Tom warned.

"I think I have a plan," John said.

"Then you'd better make it quick," Brian said. John grabbed his iPhone and called William.

"William, how many more people have to die," John demanded.

"What do I care, I'm making millions," William laughed. "Have you checked out the markets, its chaos?"

"The Secret Service is on the way to your house," John advised. "They'll be there in just a moment."

"John, I'm not there," William shouted. "What are you thinking?"

"Millions of people are dead, tell me what you know," John scolded.

"Are you sure you want to know," William seethed. "There's a second atomic bomb waiting to be released. Interested?"

"William, you can stop this. I know you can," John demanded. "What do you want?"

"It's not what I want, John. I'm just one man," William admitted. "It's too late. This is bigger than both of us."

"Where's the second bomb," John begged.

"Patience John, you'd think the world was coming to an end," William said. "Have you heard from the Chinese, Russians, or the Arabs, yet? They should be offering solutions that might be of interest. You might consider the New World Order treaties."

"What treaties," John scolded.

"It's all over the news," William replied.

"William, for God's sake, where's the second bomb," John screamed.

"Alright, John, calm down. North of Tehran is an old munitions dump left over from the war. Inside you'll find the second bomb," William acknowledged. "But John, be careful what you wish for."

"What does the world news say," John shouted turning to the news.

CNN is on the television. "At 3:30 this morning, an atomic blast occurred in Tel Aviv, Israel. The devastation is terrible. The death toll count is in the millions. This morning, stock markets around the world are opening down and still dropping," the CNN anchorman advised. "We've received word that certain nations are calling for a single world order to control the chaos. China, Russia, and the Arab nations are leading the vote at the United Nations. All eyes are watching the United States to see our response."

"The International Monetary Fund is suggesting a single world currency to stabilize the global economic collapse before it is too late," the CNN reporter pleaded.

"The United Nations has agreed to take action against Israel if any nuclear retaliation is taken against the Arab nations," the CNN reporter professed. "They're calling for a new world order to establish peace along with a single world currency to control the economic chaos created by this catastrophic event."

"Tonight, we're pushed to the brink," the CNN reporter announced. "The world is literally holding its breath." John turned to his military advisors.

"How long would it take to get marines to Tehran," John sneered.

"We have troops in Fallujah," the general replied. "They could be there in forty five minutes."

"We've a CIA operative in Tehran," Tom added. "He could coordinate the strike."

"Do it," John ordered. "Get the Prime Minister of Israel on the line and tell him we're going in. We've found the second bomb."

Outside northern Tehran, marines in helicopters flew into the abandoned munitions depot. In an all-out assault, they landed and rushed the building. A firefight broke out with a few terrorists inside. All the terrorists are killed. "Alpha Leader to Bravo One," the marine stated. "Come in Bravo One."

"Go ahead Alpha Leader," Bravo One replied.

"The area is secured. We've taken casualties but we have control of a large crate being loaded onto a truck," the marine detailed. "We're in the process of opening it now, sir."

"Good work, Sargent. Tell me what you see," Bravo One asked. "Is it a nuclear weapon?"

"Negative sir, its marijuana," the marine replied.

"Alpha Leader, are you positive," Bravo One requested.

"Affirmative, sir," the marine said. "The depot is empty, except for this crate of marijuana, that's it."

"Tend to the wounded, Sargent, over," Bravo One replied.

In the situation room inside the White House, "We didn't find the second bomb," the general whispered in John's ear.

"I can't believe it," John shouted.

"What happened," Tom asked.

"It was a trap meant to make us lose credibility and it worked," John barked. "Give me the phone." John called William on the iPhone again.

"Hello John," William laughed. "Are you chasing your tail?"

"Your little diversion worked," John snapped.

"Be careful what you wish for," William warned.

"Why William," John shouted. "When is it enough?"

"Now John, you know that answer, it's never enough," William replied. "I told you, stock markets are crashing all over the world and I'm making millions, thanks to you. I hope there's something left to spend it on."

"It doesn't matter how many people die, does it," John scolded.

"Casualties of war, John, the war that you started," William said. "You should take the United Nations offer for a New World Order; it's the only way out. By the way, we won't be speaking again, you'll understand if I'm unavailable. We'll always have Elizabeth, son." John's screen goes black, he has lost.

"We've less than twenty four hours to find the second bomb and stop it from being launched," Tom advised.

"What do you suggest," John asked.

"I'll deploy all agents to the Middle East," Tom ordered. "We have a search and destroy mission, but we need more time."

"How," John asked.

"Meet with the United Nations. Discuss their terms of a One World Government," Tom snapped. "Find out who's behind this threat."

"I know exactly who's behind it," John announced. "China, Russia, Venezuela, and the Middle East, the oil companies are behind this. It's payback for my arrogance."

"Call them out. Show them the evil behind the mask," Tom demanded. "The United Nations is in session, as we speak, you must go now."

"Will they listen to me," John said.

"John, choose your words wisely," Michael preached. "It's been written, at the time of the one world government, they will be portrayed as the solution to our problems and fool the world into believing that they'll bring about the peace."

"How can they do that," John said.

"It is a false peace," Michael assured. "Tribulation will follow, and then a worldwide crisis will cause panic. Here we are, John."

"They promise peace in order to gain power," John asked.

"By then, it's too late," Michael answered.

"I understand," John said.

"They'll be waiting for you, John," Michael assured.

"I hope so," John sneered.

In the United Nation's building in Manhattan, John walked down the United Nations hall. The mural which dominates the Security Council chamber was painted by Norwegian artist Per Krogh. It depicts a phoenix rising and the triumph of hope over war. All the countries are represented. The Prime Minister of Israel is speaking on the floor. "Our country has been attacked without provocation. We've received word from a group of terrorists that a second nuclear missile will be launched at Jerusalem, if we do not surrender our lands. I tell you now, we will never surrender. And we'll attack the nations responsible for this terrorist act of war with war in return.

I promise we'll rain a hundred nuclear warheads down upon them, without consequence."

"Sir, you cannot retaliate against any nation until we know who's responsible for this tragedy. Any escalation of a nuclear war will result in a nuclear world war," the Middle Eastern representative promised. "I speak for the countries of China, Russia, Brazil and all the Arab Nations; we must have peace, at all costs. If you follow through with your aggression, we have no choice but to view you, as the aggressor."

"Then so be it, you've twelve hours to find the second nuclear missile and the nations responsible. If not, then we're at war," the prime minister declared.

"We must preserve the peace," the United Nations representative pleaded. "The International Monetary Fund is prepared to flood the world with SDR's as a new world currency. We can stave off this economic collapse with an infusion of credit to all the world banks. The United Nations is prepared to act as a single world authority to punish the perpetrators and atone for the victims of this tragedy. We have the blessing from Pope Benedict XVI to establish a true world political authority in order to oversee this crisis, the economy, and work for the common good. With the blessing of the church, it's being called the Charity in Truth."

"This new world authority is the only solution that promised peace," the Middle Eastern representative announced. "These weapons of mass destruction, if they fall into evil hands, must be destroyed so this can never happen again."

"Prime Minister, do you not see the end of this war," John shouted. "If you sponsor a nuclear retaliation, then the countries of China, Russia, and the Middle East will destroy you with a storm of nuclear destruction. And in the name of peace, they'll establish a new world superpower, a new world order lead by fear, the fear of nuclear annihilation. That's what they want. That's why they're here."

"Treason, that's treason against the world," the Middle Eastern representative screamed. "The United States wants millions of innocent people to die, for no reason, while they do nothing."

"John Henry, you've had your chance and failed. This is our problem and we shall defeat our own enemies in this war," the prime minister commanded. "The city of Jerusalem will not fall."

"Then, we're all doomed to fall," John warned. "The Security Council is the only body which can grant permission to violate a country's sovereignty against the will of that country. If the council votes to allow an invasion of that country, for whatever reason, there is no recourse, no court of appeals. That country can do nothing but complain and prepare for the military attack." The room is electric with panic. The news spreads across the world, riots in the streets, and the entire world is now in chaos.

In the situation room, the cabinet is preparing for war. John is still inside the United Nations. They're speaking via iPhone technology on a screen. "John, the entire world is on full alert," Tom warned. "Everyone is armed and ready to launch nuclear weapons."

"We have less than twelve hours," John reminded. "If the second nuclear weapon is not found, then it's judgment day."

"John, we've had twenty reports of nuclear weapons all around the Middle East. This is insane," Tom insisted. "Every terrorist group in the world is telling us, they have a nuclear weapon and they intend to use it."

"I must speak with the President of Israel," John ordered. "I'm going to Israel."

"You do realize there's a nuclear warhead, somewhere, directed at Israel," Tom pointed out.

"How could I forget," John grinned.

In the Israeli government building, John entered the Israeli palace to speak with the President. "We must speak," John pleaded.

"You've come a long way, my friend," the President of Israel said. "You know you're in danger here."

"Frankly sir, the whole world's in danger," John admitted.

"Yes, I know. We only have three hours before the deadline," the President of Israel declared. "Then, we will proceed."

"Mr. President, God sent me here," John said reluctantly.

"What," the President of Israel said.

"He spoke to me once, and showed me the suffering at the end of the world," John admitted. "I believe he showed me this in order for me to stop it from happening."

"I see," the President of Israel said.

"We cannot play into their hands. They're hoping you will retaliate," John stated. "Then, they'll destroy you. They want to make an example of you for the world to see and fear."

"Your conviction is just, but we're an old country. For centuries, our enemies have hunted and persecuted our families. Enemies that want to take our very souls," the President of Israel divulged. "Our time has come. We cannot turn away, again."

"But...," John stammered.

"I know it is difficult for you to understand but this is our last stand," the President of Israel confessed. "If we cannot live in peace, then we'll die in triumph and go to God with open hands."

"You can't do this," John snapped.

"Of course, we can and will," the President of Israel promised.

"What if I find the second bomb and stop it from being launched," John replied.

"Then, you'll have saved our world," the President of Israel approved. "But it could be anywhere, where will you look. We've spies looking all over the Middle East. I'm afraid it's impossible."

"I'll find it," John promised.

"I'm sure the Lord walks with you," the President of Israel said. "You now have less than three hours."

"Can I borrow a jet," John asked?

"Of course," the President of Israel said. "I wish we could have met earlier; I would have liked you."

At the Israeli military airport, John is about to get into a jet with a young Israeli pilot. He gets on his headset to communicate to the White House. "Tom, is that you," John asked. "What's happening there?"

"The United Nations is voting to establish an act of war against Israel if they launch nuclear weapons against any country and it's going to pass. John, John...can you hear me," Tom repeated. "For the first time in history of the world, we are about to approve a nuclear war."

"Yes Tom," John acknowledged. "Can you get Michael?"

"John, I'm here," Michael replied.

"Michael, this is going to happen. If we don't find the bomb, it's over," John explained. "Do you understand?"

"I understand," Michael replied.

"This is a biblical moment. I need to know where evil resides in the Middle East. Where does it live," John demanded. "If the world were going to end, where would it come from?"

"Evil lives in the hearts of men, it's not a place," Michael admitted.

"Michael, we know the first nuclear launch came from somewhere near Syria, Iraq or Iran. I need you to reference the past, the Bible, anything that might give us a clue and I need it now," John explained. "We have two hours left."

"It could be anywhere in Iran," Michael guessed. "I don't know."

"Faith and courage, Michael, you taught me that," John assured. "Trust yourself, what does the Holy Spirit tell you?"

"Daniel had a vision of four beasts that tried to destroy the world. It took place in the region called Elam," Michael advised. "But there is nothing in southern Iran but desert." Michael is breaking from the pressure. "It can't be there."

"What else, think outside the box" John commanded. "It doesn't have to be Iran. It could just be another deception."

"Babylon, The ancient city of Babylon in Iraq," Michael shouted. "Babylon is the mother of all harlots and the abominations of the Earth. Revelations tells of the whore of Babylon. The whore is associated with the Antichrist and the Beast of Revelation. It marks the apocalyptic downfall of man."

"Where is it," John screamed.

"South of Baghdad, about fifty five miles south, it was once the Rome of the ancient world," Michael yelled. "If the world's to be destroyed, the evil would rise from there."

"Get Tom," John ordered.

"Yes, Sir," Tom said.

"Search and destroy mission," John ordered. "Fifty five miles south of Baghdad, do we still have forces in Iraq?"

"Yes sir, by ground they could be there in an hour," Tom shouted, "by chopper, thirty minutes."

"Send them immediately," John ordered.

"Yes sir, but where do we look," Tom asked.

"Sir, there's a closed United States airbase in southern Baghdad. A nuclear weapon could be launched from there," the general announced. "It would look like it came from us."

"And we would be getting the blame for starting World War III," John realized. "That's it."

"If it's true, the base will be heavily guarded," the general advised.

"I know this base, sir. It's a fortress."

"If it's heavily armed, then we know we've found the right place. It has to be there," John pleaded. "Tom, contact the Israeli President and inform him of what we're doing. He must not attack."

"Yes sir," Tom said.

"Report back as soon as possible," John replied. "I'm on my way to Iraq."

In an Israeli jet, John is flying to Iraq. The message came in over the radio from Tom. "John, the Israeli President said we've already had our chance. He would not wait and he'll target southern Baghdad as a first strike," Tom replied. "If you don't find the nuclear weapon at the airbase, there won't be an airbase to find. You have thirty-four minutes. Do you understand?"

"Got it, over," John closed out communication. He looks defeated. He begins to ramble to himself.

"What's that, sir," the young pilot asked. He is young brash pilot full of courage and without fear.

"Nothing, it's just such a long shot," John said.

"We'll make it sir," the young pilot promised. "We'll be in range in eight minutes."

"In range for what," John asked.

"Missile range, sir," the young pilot advised. "Our assault missiles will be in range of the airbase in seven minutes. With our US military GPS guidance system, that airbase is an easy target. I can't miss."

"If the missile hits anywhere near the base, they will return fire," John acknowledged. "If not, we just blew up an empty air force base."

"That's affirmative, sir," the young pilot said.

"Son, launch everything you've got," John shouted. "Empty this pile of bolts, now."

"Yes sir," the young pilot affirmed. The missile launched from the jet. It flew faster than the jet and reached the target with an explosion. Nothing happened.

"Did it hit the target," John asked?

"Affirmative sir, the radar shows no activity," the young pilot informed. For a moment, the radar still showed no activity. Suddenly, a bomb exploded outside the pilot's window. Several bombs exploded all around them.

"Get us out of here," John screamed.

"Mayday, Mayday. Flight GLD9er has been hit," the young pilot confirmed. "We're going down. Repeat, we are going down."

"We found it. We found it," John screamed. "Radio the location of the base."

"I've got to land this plane sir," the young pilot ordered. "You have to do it, sir. Hold down the red key."

"John Henry to US Marines, John Henry to anybody," John shouted. "Come in, come in, we've located the second nuclear weapon. It's the abandoned US airbase outside of Babylon. Seek and destroy, repeat seek and destroy, that's a direct order."

"Code Red. Seek and Destroy US air force base, target one," the young pilot ordered. "That's a direct order from the President of the United States of America, Code Red."

"Code Red," John shouted.

"Can I land the plane now sir," the young pilot asked.

"Do it," John shouted as the pilot is battling the jet downward.

"We're coming in hot," the young pilot said. The plane crash landed in the desert as the wheels came off and skid to a halt.

The perimeter of the US Air base outside Baghdad is in sight. In the distance, the military arrived at the air base with weapons blazing. Bombs go off by the dozen. Infantry attack the perimeter. The battle raged on. John gets out of the plane first. "Son, are you alright," John asked.

"I think so sir," the young pilot said. They jumped out of the plane and run toward the bombs bursting at the air base. As they reach the perimeter, the explosions stopped. They walked up behind a captain.

"Is everything under control," John asked.

"Jesus Christ," the captain said.

"It's the President of the United States," the young pilot pointed out.

"I know who he is, son. How did you...," the captain stopped.

"Have you located the nuclear weapon inside yet," John interrupted.

Sargent, have you located the prime objective," the captain demanded.

"Sir I have," the marine inside the base said. "There's a missile prepared for launch in dock bay one. I believe it to be a nuclear warhead. We have secured the area, mission accomplished."

"What time is it," John exclaimed.

"It's seven minutes past the hour," the captain reported.

"Captain, get your men out of here, right now," John demanded. "That's an order, right now."

"What do you mean," the captain asked.

"A nuclear missile is headed straight for us," John announced.

"Oh no," the young pilot said.

"Is this the radio?" John grabs the communication equipment. "This is an emergency. Get me through to General Hammond. This is the President of the United States, John Henry."

"Sir, are you alright," the general replied.

"General, contact the Israeli President. Tell him we have the second nuclear weapon in our possession," John ordered. "Abort the attack. Repeat, abort the attack."

"Yes sir," the general said. John and the pilot sat down on the ground and looked toward the night sky. A million stars in the desert sky are out in force.

"I'm really going to miss this place," John said.

"The desert," the young pilot asked.

"No, this crazy old world," John replied.

"Me too, sir," the young pilot said. They closed their eyes and waited for an explosion. Michael's voice came over the radio.

"John, come in John, can you hear me," Michael shouted.

"Michael is that you," John said?

"The Israeli President has aborted the attack," Michael shouted. "No nukes have been launched."

"Oh yeah," John shouted. "Why did he do that?"

"It was something you said to him," Michael responded. "He said if God sent the President of the United States to see him, then that had to be worth an extra ten minutes. Whatever that means, are you alright?"

"Booyah," John shouted.

"You know, it might be a good idea to put together a global treaty to keep something like this from ever happening again," Michael advised.

"Imagine that," John laughed. "How about the Treaty of Saint Christopher, we need as much protection as we can get."

"I like it, now get your butt home," Michael shouted. "The war is over."

"Affirmative sir," John said.

My name is David

In Lystra, John began to wake from his head injury. He is slow to realize

he is in the doctor's office. John has been sleeping on an operation

table full of bandages. He can hear Tom and Michael talking in a

corner, privately. "We need to think about getting out of here, quickly,"

Michael whispered.

"Not until you tell me about what happened back there," Tom

said.

"Where," Michael asked.

"In the jail with that devil," Tom replied. "What did he mean by

more than that?"

"Do you remember that night at Camp David," Michael recalled.

"I was there, Michael. How will I ever forget it? He went blind,

then crazy, and then you showed up," Tom exclaimed, "and he could

see."

"Do you know what happened to John," Michael asked.

"I know he saw something, perhaps something from God," Tom

responded.

307

"What happened to John, happened in the Bible, the book of Acts," Michael announced. "God spoke to a man named Saul. He blinded him for three days. A man named Ananias cured his blindness with just his hands. Any of this sounds familiar?"

"Are you telling me John is Saul, and Saul was blinded for three days," Tom asked. "Who is Saul?"

"Saul was the ancient world's version of Adolf Hitler. His job was to seek out and murder Christians for no other reason than they were Christians. He was judge, jury, and executioner," Michael explained. "After God spoke to him, Saul changed his name to Paul. Have you heard of him?"

"Of course, Paul's all over the new testament," Tom said. "His letters are the foundation of Christian living."

"Yes he is and that's why I'm here following John. Paul preached faith is the only road to salvation," Michael said, "salvation by the Grace of God."

"That's what John says," Tom replied.

"In the Bible, the Lord came to Paul in a vision," Michael preached. The Lord said, "Do not be afraid; keep on speaking, do not be silent. For I am with you, and no one is going to attack and harm you, because I have many people in this city."

"John does the same thing," Tom acknowledged.

"Yes, but John preaches faith and courage. Perhaps, that's what the world is looking for today. The courage to believe," Michael said. "That is why we're here."

"We've done some incredible things, but this is...," Tom stammered.

"I know, just relax. I don't think John is Paul, just similar," Michael advised. "That's all."

"I know what I saw out there. He was dead," Tom admitted. "Are you telling me John's some kind of Saint?"

"Maybe," Michael suggested.

"I hesitate to articulate...what time is it," John mumbled. He slowly began to come around. Tom looked out the window to see a crowd beginning to gather. The Major is at the front, headed toward the doctor's office.

"Time to go, John," Tom urged.

"Doctor, we need to leave," Michael stated quickly. "Is there a back door?"

"Yes, follow me," the doctor said.

"How are we going to get out of here? We don't have a car, remember," Tom panicked.

"Let's just leave now," Michael replied. They quickly exit out the back door and there is the Hummer. The little boy is sitting in the driver's seat.

"What the...," Tom said.

"Do you need a ride," the little boy asked.

"How did you get our car," Michael asked?

"Stole it," the little boy laughed.

"Awesome," John grinned.

"You're alright kid," Tom said.

"Doctor, remember what I said," Michael said. "We will come back, someday."

"I will," the doctor replied. Everyone jumps in the car and the little boy speeds away. They turn down a dark road. Tom is in the front seat with the boy.

"No one is following us," Michael said. "Let's find a place to spend the night."

"We've got to get off the road first," Tom warned. "We're not safe in any town around here."

"What's on the GPS," Michael asked.

"It shows a road that leads to a lake, up on the right," Tom advised. "We'll have water, food, and a fire for the night."

"Awesome," John replied.

"What do you want to do with the kid," Michael asked?

"Let me talk to him," John said.

"He saved us all, you know," Michael replied.

"I know," John said. "It seems we're in debt to this little boy."

At the lake side, by a fire, the group sits on the ground. "So what's for dinner," Michael asked?

"Beef jerky," Tom said.

"What no broken bread," Michael groaned.

"What do you think this is, the last supper," Tom grinned.

"It might have been," Michael said, "if not for the kid."

"It's the best beef jerky I've ever had," John proclaimed. "What's your name, son?"

"David, my name is David."

"Well, David, what's your family going to think about you spending the night away from them," John asked.

"I'm always away from them," David said. "I don't have a family. The Major killed my mother and father."

"I'm sorry, what happened," Michael said.

"He shot them for taking food from the American soldiers," David cried. "Then he took our food."

"Where do you live," Tom said.

"I sleep on the roof tops and find food where I can. Some people give me food, when they can," David said. "You gave me a dollar." The mood got quiet around the fire.

"You saved our lives because we gave you a dollar," John replied.

"Maybe," David said. "I don't know."

"David, come with me. We need to go get some water," John remarked. "Can you get our canteens?"

"Sure," David said. David walked to the back of the Hummer.

"John....," Michael said.

"I know," John interrupted.

"He can't come with us," Tom groaned. "It's too dangerous."

"We can't just leave him here, either," John whispered.

"He's here for a reason, John. Everything happens for a reason," Michael preached.

"I said I'll talk to him," John repeated.

"John, it was no accident," Michael stated. David came back with the canteens. They walked down to the lake and sat by the water.

"Can you get this," John asked.

"Sure," David said.

"I'm sorry to hear about your family," John said.

"It's okay. I hardly remember them," David replied.

"I lost my mother when I was five," John said. "I was angry and blamed God for her death."

"It's hard every day," David replied. "Some days, I don't eat. Those are the worst."

"David, have you ever heard of Jesus," John asked.

"I saw a man once wearing a robe with a cross on a string around his neck. I think it was Jesus," David said. "But, he didn't see me."

"No, he probably wouldn't, that's too bad. I was the same way, too. I knew about him, but was afraid to listen. For the longest time, I had no honor to speak of," John said. "I was there for no man, only myself."

"But, I saw what you did. You put your hands on that crippled man. He's been crippled all his life," David said. "You touched him and he walked."

"It wasn't always like that," John said. "I was once the President of the United States and all I lived for was my own selfish greed. I hated anyone that stood against me, even my best friends."

"Really," David replied.

"Then, it all changed," John said.

"What happened," David asked?

"One day, God came into my life and filled me with the Holy Spirit," John said. "Before, I was a coward, after that I feared no man."

"I saw them kill you. I followed them down the street," David replied. "Then, you came walking back into town. It was the bravest thing I've ever seen."

"When God's with you," John said, "you have nothing to fear."

"Can you teach me to be brave," David asked.

"You already are," John declared. "How would you feel about living in America?"

"America," David shouted with excitement.

"Yes," John said.

"I've never seen America," David said. "What's it like?"

"It's the land of the free and home of the brave," John answered. "Everyone there is free."

"Everyone," David said.

"Everyone has the freedom to choose their own life, to go bravely in the directions of their dreams, to live the life they've imagined. They call it life, liberty, and the pursuit of happiness," John announced.

"It sounds amazing," David replied. "Are you going too?"

"I can't right now, but I can take care of you," John promised. "I've friends in America that will make sure you're safe, warm, and eat three meals a day."

"It sounds incredible," David said.

"And I'll make sure the Lord's with you," John promised.

"How can you do that," David asked.

"You saved our lives, didn't you," John said.

"I guess so," David said.

"Then, your life's my responsibility from now on, okay," John promised.

"Okay," David grinned.

"God has a plan for everyone's life. I think he has something special planned for you, my friend," John admitted.

"Are we friends," David asked.

"Always," John promised as they walk back to the fire.

"I'm glad you gave me that dollar," David grinned.

"I am too, now get some sleep," John grinned. "We've a busy day tomorrow."

"I'll never forget you," David replied.

The sun's rising and everyone is waking up. "Can you guys help me up," John asked.

"Sure. John, we have something we need to discuss," the secret service agent admitted.

"We have orders to protect you for ten years after your Presidency," the other agent stated. "Well, the ten years are up, today."

"We have some flexibility," the secret service agent added. "We can stay as long as you need us."

"That's not necessary," John grinned. "But, I do have one final mission for you."

"Sure sir, anything," the secret service agent said.

"You name it," the other agent said.

"I need you to fly David back to America. Michael has a church in Washington, DC. The Father there will care for him," John advised. "Can you do that?"

"We'd be glad to sir," the secret service agent said.

At the airport terminal gate, the secret service and David prepare to board the plane. John walks up to David. "Can I ask you something," David said?

"Of course," John replied.

"Why are you doing this for me," David said?

"God isn't finished with me yet, either. He still has plans for me, too," John admitted. "I think he has something big for both of us to do."

"What does he want me to do," David asked.

"Right now, I believe he'd like for you to go to America and learn everything you can. In time, I'm sure he'll let you know," John promised. "But until then, have faith and courage."

"I will sir, goodbye," David said.

"Goodbye, my friend, I'll see you soon," John promised.

"Thank you," David replied. David and the two secret service agents board the American Airlines plane. Tom, Michael, and John watch from the sky deck.

The Gamble

The electric Hummer cruised down the road; John, Michael, and Tom are traveling through Northern Greece. The countryside is undeveloped and poor. They are driving down a country road with a trail of dust blowing from behind the Hummer. "John, what are we doing," Michael asked. "There's nothing here."

"I feel like a drink," John replied.

"You want some water," Tom said.

"No, something a little stronger," John suggested.

"We're in Greece," Michael said. "I'm sure we could fine some good wine."

"Actually, I was thinking more along the lines of ten-year-old blended scotch," John announced.

"That would be good, too," Michael replied.

"We might need a bar or saloon for that," Tom advised.

"Ask that guy," John said. They pull over to the side of the road. A lonely shepherd walks along with his sheep.

"Good afternoon, sir. We're looking for a place that might serve scotch," Tom proclaimed as he rolls down the window. "Do you know of any place around here?"

"There's a village just about three miles outside of Kavalla. There's a place called Luck's Tavern," the shepherd replied. "Just stay on this road, you can't miss it. But, it's not that lucky."

"What do you mean," Tom asked.

"It's a rough crowd," the shepherd said. "Mind your manners, you should be alright."

"Thanks, I appreciate it," Tom said.

"Don't thank me, yet, you haven't seen it," the shepherd laughed.

"That sounds like fun," John said as they speed away.

"Yeah, like a stick in the eye," Michael warned.

"And why are we going there," Tom asked.

"That's where the sinners are," John whispered.

"Of course, they are. I forgot," Tom urged as they pull up in front of the Luck's Tavern. It looks like a saloon from the old west. They walk in through the swinging door and sit at a table. The bar is almost empty. A waiter walks up to the table.

"What can I get for you gentleman," the waiter asked.

"Ten-year-old blended scotch and three glasses of ice," John replied.

"We don't have any scotch and we sure don't have any ice," the waiter groaned.

"Okay, how about aged bourbon," John asked.

"Nope," the waiter said.

"I guess it's not our lucky day," John admitted. "So, what do you have?"

"Whiskey," the waiter replied.

"So why do they call this place lucky," John asked.

"Gambling and girls," the waiter grinned.

"I think we'll take the whiskey please," Michael said, "a bottle of your very best."

"They're all the very best," the waiter laughed.

"Of course they are," Tom, sneered as the waiter left. Several call girls start toward them but Tom casually waved them off.

"Nice place," Michael grinned.

"Yeah, just like a Holiday Inn," Tom growled.

"Relax. What's the worst that can happen," John assured.

The waiter returns with a bottle, no label, and three glasses. He sets it on the table, grins and walks away. Tom opens it and pours the drinks. "With you, let's see," Tom replied, "what about that time in Syria, when the bounty hunter shot Michael with an arrow."

"It was a flesh wound," John laughed.

"Right," Michael recalled.

"Let's not forget the riot in Turkey," Tom said. "We barely escaped the mob, dressed like nuns."

"Yeah well, nobody said it was going to be easy," John acknowledged. "What were you expecting?"

"A little gratitude might be nice," Tom replied.

"Thank you, Tom," John responded.

"You're welcome," Tom said.

"It's been a long time since the Fraternity house days," Michael said.

"It's been thirty years but it seems just like yesterday," John stated.

"I recall you flopping around in the mud like a fool," Tom said.

"And you guys came to my rescue," John grinned.

"Somebody had to," Michael replied. "You're constantly stirring it up."

"Sleeping during vespers, drinking, and I want to be Governor of Texas," Tom laughed. "You overshot that one, just a bit."

"Imagine that," John grinned.

"I wonder what Brian's up to," Tom said. "Last I heard he was living somewhere in the Caribbean."

"He founded an orphanage in Cancun," John replied. "He oversees the children and teaches economics."

"Really, Brian," Michael questioned.

"It seems he's made all the money he'll ever need," John assured. "He wants to give something back."

"I never thought he'd give anything back," Tom said.

"Sometimes people change," John grinned.

"No offense," Tom said.

"I was a little surprised myself," John admitted.

"Surprising, I remember when I introduced you to Elizabeth. I was just looking for a wing man," Michael pointed out. "Next thing I know, it's Mrs. Henry."

"She was hot," Tom agreed.

"I do miss her. She had more testosterone then I did," John moaned. "She was a wonderful wife and mother."

"I'm sorry," Michael said. "I didn't mean to..."

"No, it is okay, it was just an amazing time to be alive," John interrupted. "So much hope, so many possibilities."

"I know," Michael agreed.

"Hey, you were the best president America has ever seen. Lincoln, Washington, Roosevelt, they had nothing on you," Tom boasted. "None of them did what you did."

"I've good friends," John said. "We've traveled the world these ten plus years converting souls to become Christians. It hasn't been easy. I couldn't have done it without you, a toast to my two very good friends." They drink their toast with whiskey.

"Oh, that was a bad idea," Michael groaned.

"Not if you like moonshine and hangovers," Tom replied.

"Thanks, guys," John said.

321

"Hey, I think that girl wants to be your friend," Tom grinned.

"Oh, man," John laughed.

A dirty nasty looking gangster of a man walked into the bar. Behind him, three men escort a woman; her skin is pale and eyes are black. They use rope to tie her hands. The group settled in at the bar. "I wonder what that's about," Michael asked.

"Call the waiter over," John demanded.

"Psst...," Tom got the waiters attention.

"Can I get you some scotch," the waiter laughed?

"Yeah, what's up with the girl, there," Tom asked.

"Mister, it's none of your business," the waiter warned.

"I'm just asking," Tom said as he slipped the waiter a twenty-dollar bill. He leaned over to clean the table.

"Some say she's possessed. She can tell the future. They use her for gambling," the waiter said. "It comes in handy, you know."

"Really," Tom replied.

"Would you like more whiskey," the waiter asked?

"Sure and send a bottle over to that gentleman," John ordered handing him a twenty.

"You sure you want to do that, mister," the waiter responded.

"What are you doing John," Michael asked.

"Remember the old man said, mind your manners," Tom warned.

"I'm just going to introduce myself," John said.

"Oh, no," Michael sneered.

"John, don't do anything crazy, again," Tom whispered.

"I won't, just relax," John replied. The waiter delivers the bottle of whiskey. He pours a drink for each man. They guzzle it down. The gangster waved John over to the bar.

"You're not from around here," the gangster said.

"No, just passing through," John replied.

"What can I do you for," the gangster asked?

"Well, I hear you're a gambling man," John said.

"Maybe," the gangster said.

"I thought you might like to make a wager or so," John offered. The other men lean in to hear what John has to say.

"How much you got," the gangster grinned.

"About a thousand dollars," John replied. The other gangsters react to the offer with arrogance.

"That's a lot of money for someone who's just passing through," the gangster said.

"Sometimes I think I can tell the future," John stated looking at the girl.

"You're playing a dangerous game," the gangster warned. "What's the wager, mister?"

"The girl, some say she's possessed by a demon," John asked. "Is that true?"

"Maybe," the gangster replied.

"Well, I bet I can chase that demon out of her, forever," John boasted. "Right here, right now." The gangster's posse laughs at John.

"You're crazy. You drink too much fool," the gangster snapped. "Go away before I have you thrown out." The gangsters turn back to the bar to drink. John reached into his jacket and pulled out a thousand dollars. He threw it onto the bar.

"Put up or shut up," John snapped.

"What's wrong with you," the gangster said. "You think you're going to beat the demon out of her."

"I just like to make money," John replied.

"You think you can drive out her demons, all by yourself," the gangster asked. "How are you going to do that?"

"Just touch her," John said.

"You're just going to touch her," the gangster laughed. "That's it."

"Just me," John declared. "Where's your money?" The gangster motions to one of his crew. The man pulls out a thousand dollars and puts it on the bar.

"Bartender, hold my money for us," the gangster said. "You think your walking out of here with my money?"

"We shall see," John grinned.

"Go for it, old man," the gangster shouted.

"My pleasure," John said. He walks slowly over to the girl. He reached out and placed his hand on her forehead. He mumbled something in Latin and removed his hand. As he stepped back, nothing happens.

"Ha, fool. You're a crazy old man," the gangster laughed. "Take your friends and go home. Don't ever come back."

"Looks like you win," John grinned. He walked back to the table. The gangster's posse laughed at John. Suddenly, the girl dropped to her knees and fell face first into the floor. She laid there motionless. Nobody moved until the gangster walked over and grabbed her hair to see her face.

"Old man," the gangster sneered. Her face was normal, again. Her skin brown and eyes clear. John walked over to the bartender past the gangster to get his money.

"Since light travels faster than sound, some people seem brighter until you hear them talk. I guess I win after all," John grinned.

"Not today," the gangster shouted as he swung at John. The posse of gangsters jumped in, as well. Tom and Michael threw themselves into the middle of the bar fight. Initially, they were winning. The fight continued and moved out of the bar and into the street. "You're going to die, mister," the gangster shouted. The posse of gangsters outnumbered them and eventually got the better of them. Two gangsters held John while a third was about to land a lethal blow. A lone loud gunshot went off.

"Not in my town," the sheriff shouted.

"This is none of your business," the gangster warned.

"I'm making it my business," the sheriff announced. "Let them go."

"No, he owed me money," the gangster replied. "He stole from me."

"Let them go," the sheriff demanded. "I won't say it again."

"Sheriff," the gangster grunted.

"They'll be in my jail," the sheriff said. "If he stole something from you, I'll get it back."

"Guess again, sheriff," the gangster threatened. "They won't be in your jail for long." The gangsters let them up and John, Michael, and Tom followed the sheriff toward the jail.

"You boys get in there," the sheriff ordered as they entered the jail. "I'll have the doctor look in on you."

"Thank you, sir. You saved our lives," Tom acknowledged.

"Don't get too happy just yet, son," the sheriff said. "You're not safe, here."

"What do you mean," Michael asked.

"It's just me and my deputies," the sheriff said. "The other officers won't be back until tomorrow." The jailer scowled at John.

"Have I offended you," John asked.

"That was my cousin in the bar. You set free his witch," the jailer remarked. "Now, he's going to take his vengeance on you."

"Vengeance is mine," John preached, "says the Lord."

"You'll need more than the Lord to save you," the jailer warned.

"I've nothing to fear from you," John replied. "The Lord sent me here to save you."

"You, save me," the jailer said. "You're cracked old man."

"Your soul, I can baptize and wash away your sins," John declared. "You can dwell in the house of the Lord, forever."

"Like you saved that witch," the jailer laughed.

"I didn't rescue that woman. The Lord did it," John replied. "He drove out the demon."

"I don't believe you. It was a trick," the jailer said. "By this time tomorrow, you'll all be dead."

"If it's God's will," John answered.

"You had best save your tricks for tonight, preacher," the jailer urged. "You'll need them."

Later that night, John, Michael, and Tom were sleeping when several gunshots went off. The door kicked in and the gangsters entered the cellblock area. The gangster walked toward the cell with the jailer behind him. "Good evening, boys," the gangster grinned. "Did you miss me?"

"Where's the Sheriff," John asked?

"The same place you're going to be," the gangster promised. "Hand over my money." John slowly hands over the money.

"Can we take them out now," the jailer pleaded?

"Not yet, they're not going anywhere," the gangster said. "Are you?"

"What do you want me to do," the jailer asked?

"Watch them closely. Tomorrow, we're going to have a hanging, that way everybody can see what happens when you defy me," the gangster said. "You're going to die, slow and painful."

"Sure," John replied.

"Sleep well, while you can," the gangster grinned.

The jailer sat with his gun and watched John while several hours pass. "You know," John said, "it's not too late."

"Too late for what," the jailer replied.

"For your soul to be saved," John said.

"Screw you old man," the jailer laughed.

"It's your funeral," John said?

"I'm not the one in jail," the jailer replied. "I'm not the one that's going to hang."

"There are worse things in life than hanging a man," John advised. "A life without faith or courage, blind to the truth, is not a life worth living."

"What truth," the jailer asked.

"The Lord's the only truth. Faith and courage is the only path to salvation," John preached. "You soul can live forever. There's still time."

"Your time's almost up," the jailer promised.

"Time is your gamble, not mine," John grinned. "I'll be a free man when the sun rises."

"A free man, that's crazy. There's no way you are getting out of this jail until I say so," the jailer demanded. "Now, shut your mouth." The jailer pointed his gun at John.

"It's your last chance," John offered as he lay back in his bed. Michael and Tom did the same.

"My last chance," the jailer laughed. "You have a busy day of hanging, tomorrow, old man."

As the sun rose, a rooster crowed and woke up the jailer. Michael shook John. "It's time to go," Michael said.

"You aren't going anywhere," the jailer laughed.

"Wait for it," John whispered. A moment passed before an earthquake hit the town. The jail started to shake and crumble. The ceiling fell on the jailer but he is still alive. The back wall of the jail is completely destroyed. They are free to escape.

"Now, it's time to go," Michael shouted. A truck horn blew. It was Brian driving a Hummer pulling up to an opening in the wall.

"Hey, you need a lift," Brian shouted.

"Brian," Tom screamed. Tom and Michael jumped out of the jail toward the Hummer. John stopped to look back to the jailer.

"Faith and courage, my friend," John advised. "It's never too late."

"Save me, please, save me," the jailer begged. John reached through the bars and touched his hand.

"It is done," John promised as the jailer died.

"John, come on," Michael shouted. "We have to go."

"Now," Tom screamed. John turned and ran to the Hummer and jumped in. Brian sped away as the earthquake continued to shake the road.

"What are you doing here," Michael asked.

"You're supposed to be in the Caribbean," Tom shouted.

"I don't know," Brian said. "Something told me I was needed."

"Well, I'm glad you're here," Tom shouted.

"I got here last night," Brian replied looking at John. "Everyone in town heard the gunfire. They told me you're still in jail. I thought I might bust you out this morning. Then, there was this earthquake. And, here I am."

"What took you so long," John snapped.

"I was hungry. I was having breakfast," Brian replied.

"Thank you, again, for saving my life," John grinned.

"Brother, you were right on time." Michael and Tom yell "booyah!" They drove off into the sunrise. The sunrise grew bigger as it engulfed the moment. The Rolling Stones, Mick Jagger is playing on the radio, "I Can't Get No Satisfaction."

The Black Pope

An electric Hummer is driving through the desert. Tom returned with Brian to his Caribbean orphanage. It seemed an occupation best suited for Tom. He has always been a protector at heart. John and Michael are alone, driving in the Hummer down a dirt road. Michael has a solid gray goatee; John's hair is completely gray. Their faces are tan from the years spent in the deserts of the world. Michael looked a bit more weather-beaten of the two. On the radio, Jagger is still playing, 'I Can't Get No Satisfaction.' "This song really takes you back, doesn't it," Michael recalled.

"You would know," John laughed.

"So where we headed," Michael asked.

"I got an e-mail from David," John said.

"Really, he must be quite the young man, by now," Michael stated. "How's he doing in the seminary?"

"Very well, he's going to make a fine priest, soon," John announced. "He's sent us a package to the Principe di Savoia hotel in Milan. It's waiting for us there."

"God bless that boy," Michael exclaimed. "I'm really looking forward to a long night in a soft bed, champagne, and a double cheeseburger with bacon. I really miss those double cheeseburgers."

"David is one of our best decisions," John acknowledged.

"He's a good kid, that's for sure," Michael agreed.

At the Principe di Savoia hotel in Milan, John and Michael parked the Hummer. Rich in tradition, the Principe di Savoia, one of the Dorchester Collection, is amongst Europe's most famous hotels. It offers a winning combination of old world luxury with the latest technology and design innovations. They are both filthy dirty and unshaven. They walk into the hotel and people stop and stare. "John Henry and guest, please," John said.

"Why am I always the guest," Michael asked?

"Mr. Henry, I mean, Mr. President. It's an honor to have you staying with us," the hostess declared. "It would be an honor to upgrade you room to the Presidential Suite?"

"What were you saying," John grinned at Michael.

"The Presidential Suite would be perfect," Michael agreed.

"That's really not necessary," John remarked.

"I insist," the hostess ordered. "Mr. President, I've a copy of your book, could I get you to autograph it for me?"

"Of course," John answered. She reached into her purse and pulled out a book. The title is *The Essence of Fatherhood: Letters from the Soul.* She

handed it to John with a pen.

"To Sharon please, thank you," the hostess replied.

"You're welcome," John said.

"The Presidential Suite will be perfect, thank you," Michael

replied.

"Yes sir," the hostess said. "And there's a package for you, too. It's

from a David Assantai."

"Yes, we're expecting it," John approved. "Thank you, it was nice

to meet you."

"If you need anything, just give me a call," the hostess giggled.

They enter the suite and Michael made a drink from the bar. It

featured Empire style, original antique furniture and an elegant working

fireplace in the living room. The elegant dining room is furnished with

French crystal, Limoges porcelain and silverware. Authentic Venetian

nineteenth century mirrors, Murano glass lamp and chandeliers, marble

and bronze wall lamps, original late nineteenth century prints and fine

objects in marble and granite complete the luxurious location. John

sits on one of the beds and opens the package. "What's not to like,"

John grinned.

"Just give me a call she says. You're twice her age, give me a break,"

Michael scolded. "What's up with David? What's he say?"

"He's studying the Roman Catholic church," John replied.

"I'll bet he has a girlfriend," Michael said.

"He seems to take issue with the new Pope Leo XX," John explained. "He says he's preaching the salvation of deeds, offering forgiveness for sale, and dictating the only route to Heaven being through the Catholic Church."

"It sounds more like he's studying ancient history," Michael replied.

"He seems to have more questions than answers," John said. "Here's a picture of the new Pope." John hands it to Michael.

"He's fine, it's just his youth," Michael reminded. "The Pope looks...,"

"Looks like what," John asked.

"Looks like he has company," Michael warned.

"What do you mean," John asked.

"In the background," Michael pointed out.

"Oh," John replied.

"John, that's Frank," Michael said. "What's Frank doing in a picture with the new Pope?"

"I'd say it has something to do with the new Pope," John suggested, "becoming the new Pope."

"John...," Michael said.

"There's more to this and you know it," John admitted. "David mentions a rumor or something about this Pope Leo being the Black Pope. What's a Black Pope?"

"It's an old derogatory term for the head of the Jesuit-Vatican connection," Michael advised. "It's just a legend, but the order is said to have ties to Lucifer."

"Lucifer," John asked, "is David saying Lucifer is the Black Pope."

"The prophecy says that Lucifer's followers will rebuild the house of the Lord so they can take control of the world," Michael quoted. "Ironically, they don't believe in Satan, but rather Lucifer, as a fallen angel. If he has risen to power, the world will not be safe."

"How could this happen," John asked.

"There would be a rise of the beast nations and the Black Pope's the beast who controls these nations. He's the dragon who spoke as a lamb," Michael preached. "They hide among the Christians waiting for their time."

"I remember when Pope Benedict called for a New World Order. A one world authority bent on controlling world peace, to keep it safe." John said sarcastically.

"It almost ended the world," Michael replied.

"We must go to Rome," John said.

"John, I'm getting too old for this," Michael emitted.

"This will be our last mission," John promised. "If this Black Pope is Lucifer, Satan, or whatever, you know we can stop it. One last adventure before we retire, for good."

"It's too much, we need help," Michael demanded.

"I remember what you once said to me," John recalled. "In Heaven there is rest."

"Are you saying, this is the last one," Michael asked. "On one condition, David and Tom must know exactly what we're doing. They might be able to help us." John agreed and began to e-mail David on his iPhone.

At the Vatican in Rome, Michael and John enter the church. The power of the place is inescapable and a long way from its humble origins as a graveyard. For nearly 2,000 years, its story has captured the imagination of millions. From here a religious faith grew to dominate the western world, crusades were launched, great inquisitions were convened, governments were made and broken. "I'm John Henry, former President of the United States. I'm here to speak with Pope Leo XX."

"Yes, Mr. Henry. The Pope will be honored to speak with you," the administrator replied. "If you would please wait inside, I'll notify him of your request."

"Thank you," John said.

"May I say what it's regarding," the administrator asked?

"The Black Pope," John remarked.

"Yes sir, you may wait in there," the administrator replied.

"That was a little too easy," Michael said as they walk into a closed room.

"Perhaps," John replied.

"Hello, Frank," Michael acknowledged as Frank enters the room.

"Long time, no see," Frank replied.

"Yeah, I see your associating with the new Pope," Michael sneered.

"You're very observant, Michael," Frank replied. "I'm impressed."

"Do you control this new Pope," John asked. "Or should I call him the Black Pope?"

"Oh, that's too bad, such a negative term," Frank expressed. "And just when I was beginning to like you, again."

"We've known each other for too many years, Frank," John snapped. "You won't get away with it, this time either."

"What will I do with you, my old friend," Frank grinned?

"Is that a threat," Michael questioned.

"Of course not, you want to speak with Pope Leo XX about the Black Pope? I'll arrange it," Frank agreed. "Where are you staying?"

"The Baglioni, room 212," John replied.

"Forgive me, I've a previous engagement," Frank announced. "It's so busy doing the Lord's work. I'll be in touch."

"The Lord's work," Michael laughed.

"Now Michael, miracles happen every day," John assured.

"You'd know about that, wouldn't you John," Frank grinned.

"Yes, I do," John agreed.

"I'll call you, tonight," Frank promised. "Have a good day."

In John's room at the Baglioni hotel, a knock at the door breaks the silence. The bell man hands John a note. "Thanks you," John said.

"What's it say," Michael asked?

"We're invited to the Pope's estate outside of town. He'll meet with us at ten o'clock this evening," John acknowledged. "The estate's about twelve miles south of the city."

"I don't like it," Michael warned.

"I don't like it either, but we have no choice," John replied. "If he's who I think he's, I need to meet him."

"I've got a bad feeling about this," Michael replied.

"You always have a bad feeling," John said.

"And I'm usually right," Michael reminded.

"We will be sure to notify Tom and David of exactly what we're doing. They'll be aware of our every move," John reminded, "right."

"That's supposed to make me feel better," Michael groaned.

In the electric Hummer, Michael and John are driving down a dark road traveling through the countryside. A car begins to follow them. The headlights are bright. "What if this Pope is Lucifer," John feared.

"Then his intentions would be to control the world, probably through war, a crisis, or economic collapse," Michael advised.

"We've had success in the past," John said.

"Yes, but this war would come about from religion. A war that pits

Christians against Muslims or Hindu's," Michael admitted. "Countries would not be involved."

"How much further," John asked.

"About three miles," Michael said.

"Can you face the devil, one more time," John asked.

"Perhaps sooner, rather than later," Michael replied. "It appears we're being followed."

"I believe you're right," John agreed.

"Can you lose them," Michael asked?

"Hold on," John ordered. The electric Hummer begins to speed away from the following car. Suddenly, a cow's standing in the middle of the road. The Hummer hits it and flips off the road. The car following stopped and two men get out. A few men with guns come out of the woods.

"Are you alright," Michael asked.

"No," John said. John pushed the speed dial on his iPhone; hides it inside his coat. The car door opens and several masked men drag John and Michael out. They are injured and quickly disarmed by the men.

"Move," the leader of the masked men ordered.

"Get rid of the car," the other masked man demanded.

"What's this all about," Michael pleaded.

"Shut up and walk," the leader of the masked men ordered. The men quickly move the car, lift the cow onto a truck, and run into the woods away from the accident.

"This is good," the other masked man ordered. One man tied John and Michael's hands behind their backs. They covered their heads with black bags.

"Why are you doing this," Michael begged?

"We almost made it to the Pope's house, didn't we," John said.

"What?" Michael answered. Two men walk behind John and Michael, they pull their guns.

"Who sent you," John demanded.

"Prepare to die," the leader of the masked men declared.

"I deserve to know, who ordered my death," John pleaded.

"Courtesy of the Black Pope," the leader of the masked men said.

"You mean Lucifer," John snapped.

"Good for you," the leader of the masked men said.

"I've prepared the world for him," John advised.

"We shall see," the leader of the masked men laughed.

"John," Michael shouted. The two men behind John and Michael bring their arms up toward John and Michaels head. At that moment, John and Michael are seen standing off in the distance with a third man. It's Gabriel standing with them.

"Can you save us," John asked?

"Not this time," Gabriel replied.

"What do you mean, not this time," Michael begged. "Do something."

"Michael, it's our time," John consoled.

"It can't be," Michael begged. "I can't die like this."

"Michael...," John ordered.

"Watch," Gabriel said. The two men pull the triggers and the execution is done. John and Michael's bodies fall to the ground.

"Bury the bodies," the leader of the masked men ordered.

"Yes sir," the other masked man replied. As they lift the bodies, John's iPhone fell out of his pocket onto the ground. The phone was still on. The leader of the masked man picked it up cautiously.

"Who is this," the leader of the masked men asked.

"My name is David," the voice on the phone announced. "Are you the Black Pope?"

"No," the leader of the masked men replied.

"Then, I'm coming for you, too," David warned. The masked man pushed the end call button and puts the phone in his pocket. He looks at the other masked man.

"Fool," the leader of the masked men barked as he points his gun at the second masked man and puts three bullets in his chest. "Bury them all, now." He walks right past John, Michael, and Gabriel without noticing them.

"I did call David," John reminded. "He knows."

"We have to do something," Michael pleaded.

"You already have," Gabriel assured.

"Well, where do we go from here," Michael cried.

"Where do you want to go," Gabriel replied.

"Anywhere, just away from here," John acknowledged.

The Prize

John, Michael, and Gabriel suddenly appear on a mountaintop looking down over a picturesque desert. Gabriel begins to walk down the mountain. John and Michael follow close behind. They walked for hours before anyone spoke a word. "Where am I," Michael asked breaking the silence. "How did I get here? Why am I here? Why am I compelled to take part in this? Who's in charge? I want to see him, now."

"Why don't you just ask him what women want," John replied.

"You can tell a clever man by his answers," Gabriel remarked, "but a wise man, by his questions."

"Why won't you answer me then," Michael asked.

"All in good time," Gabriel advised.

"I don't know who you are but…," Michael said.

"Michael, this is not the first time we've met. I have seen him several times throughout my life. He's led me through difficult times, when I had no faith," John admitted. "He gave me courage when I had none to give."

"You never said anything before," Michael expressed.

"It was none of your business," John answered. "It was between me and God."

"Oh thanks, speaking of God. When do we meet him," Michael demanded?

"When you ask a question, you're a fool for just a few moments," Gabriel advised. "If you don't ask the question, you're a fool forever."

"He knows you pretty well, too," John grinned.

"So who are you, exactly," Michael asked.

"I've had many names over the centuries. A spirit, a ghost, a guardian angel, if that makes it easier for you," Gabriel said. "I'm just a stranger, but you can call me Gabriel."

"Gabriel, the archangel," Michael replied. "The angel that told Mary her child was Jesus."

"I've had a ringside seat since the beginning," Gabriel replied.

"Well listen Gabriel, I'm hungry," Michael ordered. "And since, I'm walking through the desert, shouldn't I be hot, and we have no water. What am I supposed to drink?"

"Is he always this way," Gabriel asked. "Would you like to be hot?"

"Okay," Michael cried as he fell to his knees. "I'm sorry, my bad. I'll shut up, now." Michael brushed himself off and stood up.

"What should we be asking," John inquired?

"What's the meaning of life," Gabriel responded. "You tell me."

"To be strong, humble, and courageous," Michael replied.

"To be useful in the eyes of God," John confessed.

"Much better," Gabriel grinned.

"We're no longer of the Earth, and we're not in Heaven," John questioned. "Where exactly are we?"

"True, your journey's over and the prize awaits you," Gabriel proclaimed, "if you can answer just one small question?"

"I know this one, a bacon double cheeseburger," Michael blurted. "What's the best food in the world?"

"Did you get hit in the head," John said?

"Duh, where were you," Michael scolded.

"I like you," Gabriel assured. "I like you, both."

"Thank you," Michael replied.

"There were many that came before you and many will come after," Gabriel admitted. "But this is your time. We can take as much of it as you need. Do you a specific question?"

"What's the state of mankind," John questioned?

"I hear the call of the living and the call of the human. I feel the calls remembered in the dreams of the young and the call of the never ending spirit. But the greatest call of all is the call to a faith in people," Gabriel advised. "I've always seen that call in both of you."

"How does a man know his calling," Michael asked.

"He may fulfill his calling by asking a question he cannot answer or attempting a feat, he cannot achieve. In each case, he tests himself. Each person must answer his own question," Gabriel consoled. "No one else can answer his call."

"It's all your own," John agreed.

"We should sleep," Gabriel advised. "You must be tired."

"We're in a desert?" Michael snapped.

Gabriel points to an oasis in the distance. There are trees, a fire, water, pillows and blankets on the ground. The sun is setting over the desert. "That oasis is the word of God in the desert of humanity," Gabriel proclaimed. "Do you wish to know his word before your judgment?"

"Is this a test," Michael asked?

"It was the same offer made of the two thieves from the cross," John advised.

One thief said, "Jesus, remember me when you come into your kingdom!" And Jesus said, "Truly I say to you, today you shall be with me in paradise," Michael preached.

"Perhaps, we should rest here for the night," Gabriel replied. They walk over to the oasis and sit by the fire, relaxing for the moment and look at the night sky.

"I've never seen so many stars," John admitted.

"They've always been there," Gabriel assured.

"I never said thank you for what you did for me," John replied.

"Well, it's what you did for me, too," Gabriel acknowledged. "I thoroughly enjoyed my ringside seat at your lives. It was a real treat."

"You could have saved me, you know," Michael sneered. "That would've been nice."

"Go big or go home," Gabriel laughed. "Now get some sleep, tomorrow we'll take on the prize." Michael and John look at each other with concern when Gabriel closed his eyes.

The oasis is quite until the crowing of a rooster. "A rooster in the desert," Michael complained.

"Is that too much," Gabriel laughed.

"Not at all," John replied. "It sounds like home."

"How do you feel this morning," Gabriel asked.

"I don't feel anything," Michael said. "No pain, no hunger, or thirst, just joy."

"I feel it, too," John added.

"It's your soul. It's at peace," Gabriel announced. "Your life was an expression of your faith, so who do you have to fear?"

"Nothing," John replied.

"We're getting closer," Gabriel said.

"I'm getting a little nervous," Michael stammered.

"And this, too, shall pass," Gabriel promised.

The three begin to walk across the desert, its brilliant bold scenery. "Are we there yet," Michael asked.

"What's bothering you," Gabriel questioned.

"I keep having these questions ringing in my head, over and over," Michael groaned. "I can't stop thinking about it."

"Well, it hasn't stopped you yet," Gabriel said. "What is it?"

"I'm not sure how to ask this," Michael replied.

"If it helps, I've heard it all before," Gabriel promised. "You've nothing to be afraid of?"

"Okay, hear it is," Michael said cautiously. "What is sacred? What's the spirit made of? What, in life, is worth living for? And what's so important that we're willing to die for it?"

"I'm impressed," Gabriel admitted. "The answer to each of your questions is the same."

"What, faith," Michael asked.

"Love," John declared.

"I believe you're ready," Gabriel reassured, "both of you."

"Ready for what," Michael shuddered.

A giant fortress, like never seen by human eyes, stands over the horizon. Gabriel points to a wall great and high, it has twelve gates, and at the gates twelve angels with names written, which are the names of the twelve tribes of the children of Israel. The three of them are standing motionless in front of the gates. "We're here," Gabriel grinned. They look up to the top of the gate. Twelve angels look over the top of the wall.

"What now," Michael begged.

"You answer for your life," Gabriel replied. "Are you one of us?"

"I am," Michael feared.

"Then you have nothing to fear," Gabriel replied.

A bellowing voice echoed down from the top of the gate. "Why should I let you in," the voice demanded. They look up to the top of the wall. John and Michael turned to speak to Gabriel but he was gone. They looked at each other and paused, then smile.

"Jesus Christ is my savior," Michael proclaimed.

"He died on the cross to forgive my sins," John declared.

A deafening silence consumed the land. Suddenly, the gates cracked like thunder. They slowly began to open. Beautiful music played as the gates opened wider, you could see the paradise within. "Booyah, John," Michael shouted, "the prize."

John and Michaels parents stood in the front of a growing crowd. "Mother, Father," John shouted. Elizabeth stepped out from behind John's parents. "Elizabeth!" She began to cry, he ran to her, and they kissed. The gates continued to open showing millions of people standing behind them. They clapped and cheered. John embraced his family and cried. He looked up and saw a distinguished older man with white hair looking directly at him. This man stood like a giant among men.

"Well done, John," George Washington said proudly, "Well done."

"George...Washington?" John grinned as the crowd of a thousand voices roared like nothing he had ever heard before.

Gabriel stood alone, off in the distance, as the crowd gathered around John and Michael. "I will never forget your journey, John Henry," Gabriel whispered.

THE END

Acknowledgments

"And we're also remembering the guiding light of our Judeo-Christian tradition. All of us here today are descendants of Abraham, Isaac, and Jacob, sons and daughters of the same God. I believe we are bound by faith in our God, by our love for family and neighborhood, by our deep desire for a more peaceful world, and by our commitment to protect the freedom which is our legacy as Americans. These values have given a renewed sense of worth to our lives. They are infusing America with confidence and optimism that many thought we had lost." - Ronald Reagan

"America will never be destroyed from the outside. If we falter and lose our freedoms, it will be because we destroyed ourselves." - Abraham Lincoln

"If I could leave you with one last thought, it's this: There are no such things as limits to growth, because there are no limits on the human capacity for intelligence, imagination, and wonder. A century ago, oil was nothing more than so much dark, sticky, ill-smelling liquid. It was the invention of the internal combustion engine that turned oil into a resource, and today oil fuels the world's economy. Just 10 years ago, sand was nothing more than the stuff that deserts are made of. Today, we use sand to make the silicon chips that guide satellites through space. So, remember, in this vast and wonderful world that God has given us, it is not what is inside the Earth that counts, but what is inside your minds and hearts, because that is the stuff dreams are made of, and America's future is in your dreams. Make them come true." - Ronald Reagan

"If ever time should come, when vain and aspiring men shall possess the highest seats in Government, our country will stand in need of its experienced patriots to prevent its ruin." - Samuel Adams

APPENDICES

Book of Acts: King James Version

The Book of Acts was written to provide a history of the early church. Acts records the apostles being Christ's witnesses in Jerusalem, Judea, Samaria, and to the rest of the surrounding world. The book sheds light on the gift of the Holy Spirit, who empowers, guides, teaches, and serves as our Counselor. Reading the book of Acts, we are enlightened and encouraged by the many miracles that were being performed during this time by the disciples Peter, John, and Paul. The lust for power, greed, and many other vices are evidence of the devil in the book of Acts.

Acts 9:1-31 - The Intervention of John Henry at Camp David

And Saul, yet breathing out threatenings and slaughter against the disciples of the Lord, went unto the high priest,

[2] And desired of him letters to Damascus to the synagogues, that if

he found any of this way, whether they were men or women, he might bring them bound unto Jerusalem.

³ And as he journeyed, he came near Damascus: and suddenly there shined round about him a light from Heaven:

⁴ And he fell to the Earth, and heard a voice saying unto him, Saul, Saul, why persecutest thou me?

⁵ And he said, Who art thou, Lord? And the Lord said, I am Jesus whom thou persecutest: it is hard for thee to kick against the pricks.

⁶ And he trembling and astonished said, Lord, what wilt thou have me to do? And the Lord said unto him, Arise, and go into the city, and it shall be told thee what thou must do.

⁷ And the men which journeyed with him stood speechless, hearing a voice, but seeing no man.

⁸ And Saul arose from the Earth; and when his eyes were opened, he saw no man: but they led him by the hand, and brought him into Damascus.

⁹ And he was three days without sight, and neither did eat nor drink.

¹⁰ And there was a certain disciple at Damascus, named Ananias; and to him said the Lord in a vision, Ananias. And he said, Behold, I am here, Lord.

¹¹ And the Lord said unto him, Arise, and go into the street which

is called Straight, and enquire in the house of Judas for one called Saul, of Tarsus: for, behold, he prayeth,

¹² And hath seen in a vision a man named Ananias coming in, and putting his hand on him, that he might receive his sight.

¹³ Then Ananias answered, Lord, I have heard by many of this man, how much evil he hath done to thy saints at Jerusalem:

¹⁴ And here he hath authority from the chief priests to bind all that call on thy name.

¹⁵ But the Lord said unto him, Go thy way: for he is a chosen vessel unto me, to bear my name before the Gentiles, and kings, and the children of Israel:

¹⁶ For I will show him how great things he must suffer for my name's sake.

¹⁷ And Ananias went his way, and entered into the house; and putting his hands on him said, Brother Saul, the Lord, even Jesus, that appeared unto thee in the way as thou camest, hath sent me, that thou mightest receive thy sight, and be filled with the Holy Ghost.

¹⁸ And immediately there fell from his eyes as it had been scales: and he received sight forthwith, and arose, and was baptized.

¹⁹ And when he had received meat, he was strengthened. Then was Saul certain days with the disciples which were at Damascus.

²⁰ And straightway he preached Christ in the synagogues, that he is the Son of God.

²¹ But all that heard him were amazed, and said; Is not this he that destroyed them which called on this name in Jerusalem, and came hither for that intent, that he might bring them bound unto the chief priests?

²² But Saul increased the more in strength, and confounded the Jews which dwelt at Damascus, proving that this is very Christ.

²³ And after that many days were fulfilled, the Jews took counsel to kill him:

²⁴ But their laying await was known of Saul. And they watched the gates day and night to kill him.

²⁵ Then the disciples took him by night, and let him down by the wall in a basket.

²⁶ And when Saul was come to Jerusalem, he assayed to join himself to the disciples: but they were all afraid of him, and believed not that he was a disciple.

²⁷ But Barnabas took him, and brought him to the apostles, and declared unto them how he had seen the Lord in the way, and that he had spoken to him, and how he had preached boldly at Damascus in the name of Jesus.

²⁸ And he was with them coming in and going out at Jerusalem.

²⁹ And he spoke boldly in the name of the Lord Jesus, and disputed against the Grecians: but they went about to slay him.

³⁰ Which when the brethren knew, they brought him down to Caesarea, and sent him forth to Tarsus.

³¹ Then had the churches rest throughout all Judaea and Galilee and Samaria, and were edified; and walking in the fear of the Lord, and in the comfort of the Holy Ghost, were multiplied.

Acts 14:8-22 – The Stoning of John Henry at Lystra

⁸ And there sat a certain man at Lystra, impotent in his feet, being a cripple from his mother's womb, who never had walked:

⁹ The same heard Paul speak: who stedfastly beholding him, and perceiving that he had faith to be healed,

¹⁰ Said with a loud voice, Stand upright on thy feet. And he leaped and walked.

¹¹ And when the people saw what Paul had done, they lifted up their voices, saying in the speech of Lycaonia, The gods are come down to us in the likeness of men.

¹² And they called Barnabas, Jupiter; and Paul, Mercurius, because he was the chief speaker.

¹³ Then the priest of Jupiter, which was before their city, brought oxen and garlands unto the gates, and would have done sacrifice with the people.

¹⁴ Which when the apostles, Barnabas and Paul, heard of, they rent their clothes, and ran in among the people, crying out,

[15] And saying, Sirs, why do ye these things? We also are men of like passions with you, and preach unto you that ye should turn from these vanities unto the living God, which made Heaven, and Earth, and the sea, and all things that are therein:

[16] Who in times past suffered all nations to walk in their own ways.

[17] Nevertheless he left not himself without witness, in that he did good, and gave us rain from Heaven, and fruitful seasons, filling our hearts with food and gladness.

[18] And with these sayings scarce restrained they the people, that they had not done sacrifice unto them.

[19] And there came thither certain Jews from Antioch and Iconium, who persuaded the people, and having stoned Paul, drew him out of the city, supposing he had been dead.

[20] Howbeit, as the disciples stood round about him, he rose up, and came into the city: and the next day he departed with Barnabas to Derbe.

[21] And when they had preached the gospel to that city, and had taught many, they returned again to Lystra, and to Iconium, and Antioch,

[22] Confirming the souls of the disciples, and exhorting them to continue in the faith, and that we must through much tribulation enter into the kingdom of God.

Acts 7:54-60 – The murder of Pastor Stephen

[54] When they heard these things, they were cut to the heart, and they gnashed on him with their teeth.

[55] But he, being full of the Holy Ghost, looked up steadfastly into Heaven, and saw the glory of God, and Jesus standing on the right hand of God,

[56] And said, Behold, I see the Heavens opened, and the Son of man standing on the right hand of God.

[57] Then they cried out with a loud voice, and stopped their ears, and ran upon him with one accord,

[58] And cast him out of the city, and stoned him: and the witnesses laid down their clothes at a young man's feet, whose name was Saul.

[59] And they stoned Stephen, calling upon God, and saying, Lord Jesus, receive my spirit.

[60] And he kneeled down, and cried with a loud voice, Lord, lay not this sin to their charge. And when he had said this, he fell asleep.

Acts 6:18-19 & 26 – The gamble and escape of John Henry

And this did she many days. But Paul, being grieved, turned and said to the spirit, I command you in the name of Jesus Christ to come out of her. And he came out the same hour.

And when her masters saw that the hope of their gains was gone, they caught Paul and Silas, and drew them into the marketplace to the rulers,

and suddenly there came a great earthquake, so that the foundations of the prison house were shaken; and immediately all the doors were opened and everyone's chains were unfastened.

Resources

Blog: For Our Children

forourchildrennovel.blogspot.com

Contact the author at...

forourchildrennovel@gmail.com

Facebook Page: For Our Children, a Novel

http://www.facebook.com/tracy.mollenkopf/favorites#!/pages/For-Our-Children-a-novel-by-Tracy-Mollenkopf/52197350977

Twitter:

Tracy Mollenkopf @TracyMollenkopf